DRAWINGS
from the Collection of
Mr. & Mrs. Eugene Victor Thaw
PART II

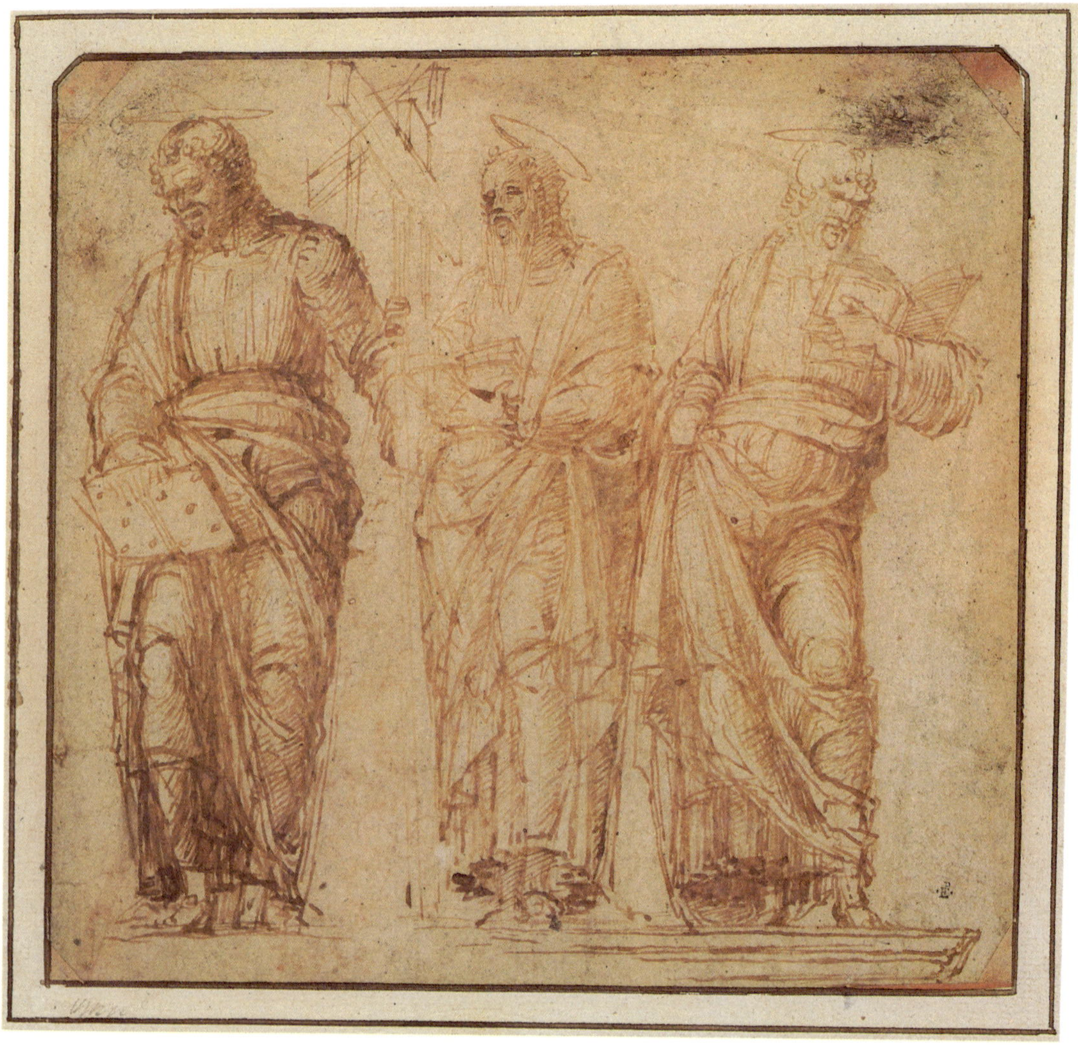

Andrea Mantegna *Three Standing Apostles*

DRAWINGS
from the Collection of
Mr. & Mrs. Eugene Victor Thaw

PART II

CATALOGUE BY

Cara D. Denison William W. Robinson

Julia Herd Stephanie Wiles

WITH INTRODUCTIONS BY

Eugene Victor Thaw and

Charles Ryskamp

The Pierpont Morgan Library

NEW YORK 1985

Exhibitions of the Thaw Collection

THE PIERPONT MORGAN LIBRARY

3 September 1985 to 10 November 1985

VIRGINIA MUSEUM OF FINE ARTS

17 February to 13 April 1986

Cover illustration: Claude Gellée, *Heroic Landscape* (cat. no. 6)

29 EAST 36 STREET, NEW YORK, N.Y. 10016

PRINTED IN THE UNITED STATES OF AMERICA

LIBRARY OF CONGRESS CATALOGUE CARD NUMBER 85-61824

ISBN 87598-082-1

TABLE OF CONTENTS

PREFACE

IT IS TEN YEARS AGO that The Pierpont Morgan Library opened an exhibition of drawings from the collection of Mr. and Mrs. Eugene Victor Thaw and they announced that the collection would be given to the Library, in stages, during their lifetimes. A significant number of the 115 drawings in the 1975 catalogue are now part of the Morgan Library. (They are indicated in the full list of drawings from the earlier catalogue which may be found on pages 101 to 103 of the present one.) Ten of the 115 drawings were from the fifteenth or sixteenth centuries, twice that from the seventeenth century, and four times as many from the eighteenth century. Forty-five were from 1800 to 1900, all but ten of these French. One was able to experience the range of European drawing over four hundred years, but the emphasis was really on the work of a few great draughtsmen: nine drawings each by Claude and Giambattista Tiepolo, eight by Degas, seven by Domenico Tiepolo, six by Rembrandt and Delacroix, five by Watteau, Guardi, and Goya, and four by Gericault, Daumier, and Cezanne. In the present catalogue, Mr. and Mrs. Thaw have added one drawing by each of these artists except Daumier, as well as two by Rembrandt, Degas, and Cézanne, and three by Delacroix. (For Degas and Cézanne there are also very important sketchbooks.) In this catalogue there is a new focus on a single artist—Fragonard, who is represented by seven drawings, six of them illustrations for Ariosto's *Orlando Furioso*.

Among the somewhat smaller group of drawings which we are publishing now, the balance tips even more towards the period after 1800. There are just three early drawings; one mannerist drawing (by Goltzius)—an aspect of art not otherwise collected by the Thaws, who also have found the Italian baroque not to their taste. There are four drawings from the seventeenth century and about twenty from the eighteenth century. More than half are from the nineteenth and twentieth centuries.

Mr. Thaw writes in his Introduction that he and his wife "have accumulated" these drawings during the past ten years. It is obvious that they followed no program, nor attempted a survey of draughtsmanship. They have pursued works which reflected their own tastes and they have as well kept in mind the strengths and weaknesses of the collection of drawings in the Morgan Library. Broad as the Morgan's collection is, it has been chiefly devoted to works before 1825. Ten years ago, the Thaws led the Library boldly into the world of drawings of the last two-thirds of the nineteenth century; above all, many of the greatest masters of France were well represented in the Thaw Collection. And with magnificent watercolors of Friedrich, Turner, and Palmer, the Thaws also established a core of masterworks of European Romanticism outside France. It is the Romantic world of all of Europe which is central to the present catalogue; this is revealed with a range and a richness beyond almost any American museum. The Morgan's own collection (of books as well as drawings and watercolors) is strong in Blake; we also have some remarkable works by Fuseli. We have a few distinguished neo-classical drawings, particularly those by Prud'hon and Ingres. Otherwise at the Morgan Library, without the drawings given and promised by Mr. and Mrs. Thaw, the first half of the nineteenth century would not have the balance and depth which is characteristic of the earlier periods for the chief European schools of draughtsmanship. Among the drawings collected by the Thaws in the past ten years are works not only by the French masters, and by Friedrich, Turner, Palmer, and Goya, but also important ones by Fuseli, Blake, Kobell, Constable, Dahl, and von Schwind.

The present catalogue reveals outstanding discernment in private connoisseurship; it also shows how such collectors can make major contributions to large public institutions. The Thaws' promised gifts here will significantly alter the future of the Department of Drawings at the Morgan Library, and the collections of New York and the United States.

There are other innovations in this second part of the Thaw Collection. Whereas the previous catalogue went from the late fifteenth century to about 1900, the drawings now go well into the twentieth century, with modern masters after Cézanne like Vuillard, Matisse (three drawings), Mondrian, Klee, Picasso (four drawings), de Chirico, and Ernst. The present catalogue also describes three remarkable sketchbooks: by Degas, Cézanne, and Jackson Pollock—the only one known by him from the 1950s. It is especially appropriate to reach beyond the other twentieth-century artists shown here, past the first three or four decades of the century, to Pollock, since Mr. Thaw's own studies of that artist have been so distinguished (the catalogue raisonné, with Francis Valentine O'Connor, of the paintings, drawings, and other works of Pollock; New Haven and London, 1978). Each of the Thaw sketchbooks has previously been fully reproduced and described, so that only selections and brief discussions are given here. These sketchbooks are also of particular interest to the Morgan Library, since, equally library and museum, it has made great efforts to collect sketchbooks from all periods. Among its earliest acquisitions of drawings was an Italian sketchbook of the late fourteenth century and a French one on boxwood leaves, from the circle of Jacquemart de Hesdin, ca. 1400. The Library on a number of occasions has bought the works of artists at the end of the nineteenth century in order to add a sketchbook to its collections, even when it did not ordinarily buy drawings or watercolors after 1825. Like the Thaws, it stretched its normal limits for the sake of a book which revealed an artist's most intimate and immediate notations.

There is one other aspect of the collecting interests of the Thaws which is shown here for the first time; that is, watercolors of European domestic interiors. The fashion for drawings of individual rooms in houses, castles, and palaces—the bourgeois world was as carefully delineated as the noble or royal—originated in France early in the nineteenth century and spread to central Europe and Russia, where it flourished. The last eleven entries of this catalogue are of such domestic interiors; they well illustrate the excellence of the collection of the Thaws, who were acquiring these watercolors some years before the collecting of them became as fashionable as in the period from 1815 to 1840 when most of them were created. These watercolors are of considerable interest in themselves, as well as of special concern to students of interior decoration. They also beautifully supplement the Morgan's group of theatre designs; with the recent gift of the collection formed by Donald M. Oenslager of sixteen hundred European theatre designs, from the earliest Italian drawings to contemporary American, the Morgan Library has one of the most notable collections in this country. Our stage designs, unlike the collections of master drawings at the Library, include works by Austrian, central European, and Russian artists. The same is true of the domestic interiors gathered by the Thaws.

There are probably as many great drawings in this as in the first catalogue, although a smaller group has been collected in the past ten years than in the more than twenty years taken for collecting those shown in 1975. The first drawing here, that by Mantegna, is a rare example, and a wonderful one, by that justly celebrated master of the fifteenth century. The Beham portrait from the first half of the sixteenth century is also an impressive work. The drawings by Jordaens, Rembrandt, and Watteau are very fine, and the Claude landscape, truly a masterpiece. So is the Fragonard portrait of a Neapolitan girl. The Guardi and Goya drawings are exceptionally beautiful, and there are many other works from the last 150 years which can stand with the finest watercolors and drawings of the century just past and that of our own. The Thaws are without question among the outstanding collectors of the present time.

The drawings in this catalogue, and the three sketchbooks, will be exhibited at The Pierpont Morgan Library and at the Virginia Museum of Fine Arts. In both places the drawings will be shown with other works of art from the Thaw Collection: ancient and Renaissance bronzes and small sculptures, Renaissance jewelry, objects in gold and silver, faience from Moustier, and small oil sketches. The Thaws have collected widely: drawings, although probably their greatest interest, constitute only a part of their art collections. All of the art has been chosen with an exceptional eye for line and form and an understanding of rarity and importance. For such connoisseurship, I am reminded of the exhibition at the Metropolitan Museum in 1962 of "Master Drawings in the Collection of Walter C. Baker." No one who was fortunate enough to see that exhibition of drawings will forget how they were made even more remarkable by being shown with some of Mr. Baker's superb small sculptures—Etruscan, Greek, and Roman. The drawings themselves went from the first half of the fifteenth century to Picasso, and beyond, to a group of contemporary artists, mostly American. I hope a similar pleasure and delight of the eye will be given to those who see the Thaw Collection as shown in New York and Richmond.

At the Morgan Library we are deeply grateful to Mr. and Mrs. Thaw for making such an exhibition possible and for promising that, as before, this collection of drawings will someday be "permanently available for the instruction and pleasure of the American people." The Thaws are among the most generous and eminent benefactors of the Library. We are thankful also to our friends at the Virginia Museum of Fine Arts who have cooperated in the plans for this exhibition and publication, especially to Mr. Pinkney Near and Mr. Richard Woodward. From the staff of The Pierpont Morgan Library, the following prepared the catalogue: Mrs. Cara D. Denison (numbers 1, 6, 9, 11–18, 21–24, 44–52, 68, 69, 71, 73), Mr. William W. Robinson (numbers 2–5, 7, 8, 30, 31, 41, 43, 53, 55–57, 60–63, 67, 75), Miss Julia Herd (numbers 25, 26, 28, 32–34, 36, 37, 42, 58, 65, 66, 76, 77), and Miss Stephanie Wiles (numbers 10, 19, 20, 27, 29, 38–40, 54, 59, 64, 70, 72); Mrs. Ilana A. Dreyer wrote number 74, and number 35 was written by Mrs. Helen B. Mules in 1980 (its bibliography and exhibition history have been revised). The photographs were taken by Mr. David Loggie, assisted by Mr. Edward Sowinski. Other members of the staff of the Library who helped were Miss Priscilla C. Barker, Mr. Timothy Herstein, Mr. Robert Riggs Kerr, Dr. Ruth S. Kraemer, Mr. Francis Mason, Mrs. Patricia Reyes, Mr. Frederick Schroeder, Ms. Nancy Seaton, Miss Diane Stiles, and Mr. David Wright. We have been assisted in various ways by Mr. Keith Andrews, Dr. Margaret Biedermann, Mrs. Barbara Buckland, Mrs. Carol Eliel, Ms. Brigitte Geerincx, Mr. Jorge Guillermo, Miss Carolyn Hicks, Mr. John Rowlands, Mr. J. Byam Shaw, Mr. Alan Shestack, Mr. Walter L. Strauss, Dr. George Szabo, Mrs. Patricia Tang, Dr. B. Woelderink, and Mr. Alexander J. Yow. We are most grateful to Mr. C. Freeman Keith, Mr. Anthony Pizzo, and Mr. Stephen Harvard of the Meriden-Stinehour Press, who worked with extraordinary skill to produce this book. The publication of this catalogue was made possible in part through endowed funds for our publications established by the Charles Engelhard Foundation and The Andrew W. Mellon Foundation.

CHARLES RYSKAMP
Director

INTRODUCTION

THIS EXHIBITION includes the bulk of the works on paper that my wife and I have accumulated since the exhibition of our drawings collection in 1975. I use the word "accumulated" with accuracy because no specific program has motivated this assemblage and, consequently, it unfolds as a much less systematic survey than the collection we showed ten years ago.

In many cases we have simply added a new example to the groups of works by favorite artists we already possessed: a new Watteau; a Claude which overshadows but enhances the nine we had; a very unusual Guardi; a unique Gericault; a Goya of a different period than the ones we owned, etc., etc.

We have continued to avoid those same sections of art history towards which, in the catalogue of 1975, I confessed to harbor unreasonable prejudice. A personal collection, after all, unlike a museum, can and probably should reflect private tastes, even eccentric preferences. In that same catalogue, I expressed the desire to find more of the rare early drawings about which one dreams. On the whole they still elude me, but I am certainly proud of the Mantegna sheet; the little German silverpoint drawing from Chatsworth; and the rare Hans Sebald Beham that will have to serve as a surrogate for the Dürers and Altdorfers which never came our way.

What continued to come our way, however, were works by great nineteenth-century artists whom we particularly favored. As this area is the one in which our activity can ultimately strengthen the Morgan Library collection most significantly, we have had no hesitation in pursuing the opportunities offered. Two large Turner watercolors, both first owned by Ruskin, two Constable drawings, two Redon fusains, two more late Cézanne watercolors, two Degas drawings, and a group of German Romantics have strengthened the representation of this period. In addition, we have, at last, found an Ingres portrait of the Roman period to add to the merely respectable later one we previously exhibited and also a large reed-pen Van Gogh drawn near Arles of the sort we had always hoped to possess.

A lucky chance enabled us to acquire the famous Fragonard *Neapolitan Girl* from the Stralem Collection several years before the rest of that group of eighteenth-century drawings was dispersed at auction. But, since I am an art dealer in my professional life, that drawing as well as several others, which I ought not to identify, entered our private collection only after I had tried unsuccessfully to interest museums and private clients in buying them. After more than thirty-five years in the business of selling art, I am still amazed at how slow to react many collectors and institutions are even when confronted with something that is the best of its kind.

A totally new development in this second collection is our plunge into the twentieth century. The late Cézannes we exhibited in 1975–76 are technically and esthetically twentieth-century works, but we are showing this time eleven representative drawings by Picasso and other leading figures of early modernism. Once again, this is an area that must eventually be taken account of by the Morgan Library—at least with selected highlights—so that it will, like the British Museum and the Albertina, be able to document the whole history of draughtsmanship in Western Art. It is our hope that someone else will continue our tentative step forward in time with a more comprehensive twentieth-century group which one day will complement the Morgan's collections of books and literary and musical manuscripts.

My wife, Clare, was an early enthusiast for watercolors of domestic interiors which have lately become so popular with collectors. We have, by occasional gifts to each other, assembled a fair number of these and somewhat hesitantly, encouraged by Charles Ryskamp, are showing a selection of eleven to demonstrate another phase of our interest in drawings.

When the tour of the earlier selection of "Drawings from the Thaw Collection" ended in 1976, we were rather exhausted by the whole idea of strenuous collecting. The publication of a definitive catalogue and the absence of the drawings from our walls for so long a time seemed to write *finis* to our activities in this field. We were even reluctant to rehang the drawings, allowing them to remain in storage at the Library for nearly a year. The habits of a lifetime are not easily discarded, however, and it was not long before one or two irresistible opportunities presented themselves and we were off and running again.

I have found that emotional collecting can have a therapeutic result in spite of its suspicious psychotic aspects. At a particularly low point in my life, when I believed I had lost my abilities and my luck, Leigh Block visited my office carrying under his arm a package containing his famous sketchbook by Cézanne. I closed the office door, vowing to stay cool and not to emerge until I possessed it. Mr. Block, now a good friend, made that possible, and, like the sun bursting forth after a storm, all my fortunes seemed to change and my crisis and depression quickly ended.

More recently, I was able to buy a Degas sketchbook and Lee Krasner Pollock gave to my wife and me a very moving and beautiful sketchbook by Jackson Pollock in which he drew some of the last images of his life.

A considerable number of the drawings included in the 1975 catalogue have now entered the Morgan collection. We have consistently pursued this transfer and the Library has called upon numerous "promised gifts" for inclusion in several of its major exhibitions, causing us great pride in our place in such company. Recently, we were able to add a footnote to the story I told in 1975 about my admiration for Janos Scholz and my gratitude for his early encouragement of my collecting career. The great Goya drawing which he found for us many years ago we were pleased to give to the Morgan Library in 1983 in honor of Janos' eightieth birthday.

I have not yet said anything about the special pleasures that living with these drawings provide. As well as we have gotten to know them, their magic and their secrets are still not exhausted. Like most collectors of drawings we constantly shift them around on our walls trying new arrangements and juxtapositions, each new placement provoking new insights into the essence of the work. But it is a particular quality of drawings, their kinship to handwriting, which most attracts us to them as evidence of the authentic touch of the artist's own hand. In this age of computers, multiples, and other devices for graphic programming and duplication, the artist's hand seems to be getting less and less important. All the more reason to cherish such survivals from other times when the hand of genius was a sign of civilization.

Our deepest thanks to all of our friends at the Morgan Library and at the Virginia Museum of Fine Arts for their kindness and care in preparing this exhibition.

Once again we share an important part of ourselves—our obsession you might call it—with the public, and weaknesses as well as strengths will be only too apparent. However, as most of these sheets of paper will one day belong to the public, we hope some of the enjoyment they have given us continues to emanate from them.

EUGENE VICTOR THAW

LIST OF ABBREVIATIONS

A.S.M.
Odilon Redon, *A Soi-Même, Journal (1867–1915)*, Paris, 1922.

Bartsch
Adam Bartsch, *Le Peintre-graveur*, 21 vols., Vienna, 1803–21.

Beau
Marguerite Beau, *La collection des dessins d'Hubert Robert au Musée de Valence*, Lyons, 1968.

Bénézit
Emmanuel-Charles Bénézit, *Dictionnaire critique et documentaire des Peintres, Sculpteurs, Dessinateurs et Graveurs*, 10 vols., Paris, 1976.

Briquet
C. M. Briquet, *Les Filigranes. Dictionnaire historique des marques du papier*, 4 vols., Geneva, 1907.

Churchill
W. A. Churchill, *Watermarks on Paper*, Amsterdam, 1935.

Cohen & de Ricci
Henry Cohen and Seymour de Ricci, *Guide de l'amateur de livres à gravures du XVIIIe siècle*, 6th ed., Paris, 1912.

Heawood
Edward Heawood, *Watermarks, Mainly of the 17th and 18th Centuries*, Hilversum, Holland, 1950.

Lemoisne
P. A. Lemoisne, *Degas et son oeuvre*, 4 vols., Paris, 1946.

Lugt
Frits Lugt, *Les Marques de collections de dessins et d'estampes . . .* , Amsterdam, 1921.

Lugt S.
Frits Lugt, *Les Marques de collections de dessins et d'estampes . . . Supplément*, The Hague, 1956.

Mongan, Hofer, and Seznec, 1945
Elizabeth Mongan, Philip Hofer, and Jean Seznec, *Fragonard Drawings for Ariosto*, New York, 1945.

Morgan Library, Thaw exhibition, 1975–76
The Pierpont Morgan Library, New York and elsewhere, *Drawings from the Collection of Mr. and Mrs. Eugene V. Thaw*, catalogue by Felice Stampfle and Cara D. Denison, New York, 1975.

Rubens and Rembrandt, 1979–80
The Pierpont Morgan Library, New York and elsewhere, *Rubens and Rembrandt in their Century*, catalogue by Felice Stampfle, 1979–80.

Thieme-Becker
Ulrich Thieme and Felix Becker, *Allgemeines Lexikon der bildenden Künstler von der Antike bis zur Gegenwart*, 37 vols., Leipzig, 1907–50.

Washington, Fragonard Exhibition, 1978–79
National Gallery of Art, Washington and elsewhere, *Fragonard Drawings in North American Collections*, catalogue by Eunice Williams, 1978–79.

CATALOGUE

ANDREA MANTEGNA

ISOLA DI CARTURO 1431 – 1506 MANTUA

1 *Three Standing Apostles*

Pen and brown ink with traces of red chalk, possibly an offset from another sheet; corners cropped diagonally. 7×7½ inches (175×188 mm.). Watermark: none visible through lining. Inscribed in pen and brown ink on back of old mount in an eighteenth-century hand, *H 4 / Three Apostles.*

Very few drawings by Andrea Mantegna, one of the greatest masters of the fifteenth century, are known to exist, and only a small number have made their way into American collections such as the Fogg Art Museum, Harvard University; the Metropolitan Museum of Art, New York; and the National Gallery of Art. Within four years, however, two outstanding drawings emerged on the London art market and were bought by Americans. The drawing of *Three Standing Apostles*, arguably the more powerful of the two, was acquired by Mr. and Mrs. Thaw in the Hatvany sale of June 1980, while in July 1984, the Getty Museum purchased the *Four Saints* in the Chatsworth sale. Although it has been shown that the Chatsworth drawing is connected with the left-hand panel of the S. Zeno altarpiece which Mantegna completed in 1460, the Thaw study cannot be related with certainty to any known painting. These two drawings offer many points of comparison, notably in subject and the treatment of the figures, which are presented as a compact mass rather than isolated individually. The *Three Standing Apostles*, however, appears to be later than the Chatsworth sheet, especially in the more advanced and fluent treatment of the saints' drapery.

When the Thaw drawing first appeared in 1959, A. E. Popham connected it with the *Study of a Saint Reading* in the British Museum. At that time the British Museum sheet was attributed to Giovanni Bellini (A. E. Popham and Philip Pouncey, *Italian Drawings in the Department of Prints and Drawings in the British Museum*, London, 1950, no. 11, repr.). Given certain parallels between the two which are almost identical in style, it is believed that both are related to the same project.

The same hand is evident in the Chatsworth sheet (sale, London, Christie's, 3 July 1984, lot 26, repr.); the Gathorne-Hardy *St. James Led to Execution*, a preparatory drawing for the Eremitani Chapel in Padua, now also in the British Museum; the *Christ at the Column* from Count Seilern's collection, now in the Courtauld Institute Galleries, London, which is demonstrably a preliminary study for Mantegna's *Flagellation*, a work now known only in two fifteenth-century engravings (*Addenda to the Italian Paintings and Drawings in the Seilern Collection*, 1969, repr.); a sheet of studies for a *St. John the Baptist* formerly in the Koenigs Collection (Hadeln 58); and the *Pietà* in the Accademia, Venice (Hadeln 62).

For many years the authorship of this group of drawings has been the subject of debate but the consensus among scholars now is that Mantegna rather than Bellini was in fact the author. The definitive argument for the reattribution of the entire group to Mantegna was advanced in Johannes Wilde's detailed discussion of *Christ at the Column* in Count Seilern's collection (*ibid.*, pp. 37 ff.).

PROVENANCE: Edward Pearf or Edmund Prideaux (Lugt 893); sale, London, Christie's, 7 July 1959, lot 70, repr.; Baron Hatvany; his sale, London, Christie's, 24 June 1980, lot 3, repr.

BIBLIOGRAPHY: Fritz Heinemann, *Giovanni Bellini e i Belliniani*, Venice, [1959], I, no. 338 bis, II, fig. 147 (as Bellini of the same date as the Koenigs drawing); Giles Robertson, *Giovanni Bellini*, Oxford, 1968, p. 25, no. 4 (noting its superiority to the Koenigs drawing); Bernhard Degenhart and Annegrit Schmitt, *Corpus der Italienischen Zeichnungen, 1300–1450*, Berlin, 1968, II, p. 363, n. 13 (as Mantegna); J. Byam Shaw, *Biblioteca di Disegni*, 3, 1979 (as Mantegna), illustrated in facsimile.

GERMAN SCHOOL

ca. 1520

2 *Sheet of Studies with a Seated Man and Farmhouses in a Landscape*

Metalpoint on paper prepared with a cream ground. $6^3/_8 \times 4^3/_8$ inches (163×112 mm.). Watermark: none visible through lining.

This sheet belonged in the collection of the Duke of Devonshire until it was sold in July 1984 in the sensational auction of drawings from Chatsworth. A closely related study of an executioner poised to swing his sword also figured in the sale and is now in private hands in Chicago (see Washington, 1969, no. 105b). Both drawings are by the same artist, have identical dimensions, and are similar in technique, although the pale lilac ground of the sheet in Chicago differs in tone from the cream preparation of the Thaw work. (The use of metalpoint requires a ground that is applied to the paper and to which the metal medium adheres.)

It is possible that these studies formed part of a small sketchbook of metalpoint drawings similar to the one Albrecht Dürer used on his journey to the Netherlands in 1520–21. Like many early German drawings, they are probably copies after details in other works of art. The abrupt truncation of the tall tree in the sheet exhibited here suggests that it is such a copy rather than a study from nature, while the executioner in the companion piece is less likely to have been observed from life than from a contemporary German or Netherlandish scene of martyrdom, where the headsmen often strike similar poses.

The author of the two drawings has not been identified. Byam Shaw, having dismissed the earlier, groundless attribution to Lucas van Leyden, ascribed them tentatively to Hans Baldung on the strength of their similarities to the later works in an album of metalpoint sketches by Baldung at Karlsruhe and the related sheets in Copenhagen (Karl Koch, *Die Zeichnungen Hans Baldung Griens*, Berlin, 1941, nos. 160–252). Although the broad, dynamic strokes of Baldung's studies, as well as their comparatively massive forms, rule out the possibility that he was the draughtsman of the delicate and minutely executed Thaw work, the general resemblance to Baldung's metalpoint drawings confirms that it was produced by one of his German contemporaries. Moreover, the graphic conventions used to represent foliage bring to mind landscapes by other South German masters of the early sixteenth century: the rendering of the billowing crowns of the lower trees at the right recalls the similarly generalized woods in many of Dürer's drawings and prints, while the drooping foliage of the tall tree probably derives from works by Albrecht Altdorfer or another artist of the Danube School.

Three smaller metalpoint drawings still at Chatsworth have been associated with the two discussed thus far. These three sheets, which bear studies of various heads, a grasshopper, and a goat, had been assigned to Pisanello and even to Leonardo da Vinci until Campbell Dodgson convincingly restored them to the German School of the early sixteenth century (*The Vasari Society*, Second Series, Part VI, Oxford, 1925, nos. 13–16). Edmund Schilling gave two of them to Baldung in a note in the manuscript catalogue of the Chatsworth drawings, but neither Dodgson nor Schilling related them to the Thaw work and its companion in Chicago. This step was taken by Byam Shaw, who thought all five drawings were by the same hand—possibly Baldung's—and may have come from a single sketchbook. Judging from reproductions of the three Chatsworth studies, the suggestion that the five works are by the same hand is plausible. However, comparison of the study of a goat at Chatsworth with the goat sketched by Baldung in the Karlsruhe album (Koch, no. 200) once again underscores the greater dynamism and economy of Baldung's draughtsmanship.

PROVENANCE: The Duke of Devonshire, Chatsworth, Derbyshire; his sale, London, Christie's, 3 July 1984, lot 69, repr.

EXHIBITIONS: National Gallery of Art, Washington and elsewhere, *Old Master Drawings from Chatsworth II*, catalogue by James Byam Shaw, 1969–70, no. 105a; Victoria and Albert Museum, London, *Old Master Drawings from Chatsworth*, catalogue by Byam Shaw, 1973–74, no. 105a; National Museum of Western Art, Tokyo, *Old Master Drawings from Chatsworth*, catalogue by Byam Shaw, 1975, no. 90.

HANS SEBALD BEHAM

NUREMBERG 1500 – 1550 FRANKFURT AM MAIN

3 *Portrait of a Man*

Red chalk, heightened with white bodycolor. $10\frac{5}{8} \times 7\frac{7}{16}$ inches (270×190 mm.). Watermark: Bull's head surmounted by a cross and serpent (Briquet 15405). Monogram at left, in red chalk, *H*[?]*S B* (in ligature).

This vigorously executed portrait is an important addition to the extensive but insufficiently studied corpus of drawings by Hans Sebald Beham, a follower of Albrecht Dürer best known for his numerous small engravings.

Although Beham made several expressive head studies and portrait drawings, few are drawn with chalk and none is closely related in style to the Thaw example. Were it not for the presence of Beham's monogram—which appears, slightly truncated, at the left side of the sheet—the work might never have been attributed to him. It certainly dates from after 1531, the year Beham altered the last letter of his monogram from P to B. The change in spelling is related to Beham's emigration in 1531 from southern Germany to Frankfurt am Main, where he settled in 1532. The watermark in the Thaw sheet occurs in papers in Switzerland and the Rhineland, among other locations, between 1519 and about 1535.

Comparison of the swirling, impetuous strokes of the Thaw drawing with the fine, regular hatchings of a formal black chalk portrait in the Albertina, which dates from before 1531 (Joseph Schönbrunner and Joseph Meder, *Handzeichnungen alter Meister aus der Albertina und anderen Sammlungen*, Vienna, 1896–1908, IV, no. 412), reveals the remarkable diversity in Beham's style and handling of the chalk. The spontaneous touch of the Thaw work is anticipated in another head study, which is dated 1523 and executed with a similar freedom and graphic energy (Edmund Schilling, *Städelsches Kunstinstitut, Frankfurt am Main. Katalog der deutschen Zeichnungen. Alte Meister*, 1973, Munich, I, no. 39, II, pl. 11). It is possible that Beham employed this vigorous style for expressive character heads, while reserving the restrained manner of the Albertina sheet for formal portraits from life.

The use of red chalk was rare in German art during the first half of the sixteenth century, although Hans Baldung, Hans Schäufelein, and Wolf Huber also utilized it for portrait studies.

The interpretation of the Thaw drawing poses manifold problems. First of all, it is difficult to determine whether the study represents an actual person, as does the black chalk portrait cited above, or depicts an ideal type or character head of the kind that occurs elsewhere in Beham's work and in the drawings of his contemporaries such as Baldung, Schäufelein, and Huber. Dr. George Szabo has noted in correspondence that the sitter's aquiline features and forked beard resemble portraits of Emperor Sigismund of Luxembourg (1361–1437), especially the painting Dürer made for the Rathaus in Nuremberg between 1511 and 1513 and the preparatory drawing for it, where Sigismund appears in imperial regalia (see Johannes Wilde, "Ein zeitgenössisches Bild des Kaisers Sigismund," *Jahrbuch der Kunsthistorischen Sammlungen in Wien*, Neue Folge, IV, pp. 213–22, and Walter L. Strauss, *The Complete Drawings of Albrecht Dürer*, New York, 1974, III, no. 1510/5). The decorated collar worn by the man in the Thaw work also suggests the costume of an important personage. However, the resemblance to the portraits of Sigismund, who died a century earlier, is not absolutely compelling, nor is it clear why Beham should have shown the emperor without any attributes except for the curious collection of objects he delineated along the upper left side of the sheet.

That these objects add a satirical slant to the drawing is certain, but their precise meaning remains elusive. Impaled on a rod at the very top are the cap and bells worn by professional fools. The rod and a pair of asses' ears, another attribute associated with folly, seem to grow out of a chamber pot that rests upon a dome-shaped vessel, probably a beehive. Further below is a pile of dung on a cushion. This latter motif, as Walter Strauss pointed out in conversation, figures prominently in two woodcuts by Erhard Schoen that satirize those who dissipate time and money in excessive eating and drinking (Walter L. Strauss, *The Illustrated Bartsch*, XIII, Commentary, New York, 1984, nos. 196–97). It also appears, with drinking vessels, asses' ears, cap and bells, and other attributes of gluttony and folly, in the side borders of the first pages of Thomas Murner's *Narrenbeschwörung* (Strassburg, 1512), which John Rowlands related in conversation to Beham's drawing. The vertical arrangement of the objects in the woodcut borders of Murner's book recalls the disposition of the items in the margin of Beham's study. The significance of the beehive—if it is a beehive—in the context of these symbols of gluttony and folly is particularly obscure. In Pieter Bruegel's *The Ass in the Schoolhouse* of 1556, one of the ineducable pupils affirms his stupidity by thrusting his head in an active beehive, but whether it conveys a similar idea in Beham's drawing remains to be seen (Ludwig Münz, *Bruegel, The Drawings, Complete Edition*, London, 1961, no. 129).

Finally, the connection between these objects and the man or character type portrayed here also requires clarification. It is possible, though unlikely, that he is a jester. The cap and bells and asses' ears probably allude to the folly of mankind in general, as they do repeatedly in Sebastian Brant's *Ship of Fools* and other moralizing literature of the period, rather than to the occupation of a professional jester of the court or stage, and the same very likely holds true for the other attributes shown at the left.

PROVENANCE: W. J. Goldsmith, Ochiltree Castle near Linlithgow, Scotland; Baskett & Day, London.

HENDRICK GOLTZIUS
MÜHLBRACHT 1558 - 1617 HAARLEM

4 *The Sense of Smell*

Black chalk, some stumping, heightened with white chalk and white lead pigment (oxiized); border in pen and brown ink. Verso: Drapery study in black chalk, some stumping, and traces of heightening in white lead pigment (oxidized). 12 5/16 × 7 7/8 inches (313 × 201 mm.). Watermark: none. Inscribed on verso, at left, in pen and brown ink, *59*, and at lower center, in graphite, *600*(?).

The Sense of Smell belongs to a series of five drawings of loosely draped female figures accompanied by attributes that identify them as personifications of the Senses. Closely related in size, media, and composition, the studies form a suite that Goltzius probably intended to translate into engravings. However, the contours have not been incised for transfer to a copper plate and no prints after these designs have been identified.

When E.K.J. Reznicek published his monograph on the drawings of Goltzius in 1961, he knew only one work from the series, *The Sense of Sight* now in the Fitzwilliam Museum, Cambridge (E.K.J. Reznicek, *Die Zeichnungen von Hendrick Goltzius*, Utrecht, 1961, I, no. 173, II, fig. 346). The remainder have come to light during the past decade. *Lucretia as the Sense of Touch* entered The Pierpont Morgan Library in 1974 (Acc. No. 1974.5; *Rubens and Rembrandt*, 1979–80, no. 38, repr.), and *The Sense of Taste* was sold at Sotheby Mak van Waay, Amsterdam, 15 November 1983, lot 248. The present drawing and *The Sense of Hearing* surfaced together at a Belgian auction in 1984. The latter is now in a private collection in Belgium.

Like the other studies in the group, the Thaw drawing depicts the artfully posed figure against the foliage and trunk of a nearby tree. A dog, whose olefactory acuity makes him the perfect embodiment of Smell, sits at her side, his nose attracted to a flower that protrudes from her drapery. The woman, too, inhales the fragrance of a blossom presumably taken from the elegant, lobate-style metal bowl she balances on the bank at the right. Both the attendant dog and the act of sniffing a flower figure in many sixteenth- and seventeenth-century Netherlandish allegories of the Sense of Smell, including three prints by or after Goltzius that belong to series of the Senses designed ca. 1578, ca. 1586, and ca. 1595–96 (see Reznicek, I, nos. 169, 177, II, figs. 307, 61; and Walter L. Strauss, ed., *Hendrik Goltzius, Complete Engravings, Etchings, Woodcuts*, New York, 1977, I, no. 34, repr.).

Reznicek dated the Fitzwilliam sheet around 1600 on the basis of its relatively realistic representation of the body and its free, painterly execution, and his observations remain valid for the rest of the drawings in the series. The dog in the Thaw study—a Drente setter that was probably the artist's pet—appears in several works by Goltzius, among them another drawing of the Sense of Smell and the engraving after it (Reznicek, I, nos. 11, 169, 412–15, II, figs. 295–300, 307, 345; and Strauss, II, no. 344). As these other works are all ca. 1595/96–ca. 1600, the animal's presence here corroborates the date Reznicek assigned to the related Fitzwilliam work.

The drapery study on the verso, if by Goltzius, would be unique in his *oeuvre*. However, its soft modeling and delicate light suggest that it is not by him but by a later seventeenth-century Dutch draughtsman.

PROVENANCE: Private collection, Belgium; sale, Brussels, Galerie Moderne, August 1984 (according to Brigitte Geerincx); Brigitte Geerincx, Brussels, 1984.

JACOB JORDAENS

ANTWERP 1593 – 1678 ANTWERP

5 *Mother and Child*

Black and red chalk, gray wash, heightened with white chalk. 6$\frac{13}{16}$ × 8$\frac{1}{8}$ inches (176×205 mm.). Watermark: none. Inscribed at upper right, in black chalk, *dichten bij de . . .*

Jordaens adapted this attractive study for his painting *The King Drinks*, ca. 1638–40, now in the Louvre (R. A. d'Hulst, *Jacob Jordaens*, Ithaca, New York, 1982, p. 179 and pl. 139). There, the woman and her daughter are seated at a table, celebrating the Feast of the Epiphany with six other merrymakers. The traditional Epiphany meal began with a cake, baked with a single bean concealed in it, and the reveller whose portion contained the bean was crowned king and exercised the privilege of drinking the first glass.

Jordaens changed the direction of the woman's glance in the painting, so both mother and child look to the left, where the elderly Bean King takes a draught. In addition, he dressed the woman in the Louvre canvas in a fancy costume, which includes earrings, a feathered hat, a pearl choker, and a diaphanous *fichu* over her *décolletage*. Not indicated in the study is a man in a jester's garb who leans over her right shoulder, rests a hand on her left shoulder and smiles at the viewer. The girl also wears a pearl necklace in the picture, details of her dress differ slightly from the drawing, and a pewter tankard on the table obscures her left hand and shoulder, but her facial expression and the position of her head are reproduced as they appear in the study. The object she holds is her piece of the festival cake. In the painting a bite has been taken from it.

During the period ca. 1628–41 Jordaens designed many of his most original and characteristic compositions, including genre scenes such as *The King Drinks*, of which he produced several variants. Before executing these works in oils, he often drew studies of the principal figures from life. Like the Thaw sheet, many of them are in red and black chalk with white heightening, a technique he learned from Rubens. Jordaens occasionally used members of his household as models, and it is likely that the drawing depicts his wife Catharina van Noort (born 1589) and their daughter Anna Catharina (born 1629). A study for the head of the old woman seated to the right of the girl in the painting, also in black and red chalk heightened with white, is preserved in Copenhagen (d'Hulst, 1974, cat. no. 160).

Although Jordaens sometimes inscribed Biblical passages on his drawings of religious subjects and proverbs on his genre studies, he rarely wrote color notes or other directions to assist him in the execution of the projected painting. The drawing exhibited here may be an exception. D'Hulst read the inscription tentatively as *de groen bij de rood* (the green next to the red), but it certainly begins with the word *dichten*, which means to fill or stop up. Perhaps the note indicated how in the painting Jordaens planned to fill in the area beside or behind the figures, where there is empty space in the study.

PROVENANCE: Emile Wauters, Paris (Lugt 911 and 912); his sale, Amsterdam, Frederick Muller, 15–16 June 1929, lot 89, repr.; Paul Cassirer, Berlin; Otto Wertheimer, Paris and Zurich.

BIBLIOGRAPHY: R. A. d'Hulst, *De Tekeningen van Jacob Jordaens*, Brussels, 1956, pp. 192, 244, 350, cat. no. 75, fig. 123; National Gallery of Canada, Ottawa, *Jacob Jordaens*, catalogue by Michael Jaffé, 1968–69, p. 108, under no. 64; D'Hulst, *Jordaens Drawings*, London-New York, 1974, p. 222, no. A130, fig. 143.

EXHIBITION: Brussels, *Exposition d'Art Ancien, L'Art Belge au XVIIe Siècle*, 1910, no. 60.

CLAUDE GELLÉE, called CLAUDE LORRAIN
CHAMAGNE near MIRECOURT 1600 – 1682 ROME

6 *Heroic Landscape*

Black chalk, pen and brown ink, brown, gray and some blue wash. Verso: Landscape with a coastal town in the distance in black chalk. 10 1/16 × 15 11/16 inches (254 × 396 mm.). Watermark: fragment of *tête de boeuf*.

Claude apparently drew this poetic landscape *en plein air* in black chalk, later strengthening it in his studio with pen and wash. While it is clearly one of the artist's most beautiful nature studies, its composition is strikingly close to that of *The Journey to Emmaus*, which Claude painted in 1652, known today only from the artist's record drawing in the *Liber Veritatis* (see Roethlisberger, *Claude Lorrain, The Paintings*, New Haven, 1961, LV 125, repr.). The framing trees of the foreground as well as the view of the distant castle or fortified city correspond well to these same elements in the copy of the painting in the *Liber Veritatis*. Only the figures of Christ and the Apostles are not indicated in the drawing.

However, two drawings for this figure group survive, one of which is in the Thaw collection (Morgan Library, Thaw exhibition, 1975–76, no. 20, repr.). The other drawing was in the same album as the Thaw landscape, following it in the original sequence.

This album, best known as the Wildenstein Album, has been studied in detail by Marcel Roethlisberger since its purchase by Georges Wildenstein in 1960. Because of the exceptional beauty of its contents, which range over the entire span of Claude's working career, it is supposed that the artist himself selected and arranged the drawings in the album as an anthology of his best work for Queen Christina of Sweden. It would then have passed to her heir, Cardinal Decio Azzolini, whom Christina predeceased by only a few months. It was subsequently purchased by Livio Odescalchi, Duke of Bracciano, in whose family it remained for many years. In addition to the consistently high quality of these drawings, they are remarkably fresh, owing to their preservation for almost three centuries in album format; unlike most of Claude's drawings, they had not been exhibited and exposed to light until quite recently. This drawing was one of the three largest drawings contained in the album, which was originally supposed to contain sixty drawings, including twenty-four nature studies, twenty-one composition drawings, and fifteen figure drawings. Subsequent to its early publication, it has come to light that eight drawings were detached from the album by Hans Calmann in 1957/58, and that another thirteen drawings were retained by the Odescalchi family until the mid-1970s, making a total of eighty-one. This figure corresponds exactly to the number in the 1713 Odescalchi inventory, as well as the number "81" which is at the top of the first page of the album. In 1959 the Morgan Library acquired one of the eight sheets from Hans Calmann, *Alexander Refusing the Waters* (Acc. No. 1959.9).

The sketch on the verso was apparently not used by the artist in any known composition.

PROVENANCE: Queen Christina of Sweden(?) (1629–1689), in Rome from 1655 to 1689; Cardinal Decio Azzolini(?) (1623–1689), Rome; Don Livio Odescalchi, Duke of Bracciano (1652–1713), Rome; by descent; Georges Wildenstein, Paris, 1960; Norton Simon, Pasadena, 1968.

BIBLIOGRAPHY: Marcel Roethlisberger, *L'Album Wildenstein*, Paris, 1962, pp. 6, 7, no. 35, repr. in color; Roethlisberger, "Claude Lorrain: ses plus beaux dessins retrouvés," *Connaissance des Arts*, 1962, pp. 144, 147, no. 7, repr.; Roethlisberger, *Claude Lorrain: The Drawings*, Berkeley and Los Angeles, 1968, no. 709, repr.; Roethlisberger, *The Claude Lorrain Album in the Norton Simon, Inc. Museum of Art*, Los Angeles, 1971, p. 7, no. 34, pl. 34 in color, verso repr. pl. 62.

EXHIBITION: National Gallery of Art, Washington, D.C. and Grand Palais, Paris, *Claude Lorrain 1600–1682*, catalogue by H. Diane Russell, 1982–83, D 47, repr.

REMBRANDT VAN RIJN

LEIDEN 1606 – 1669 AMSTERDAM

7 *The Rest on the Flight into Egypt*

Reed pen and quill pen in brown-black ink, smudged in places with the finger. 6 13/16 × 9 3/16 inches (173 × 234 mm.). Watermark: illegible (eagle?). Inscribed at upper right, in graphite, *12*; on verso, at lower left, in graphite, *18*, and at lower center, *313*.

The largest category of Rembrandt's drawings—about one-third of those known today—consists of independent studies of Biblical and other historical subjects. Like *The Rest on the Flight into*

Egypt, many of them are fully resolved compositions. Rembrandt sketched and resketched the familiar—and occasionally unfamiliar—themes in order to gain proficiency in composition, to improve his ability to represent emotion through gestures, facial expression, and the manipulation of light, and to study the appropriate costumes and ambience for the historical event. Nearly all these drawings were made for practice. They were not intended for sale, and only a small number of them served as preparatory studies for paintings or prints. In the Thaw sheet he concentrated particularly on the placement of the Holy Family, the disposition of light and shadow around them, and the poetic harmony between the reposing figures, the grazing mule, and the grand, yet idyllic, landscape.

Scholars agree on dating *The Rest on the Flight into Egypt* ca. 1655. During the first half of the 1650s Rembrandt produced his most realistic and evocative sketches of the Dutch countryside. However, in several studies of Biblical themes in outdoor settings, which he composed in the workshop, he adapted the landscape backgrounds not from nature but from sixteenth-century Venetian drawings and prints. While the Thaw work clearly betrays the influence of Titian and Domenico Campagnola, the example of the Venetian masters has been translated into Rembrandt's broad, impetuous drawing style and transformed to suit his vision of the historical landscape. Included in this vision is a distant city that recalls Jerusalem as it was commonly represented in Western art.

Rembrandt depicted the Rest on the Flight in five securely attributed works, of which the Thaw sheet is the latest in date and the sole authentic drawing. In the etchings Bartsch 57–59, the figures of Mary and Joseph dominate the summarily described outdoor setting. Only in the Thaw drawing and the painting of 1647, a night piece based loosely on Adam Elsheimer's famous picture (Abraham Bredius and Horst Gerson, *Rembrandt, The Complete Edition of the Paintings*, London, 1969, no. 576), does landscape play a major role.

PROVENANCE: Sir Joshua Reynolds (Lugt 2364); Rodolphe Kann, Paris; Dr. A. Hamilton Rice, New York; Louis H. Silver, Chicago; Norton Simon Foundation, Fullerton, California.

BIBLIOGRAPHY: Wilhelm R. Valentiner, *Die Handzeichnungen Rembrandts*, New York, 1925, I, no. 343, repr.; Otto Benesch, *Rembrandt, Werk und Forschung*, Vienna, 1935, p. 55; Benesch, *The Drawings of Rembrandt*, London, 1954–57, V, no. 965, fig. 1179; Kenneth Clark, *Rembrandt and the Italian Renaissance*, London, 1966, p. 113, fig. 102; Benesch, *The Drawings of Rembrandt*, 2nd ed., London, 1973, V, no. 965, fig. 1248; Marianne Bernhard, *Rembrandt Handzeichnungen*, Munich, 1976, p. 515, repr.

EXHIBITION: The Art Institute of Chicago, Chicago and elsewhere, *Rembrandt after Three Hundred Years*, catalogue by J. Richard Judson, Egbert Haverkamp-Begemann, and Anne-Marie Logan, 1969–70, no. 132, repr.

8 *Old Scholar at his Writing Table*

Reed pen and brown ink, smudged with the finger, some brown wash, corrections in white bodycolor. $5\frac{1}{8} \times 4\frac{3}{16}$ inches (129×105 mm.). Watermark: illegible fragment (repr. in *Rubens and Rembrandt*, 1979–80, watermark no. 57).

Between the middle of the 1650s and his death in 1669, Rembrandt made fewer drawings than he had during the first three decades of his career. His rare late sketches are distinguished by their unprecedented pictorial effects, which recall the broad, vigorous brushwork and luminous shadows of his paintings of the 1660s. In *Old Scholar at his Writing Table*, Rembrandt summarized the structure of the figure, the table, the chair, and the globe with thick strokes of the reed pen, but, when he smudged the ink with his finger and made corrections in white bodycolor, linear description gave way almost entirely to a painterly impression of the scene. Otto Benesch placed the Thaw work about 1661–62, comparing its style and technique with those of one of the studies for the *Syndics of the Cloth Drapers' Guild* of 1662 (Benesch, 1973, no. 1178).

A scholar writing at his desk is the subject of many works by Rembrandt and his followers, including genre scenes, commissioned portraits, and, with the appropriate attributes, portrait-like representations of saints. The stacks of heavy books, the globe, and the pen poised to record the next thought are constant features of these paintings, drawings, and prints. For examples of the various types, see: Werner Sumowski, *Gemälde der Rembrandt-Schüler*, Landau/Pfalz, 1983, I, nos. 62 and 127, and pp. 290 and 521; Sumowski, *Drawings of the Rembrandt School*, New York, 1979, I, no. 211x; Rembrandt's painting of 1634, Bredius, no. 432; and Rembrandt's etching *St. Jerome in a Dark Chamber*, Bartsch 105.

PROVENANCE: Friedrich August II of Saxony, Dresden (Lugt 971); A. & R. Ball, New York; L. V. Randall, Montreal; his sale, London, Sotheby's, 6 July 1967, no. 5, repr.; Eugene and Clare Thaw Charitable Trust.

BIBLIOGRAPHY: Cornelis Hofstede de Groot, *Die Handzeichnungen Rembrandts*, Haarlem, 1906, no. 305; Hans Wolfgang Singer, *Zeichnungen aus der Sammlung Friedrich August II . . .*, 1921, no. 46; Kurt Freise and Heinrich Wichmann, *Rembrandts Handzeichnungen, III: Staatliches Kupferstichkabinett und Sammlung Friedrich August II zu Dresden*, Parchim a. M., 1925, no. 113; Hans Hell, "Die späten Handzeichnungen Rembrandts, II," *Repertorium für Kunstwissenschaft*, 1930, LI, p. 127; Benesch, 1935, p. 67; Benesch, 1954–57, V, no. 1151, fig. 1373; Benesch, 1973, V, no. 1151, fig. 1447.

EXHIBITIONS: Wildenstein and Co., New York, *Rembrandt*, 1950, no. 39; Museum Boymans-van Beuningen, Rotterdam and Rijksmuseum, Amsterdam, *Rembrandt: Tekeningen*, 1956, no. 252; The Pierpont Morgan Library, New York and Fogg Art Museum, Harvard University, Cambridge, Massachusetts, *Rembrandt Drawings from American Collections*, catalogue by Felice Stampfle and Egbert Haverkamp-Begemann, 1960, no. 77, pl. 67; The Pierpont Morgan Library, New York and elsewhere, *Rubens and Rembrandt in their Century*, catalogue by Felice Stampfle, 1979–80, no. 78, repr.

JEAN-ANTOINE WATTEAU

VALENCIENNES 1684 – 1721 NOGENT-SUR-MARNE

9 *Study of a Young Man Seen from the Back and Another Study of his Right Arm*

Black, red and white chalk on light brown paper. 8 3/16×9 inches (208×227 mm.). Watermark: none visible through lining.

Watteau's sketch of an elegantly disposed young man seated on the ground epitomizes the artist's gift for drawing the human figure with effortless grace. The assured execution of this rapid life sketch is typical of the artist's work in the latter half of the second decade of the eighteenth century, and Margaret Morgan Grasselli, author of the most recent monographic study of Watteau's draughtsmanship, dates it 1717 by reason of its apparent relation to the painting *The Pleasures of the Ball,* in the Dulwich Picture Gallery. The young man's pose is repeated in a full composition study in Dresden (see *Watteau,* 1984–85, D 98, repr.). In the Dulwich picture, the artist modified the pose of this figure and employed the sketch of his right arm and shoulder, also on the Thaw sheet, for another young man who appears in the lower right *tête-à-tête* with a young woman toying with a fan.

The drawing has a distinguished provenance; its earliest known owner was the painter-connoisseur, Sir Thomas Lawrence (1769–1830). It passed from his collection into that of Miss James which was sold at Christie's in 1891. From English collections it returned to France where it remained for nearly a hundred years until its purchase by the Thaws in 1982. While it may be said that Watteau executed the drawing in the *trois crayons* technique, that is, in a combination of black, red, and white chalk, a method of drawing perfected by the artist, here he drew primarily in black chalk, with some work in red and much less in the white chalk. The slight darkening of the paper is a measure of the high regard it has been held in by its previous owners who must often have had it on view for their private enjoyment. Nonetheless, the work remains essentially fresh with all its chalk surfaces and accents in perfect equipoise. It was first exhibited publicly in 1984.

PROVENANCE: Sir Thomas Lawrence (Lugt 2445); Miss James; her sale, London, Christie's, 22–23 June 1891, lot 300; Camille Groult, Paris; his descendant, Pierre Bordeaux-Groult; sale, Paris, Palais Galliera, 30 March 1963, no. 17; Henri Farman; his sale, Paris, 15 March 1973, lot G; Otto Wertheimer, Paris and Zurich.

BIBLIOGRAPHY: Karl T. Parker and Jacques Mathey, *Watteau,* Paris, 1957, no. 641, repr.

EXHIBITION: National Gallery of Art, Washington, D.C., and elsewhere, *Watteau,* catalogue by Pierre Rosenberg and Margaret Morgan Grasselli, 1984–85, no. D 95, repr.

JEAN-BAPTISTE OUDRY

PARIS 1686 – 1755 BEAUVAIS

10 *The Rat and the Oyster*

Pen and point of brush and black ink, gray wash, heightened with white gouache, on blue paper. Full sheet: 12¼×10 5/16 inches (309×261 mm.). Design area: 9½×7 7/16 inches (239×189 mm.). Watermark: none. Signed and dated at lower right, in brush and black ink, *JB. Oudry / 1732*. Inscribed on verso, in pen and brown ink, *27.t.2*.

Between the years 1729 and 1734, Oudry completed a series of drawings for Jean de la Fontaine's *Fables choisies mises en vers*, 4 volumes, Paris, Desaint et Saillant, 1755–59; *The Rat and the Oyster* is preparatory for the engraving "Le Rat et l'Huitre," Fable CLI, no. IX, Book 8, vol. III. Originally bound together in two albums, probably after being engraved, the series consists of 276 drawings for the 245 fables, including a frontispiece designed by Oudry in 1752 for the printed edition. The first album is now in the possession of the British Rail Pension Fund; the second was dismembered and the drawings were sold individually.

The actual publication of the printed edition must be credited to the *amateur* Montenault. Opperman, however, surmises that Oudry himself probably intended to have this set of drawings engraved because of his systematic method of illustrating all the fables in order. Montenault bought the drawings from Oudry in 1751 and, at the end of that year, began to look for engravers, printers, typefounders, booksellers, and patrons for the publication. Charles-Nicolas Cochin, le fils (1715–1790), whom Montenault put in charge of the illustrations, redrew Oudry's original drawings in lead pencil in a more finished form. The Cochin drawings used by the engravers are also widely dispersed today. (For an extensive study of this complex project see Marquis de Girardin, 1913.)

The drawings for the *Fables* are all executed in pen and brush with wash and white gouache on blue paper. Several earlier authors, possibly misled by the spontaneous quality of Oudry's brush technique, mistakenly described these drawings as a series of chalk sketches. Oudry's summary handling of the details of the composition, seen in the boats, the trees, and the coastline, was presumably elaborated upon by Cochin in his rendering of the subject. The engraving, executed in reverse of the drawing, by Pierre-Quentin Chedel (1705–1763) for the Montenault edition, follows Oudry's original design very closely while supplying a fuller rendering of the above-mentioned details.

Oudry's drawing illustrates La Fontaine's fable about a rather dull rat who decides to leave his home to travel. Coming upon a group of appetizing oysters on a beach, one of whom is sunning himself, the rat sticks his head in the open shell and the oyster snaps shut his shell catching the rat's head. The fable ends with the moral:

> Cette Fable contient plus d'un enseignement.
> Nous y voyons premiérement,
> Que ceux qui n'ont du monde aucune expérience,
> Sont au moindres objets frappés d'étonnement;
> Et puis nous y pouvons apprendre
> Que tel est pris qui croyoit prendre.

PROVENANCE: Sold by the artist to Montenault (publisher of the 1755–59 edition of the *Fables*); the brothers de Bure, Paris; sale of J. J. de Bure, Paris, 1–18 December 1853, part of lot 344; Count Adolphe-Narcisse Thibaudeau; Félix Solar; his sale, Paris, 19 November – 8 December 1860, part of lot 627; Baron Isidore Taylor, Paris; Librairie Morgand et Fatout, Paris; Emile Péreire; Louis Olry-Roederer, Rheims; Rosenbach Company, New York; Raphael Esmerian, New York; his sale, Paris, Palais Galliera, 6 June 1973, part of lot 46; Claus Virch (Art Associates Partnership), Bermuda.

SELECTED BIBLIOGRAPHY (references are to the albums and not specifically to the Thaw sheet, except where noted): Jacques-Charles Brunet, *Manuel de libraire*, Paris, 1862, III, col. 753; *Bulletin de la librairie Morgand et Fatout*, no. 6 (January 1877), p. 482, no. 2904; Baron Roger de Portalis, *Les Dessinateurs d'illustrations au dix-huitième siècle*, Paris, 1877, II, pp. 483ff.; Dr. A. Després, *Les éditions illustrées des Fables de La Fontaine*, Paris, 1892; Henry Cohen, ed., *Guide de l'amateur de livres à gravure de XVIIIème siècle*, Paris, 1912, col. 548ff.; Jean Locquin, *Catalogue raisonné de l'oeuvre de Jean-Baptiste Oudry (1686–1755)*, 1912, pp. 152–53, no. 1099 (this drawing only); Marquis de Girardin, "L'édition des Fables de la Fontaine, dite d'Oudry," *Bulletin du Bibliophile*, 1913, p. 217ff.; Hal N. Opperman, *Jean-Baptiste Oudry*, New York, 1972 [1977], I, pp. 99–101, 128, and 143, II, 682–85 and 700, no. D386 (this drawing only). [For a full bibliography of the albums see: The Kimbell Art Museum, Fort Worth, *J.-B. Oudry, 1686–1755*, catalogue by Hal N. Opperman, 1983, p. 146.]

JEAN-HONORÉ FRAGONARD
GRASSE 1732 – 1806 PARIS

11 *Portrait of a Neapolitan Girl*

Brush and brown wash over slight traces of black chalk. 14 7/16 × 11 1/8 inches (367 × 282 mm.). Watermark: Van der Ley (*cf.* Churchill 321). Inscribed in pen and brown ink at lower right, *Naples 1774 – femme de / St.t Lucie.*

Ten years after his student days in Rome had passed, Fragonard returned to Italy with his friend and patron, Bergeret de Grancourt. In this instance the artist acted as guide for Bergeret, who had never before visited Italy. The two men set out in the autumn of 1773 and did not return to France until the summer of 1774. During the course of this extended trip, Fragonard made numerous on-the-spot drawings of the people and places they saw. This beautiful wash drawing of a young Neapolitan woman was executed in May of 1774 when they visited Naples. Eunice Williams has pointed out that Fragonard's inscription indicates that the drawing was made on the *passegiata di Santa Lucia*, a favorite gathering place on Sundays. Although it is not specifically mentioned in Bergeret's journal, Vincent, who visited them earlier in Rome, must have accompanied the two men to Naples for he also drew the same young woman in preparation for the painting, once owned by Bergeret, and now in the collection of Jacqueline and Matt Friedlander of Moultrie, Georgia (repr. in color in *The Rococo Age*, 1983, no. 35). The full details of the woman's distinctive Neapolitan costume can be fully appreciated in the painting. Since it was during the feast of Januarius, she wore her best clothes, a black velvet jacket and red skirt trimmed with much gold lace. Fragonard's portrait is a study of her head and shoulders, concentrating on her face. Charming as Vincent's portrait of her is, Fragonard's drawing—worked almost exclusively in brush and brown wash—captures something of the psychological presence of the sitter as well as her features and interesting clothes and is one of the most memorable drawings by the artist.

PROVENANCE: Antoine Marmontel (sale, Paris, Hôtel Drouot, 28 March 1868, no. 24); E. M. Hodgkins (sale, Paris, Galerie Georges Petit, 30 April 1914, no. 28); Mrs. C. I. Stralem, New York; her son, Mr. Donald S. Stralem; his wife, Mrs. Donald S. Stralem, New York.

BIBLIOGRAPHY: Roger de Portalis, *Fragonard, sa vie et son oeuvre*, Paris, 1889, p. 314; Regina Shoolman and Charles E. Slatkin, *Six Centuries of French Master Drawings in America*, New York, 1947, p. 92; Louis Réau, *Fragonard, sa vie et son oeuvre*, Brussels, 1956, p. 215; Alexandre Ananoff, *L'Oeuvre dessiné de Jean-Honoré Fragonard (1732–1806)*, Paris, 1961–70, I, no. 119, III, fig. 495; High Museum of Art, Atlanta, Georgia, *The Rococo Age*, exhibition catalogue by Eric M. Zafran, 1983, under no. 35, fig. III. 6.

EXHIBITIONS: Musée des Arts Décoratifs, Paris, *Exposition d'oeuvres de Jean-Honoré Fragonard*, 1921, no. 173; Jacques Seligmann, Paris, 1931, no. 64; Musée de l'Orangerie, Paris, *De Clouet à Matisse, dessins français des collections américaines*, 1958–59, no. 50, pl. 63; Museum Boymans-van Beuningen, Rotterdam, *Van Clouet tot Matisse*, 1958, no. 50, pl. 66; Metropolitan Museum of Art, New York, *French Drawings from American Collections, Clouet to Matisse*, 1959, no. 50; Royal Academy of Arts, London, *The Eighteenth Century*, 1968, no. 270; Metropolitan Museum of Art, New York, *French Drawings and Prints of the Eighteenth Century*, 1972, no. 20; Washington, Fragonard Exhibition, 1978–79, no. 33, repr.

SIX DRAWINGS FOR ARIOSTO'S *ORLANDO FURIOSO*

12 *Ruggiero and Alcina at the Bath (?) (VII, 31)*

Black chalk, brown wash. 15½×9½ inches (394×241 mm.). Watermark: Maltese cross within a circle surmounted by a crown.

During the 1770s and 80s, Fragonard produced a remarkable series of nearly 150 brush-and-wash drawings illustrating the epic poem *Orlando Furioso* written by Ariosto early in the sixteenth century. The epic utilized legends that had their origin in the distant past of the mediaeval period. But Ariosto's own period, the Italian Renaissance, was a time when his contemporaries were taken with a new vision of classical antiquity, an obsession with ancient culture which would persist through succeeding centuries. In Fragonard's time, however, the trend towards Romanticism was to invest the Middle Ages with much of the archaistic glamor which the Renaissance had bestowed on Greece and Rome. For the artist the chivalric tradition had assumed an aesthetic force that enabled him to depict Ariosto's scenes and characters with a conviction that is highly persuasive.

Although some of Fragonard's Ariosto drawings were dispersed during the nineteenth century—six of them are in the Louvre—the majority, or specifically 137 of them, came to the United States in 1923 when they were acquired *en bloc* by Dr. A. S. W. Rosenbach of Philadelphia. Nineteen of these found their way into other American collections, including those of John Nicholas Brown and Lessing J. Rosenwald. From 1947 until some were offered for sale in 1978, the remaining 118 drawings were in a private New York collection. In 1945 Fragonard's Ariosto illustrations were the subject of a book by Elizabeth Mongan, Philip Hofer, and Jean Seznec, which discussed them in relation to the artist's *oeuvre*, their place in the history of illustrations of *Orlando*, and their correlation with scene and character in the poem. According to the latest count by Gabriel Naughton, at least sixty-three of the Ariosto drawings are still in this country, including the six drawings acquired by Mr. and Mrs. Thaw in 1978.

Even though they have been studied carefully, it is not known to what practical purpose Fragonard prepared them. It is almost certain that the artist read the epic in the original Italian. He was fluent in the language and the illustrations correspond closely to the text. It has been remarked that Fragonard's verve and imaginative style are well suited to Ariosto's quick-witted and colorful poem with all its narrative sweep. Unlike most eighteenth-century drawings for book illustration, Fragonard's drawings are so rapid and spontaneous, it seems unlikely that in this state they could ever have been intended to serve as preparatory drawings for an engraver.

It is unfortunate that, given his natural flair for narrative illustration, very few of the artist's drawings for book illustration were ever utilized for this purpose. (His drawings for the *Contes de La Fontaine* and *Don Quixote*, likewise, were never realized in printed form.) Various factors, including the growing revolutionary climate and the lack of private patrons, probably contributed to his failure in this area. Also, around the same time that Fragonard was working on his Ariosto illustrations, Cochin was preparing the plates for the sumptuous Baskerville edition which was printed in Paris. For all of these reasons it seems probable that Fragonard lost interest in the project and the surviving drawings cover only about twenty-five of the forty-six cantos of the poem. In fact only the first third of the epic was illustrated extensively; the artist prepared just a few drawings for the remainder of the poem.

The six drawings shown here represent a wide range of mood and subject, from amusing and ebullient, to active or contemplative. Jean Seznec's work on identifying the subjects still stands today and has been used here. The subjects of only two of the six drawings are unclear and have identifications open to question. The first drawing is a case in point and has been tentatively identified as Alcina, the sorceress who embodies carnal desire, standing at Ruggiero's bath.

PROVENANCE: Hippolyte Walferdin (who probably purchased the complete set of the Ariosto drawings direct from the Fragonard family); his sale, Hôtel Drouot, Paris, 12–16 April 1880; Louis-Olry Roederer, Rheims; A. S. W. Rosenbach, Philadelphia; private collection, New York; Thos. Agnew & Sons Ltd., London.

BIBLIOGRAPHY: Roger de Portalis, *Les dessinateurs d'illustration au dix-huitième siècle*, Paris, 1877; Portalis, *Fragonard, sa vie et son oeuvre*, Paris, 1889, p. 311; Cohen and De Ricci, p. 97; Seymour de Ricci, *The Roederer Library of French Books*, Philadelphia, 1923, n.p.; Mongan, Hofer, and Seznec, 1945, pl. 34; Thos. Agnew & Sons Ltd., London, *Old Master Paintings and Drawings*, 1980 (not included in exhibition).

EXHIBITIONS: Thos. Agnew & Sons Ltd., London, *Fragonard Drawings for Orlando Furioso*, 1978, no. 9, repr. (*Ruggiero and Alcina at the Bath*?); Washington, Fragonard Exhibition, 1978–79 (discussed but not exhibited).

13 *With Logistilla's Guidance, Ruggiero Masters the Hippogryph (X, 67)*

Black chalk over brown wash. 15 3/8 × 10 3/16 inches (391 × 259 mm.). Watermark: letters R M.

Alcina's sister, Logistilla, who embodies Reason, instructs Ruggiero to ride the Hippogryph, a marvelous winged horse (see No. 12).

PROVENANCE: Same as No. 12.

BIBLIOGRAPHY: Mongan, Hofer, and Seznec, 1945, pl. 65.

EXHIBITION: Washington, Fragonard Exhibition, 1978–79, no. 65, repr.

14 *Ferrau and Orlando Part to Look for Angelica (XII, 55–56)*

Black chalk and gray-brown wash; lightly sketched framing line in black chalk. 17 5/16 × 11 5/16 inches (442 × 287 mm.). Watermark: letters illegible within a circle.

In this lightly sketched scene, Ferrau, the fiery Saracen who also loves Angelica, and Orlando gallop off in different directions in search of her (see No. 12).

PROVENANCE: Same as No. 12.

BIBLIOGRAPHY: Mongan, Hofer, and Seznec, 1945, pl. 88.

15 *After the Shipwreck, Isabella is Rowed to Shore (XXII, 17)*

Brown wash over black chalk; lightly sketched framing line in black chalk. 15 7/16 × 10 3/16 inches (390 × 258 mm.). Watermark: letters (illegible).

In the midst of a terrific storm at sea, Isabella, daughter of the king of Galicia, is rowed to safety in a shell-like barque (see No. 12).

PROVENANCE: Same as No. 12.

BIBLIOGRAPHY: Mongan, Hofer, and Seznec, 1945, pl. 92.

16 *Orlando Discovers the Names of Angelica and Medoro Carved in the Rock (XXIII, 107, 111)*

Brown wash over black chalk. 15¼×9⅞ inches (387×251 mm.). Watermark: letters R M.

When Orlando sees Angelica and Medoro's names carved in the rock, he goes mad with jealousy (see No. 12).

PROVENANCE: Same as No. 12.

BIBLIOGRAPHY: Mongan, Hofer, and Seznec, 1945, pl. 126.

17 *Bradamante Weeps upon Reading the Letter of Ruggiero (XXX, 78–80)* or *Astolfo Reads the Magic Book (XV, 13–14)*

Black chalk and gray-brown wash; lightly sketched framing line in black chalk. 17¼× 11 9/16 inches (438×292 mm.). Watermark: letters R M.

This scene has been identified as showing Bradamante, the girl warrior who is Rinaldo's sister, reading Ruggiero's letter, or alternately, Astolfo, son of the king of England, reading the magic book. Astolfo has many adventures including trips to the Inferno by Hippogryph and to the moon where he recovers Ruggiero's lost wits as well as his own (see No. 12).

PROVENANCE: Same as No. 12.

BIBLIOGRAPHY: Mongan, Hofer, and Seznec, 1945, pl. 132.

EXHIBITION: Washington, Fragonard Exhibition, 1978–79, no. 68, repr.

HUBERT ROBERT
PARIS 1733 – 1808 PARIS

18 *Roman View with Horsemen Passing through the Arch of Titus*

Red chalk. 14 11/16×19½ inches (371×496 mm.). Watermark: none visible through lining.

It is not certain what influences—taste and native ability aside—shaped Robert's interest in architectural painting. By the time he reached Rome in 1754 when he was twenty-one, his talents in this direction were clearly established. The depiction of architecture, especially antique monuments, was to become a lifelong preoccupation, earning him the epithet "*Robert des Ruines*" from his contemporaries. Thanks to the influence of the Marquis de Stainville, the young artist secured a place at the French Academy in Rome where he was to remain for eleven years. There is no doubt that the Director of the Academy, Charles-Joseph Natoire, a strong advocate of sketching directly from nature, as well as Giovanni Paolo Pannini, whose own reputation as a painter of classical ruins well-qualified him for his role as Professor of Perspective at the Academy, strongly influenced the young artist's development along these lines. Also, a good deal of interest in classical antiquity was being generated at this time by the recent excavations at Pompeii and Herculaneum. Although Robert visited many archaeological sites throughout Italy, as is well-documented by his work on the *Voyage pittoresque*, the celebrated travel book of the Abbé de Saint-Non, Rome itself was the center of his interest in antiquity.

The Roman Triumphal Arch was a very natural subject for artists. The Arch of Titus, on the Velia at the top of the Via Sacra looking through to the Forum or the Coliseum, was frequently depicted by them. It figures in several of Robert's works, notably a painting in the Uffizi, Florence. Although Robert often invented views of ruins, the arch of Titus actually appeared in the eighteenth century as it does in this drawing. This is well documented by the work of other contemporary artists such as Piranesi. Built by Domitian some time after 81 A.D. to commemorate the victory of Titus and Vespasian in the Judean War in 70 A.D., it was severely damaged in the succeeding centuries. Many of its stones were stolen and in the Middle Ages it was built into the structures of other buildings. When these buildings, which acted as a support for the arch, were destroyed, it fell into a state of greater dilapidation. Although near collapse, it was not until 1821 that its restoration was undertaken.

Since the Thaw drawing is sketchy, it is not clear which side Robert studied. Only one of the two side reliefs in the passage is indicated, and it is so summarily sketched that it is not possible to identify it either with the panel with Titus riding in the triumphal chariot or that of the panel showing the procession carrying the spoils of the Temple. The imperial eagle is centered in the coffered vault of the arch and the pairs of winged victories with wreaths in the spandrels of both façades are visible. There is, moreover, no distant view of the Coliseum or the Forum.

Three other drawings show different aspects of the arch. A view of the west side looking through to the Coliseum is in the Musée des Beaux-Arts in Valence (Marguerite Beau, *Dessins d'Hubert Robert*, 1968, no. 5, repr.). Robert sketched a similar view in the drawing now in the Musée Marmottan, Paris (see also Beau, no. 5d). The third drawing, which is now in the Wallraf-Richartz Museum, Cologne, shows a detail of the arch by moonlight. As the Thaw drawing corresponds most closely to the painting in the Uffizi, it may properly be considered a preliminary sketch. The two works have many points of comparison, but in the painting the artist moves the viewpoint sharply to the right.

PROVENANCE: Private collection, Massachusetts.

PIERRE-PAUL PRUD'HON
CLUNY 1758 – 1823 PARIS

19 *Portrait of Count Giovanni Battista Sommariva*

Black chalk, heightened with white, some stumping on blue paper; framing line in black chalk. Full sheet: 11 7/8 × 8 15/16 inches (301 × 225 mm.). Design area: 9 15/16 × 7 inches (249 × 178 mm.). Watermark: none visible through lining. Signed at left below design area, in black chalk, ***P.P. Prud'hon.***

This drawing is one of a series of preliminary studies for the painting *Portrait of Count Sommariva,* which was exhibited unfinished at the Salon of 1814 and is now in the Brera, Milan. In his catalogue of Prud'hon's work, Jean Guiffrey records eight preparatory drawings for this painting, including one portrait of the Count formerly in the Féral collection. In the Thaw sketch, Prud'hon does not attempt to elaborate on the details either of the figure or the landscape, and this lack of detail is most noticeable in the Count's face. Here Prud'hon concentrates on the pose of the count who is seen seated, full-face, his body turned to the right, and holding a book in his left hand, virtually the same position as in the painting. The use of white heightening in the drawing suggests that Prud'hon was also concerned with the disposition of light and shade. With the exception of the left side of the bench, the lighting of the Thaw sketch corresponds very closely to the finished painting.

Born in Milan, Giovanni Battista Sommariva (1760–1826) sided with the French when they invaded Italy in 1796. He was appointed secretary-general of the Cisalpine Republic in June of 1797. After the battle of Marengo, Napoleon appointed him to the new Directory of the Cisalpine Republic and, when it became the Italian Republic on 26 January 1802, Sommariva retired from public life and moved to Paris. There Count Sommariva made his fortune through speculation and actively supported the arts both as patron and collector. His collection included several important works by Prud'hon and is partly reunited today in his former home, now a museum, in the Villa Carlotta at Cadenabbia on Lake Como.

PROVENANCE: Camille Marcille; his sale, Paris, 6–7 March 1876, lot 130; Camille Groult; his sale, Paris, 21 March 1952, lot 49, repr. (under the title *Le Repos dans le Parc*); Galerie Cailleux, Paris, 1957; Benjamin Sonnenberg, New York; his sale, Sotheby's, New York, 5–9 June 1979, lot 24, repr.; Hirschl & Adler Galleries, Inc., New York.

BIBLIOGRAPHY: Edmond de Goncourt, *Catalogue raisonné de l'oeuvre de P.P. Prud'hon*, Paris, 1876, pp. 43 and 323; Jean Guiffrey, "L'Oeuvre de Pierre-Paul Prud'hon," *Archives de L'Art Français*, Nouvelle Période, 1924, XIII, no. 620, p. 235; Agnes Mongan, *Great Drawings of All Times*, New York, 1962, III, no. 713, repr.; Mahonri Sharp Young, "Treasures in Gramercy Park," *Apollo*, LXXXV, no. 61, 1967, p. 181.

EXHIBITIONS: Societé Archéologique d'Eure-et-Loire, Chartres, *Exposition Archéologique et d'objects d'Art*, 1858, no. 91; Ecole des Beaux-Arts, Paris, *Exposition des Oeuvres de Prud'hon*, 1874, no. 140; Paris, *Exposition Universelle de 1900*; Vassar College, Poughkeepsie, New York, and Wildenstein and Co., New York, *Centennial Loan Exhibition*, 1961, no. 75; The Pierpont Morgan Library, New York, *Artists and Writers: Nineteenth and Twentieth Century Portrait Drawings from the Collection of Benjamin Sonnenberg*, catalogue by Felice Stampfle and Cara Dufour, 1971, no. 2, repr.; The Royal Academy and the Victoria and Albert Museum, London, *The Age of Neo-Classicism*, 1972, no. 740.

LOUIS LÉOPOLD BOILLY
LA BASSÉE 1761 – 1845 PARIS

20 *Les Fiancés*

Black and white chalk, which has been moistened, on paper darkened to a light brown; black chalk *pentimenti* in the area of the woman's hair. Verso: Study of a seated woman nursing a child, in black chalk with slight touches of white. 9 7/16×6 5/8 inches (239×168 mm.). Watermark: none.

In 1785, after his schooling at Arras and Douai, Louis Léopold Boilly established himself in Paris where he produced paintings, drawings, and lithographs, specializing in portraits and genre scenes. He often painted events from the French Revolution, focusing only on the positive aspects of war. Between the years 1791 and 1824, Boilly participated in fourteen salons at the Louvre and, in the salon of 1808, he exhibited six paintings, including *La lecture du Bulletin de la Grande Armée* (present location unknown). An engraving after the painting is published in Roger Raymond Peyre's *Napoleon 1er et son temps*, Paris, Firmin-Didot, 1888. (We are grateful to Carol Eliel, who recently completed a dissertation on Boilly, for giving us this reference.) The Thaw sheet is one of several preparatory studies executed for this painting. A large compositional drawing, whose location is also unknown, is signed and dated 1806 and depicts a room filled with members of a large family with a group of men gathered around a table following the progress of the French imperial army on a map of Europe. The woman and young man in the Thaw sheet correspond to the standing woman and seated youth found on the right side of the large compositional study. In the latter work, however, the young man seated at the table avidly inspects the map while the woman is shown with her right arm around the young man's shoulder. The study on the verso of the Thaw sheet depicts a seated woman nursing; it, in turn, is preparatory for the woman on the left side of the large drawing, who nurses her baby by the fireside.

PROVENANCE: Artemis (David Carritt, Ltd.), London.

EXHIBITIONS: Rouen, *Exposition de l'art du XVIII siècle*, 1929, no. 74; Société des Amis du Musée Carnavalet, Paris, *Exposition L.-L. Boilly*, 1930, no. 146 (under the title *Étude de jeune femme et de jeune homme* and described as the portrait of the second wife of Houdon); Galerie Charpentier, Paris, *La vie familiale, scènes et portraits*, 1944, no. 17.

GIOVANNI BATTISTA TIEPOLO
VENICE 1696 – 1770 MADRID

21 *Caricature of a Sleeping Man*

Pen and black ink, gray wash. 6 1/16×8 15/16 inches (154×228 mm.). Watermark: trefoil surmounting [cut off].

Since the tradition of figural caricature drawing in Italy goes back as far as the seventeenth century, it is not surprising that the most accomplished draughtsman of his generation, Giovanni

Battista Tiepolo, occasionally drew these quick satirical studies for his own and others' diversion. It is assumed that he filled at least three volumes with single figure caricatures, an assumption based on the title of one of these albums, *Tomo Terzo di Caricature*, at one time in the collection of Arthur Kay of Glasgow. This volume, which was broken up and sold in ten lots at Christie's in 1943, consisted of 106 drawings, including the Thaw caricature.

As Byam Shaw has pointed out, Giambattista's son, Domenico, borrowed a number of these amusing figures, recycling them into large-scale drawings of genre subjects. This particular drawing of a sleeping man in a conical hat lent itself readily to the figure of Punchinello in Domenico's composition, *The Last Illness of Punchinello*, a drawing acquired a number of years ago by Mr. and Mrs. Thaw and included in the previous exhibition of their collection at the Library.

Domenico turned to the Punchinello series late in life, when he was comfortably off and no longer in demand as a history painter. Earlier he had decorated a room in the family villa at Zianigo with Punchinello subjects. For the series of drawings, he produced 102 compositions, now scattered in various public and private collections, recounting the adventures of the popular Commedia dell'Arte figure, and dedicating the series to children with the title, *Divertimento per li Regazzi*. Perhaps the most charming of all his drawings, the Punchinello subjects are also the most eagerly sought after by collectors. In 1971 an entire exhibition was devoted to these drawings (Indiana University Art Museum and elsewhere, *Domenico Tiepolo's Punchinello Drawings*, introduction by Adelheid M. Gealt, catalogue by Marcia E. Vetrocq).

Nearly twenty Punchinello drawings by the elder Tiepolo are known, including the foreshortened recumbent figure of a *Drunken Punchinello* owned by Mr. and Mrs. Thaw (Morgan Library, Thaw exhibition, 1975–76, no. 48, repr.). Tiepolo has always held a special interest for New York collectors; the Thaws exhibited nine drawings by Giambattista in the previous show as well as seven by Domenico.

PROVENANCE: Arthur Kay, Glasgow; his sale, London, Christie's, 8–9 April 1943, part of lot 246; art market, Rome.

BIBLIOGRAPHY: J. Byam Shaw, *The Drawings of Domenico Tiepolo*, London, 1962, p. 49; Morgan Library, Thaw exhibition, 1975–76, under no. 63.

EXHIBITION: Arcade Gallery, Ltd., London, *Giovanni Battista Tiepolo, Twenty-Five Caricatures*, introduction by Osbert Lancaster, 1943, pl. 25.

FRANCESCO GUARDI

VENICE 1712 – 1793 VENICE

22 *View of Lévico in the Valsugana*

Pen and brown and black ink, brown wash, over black chalk; vertical crease at center. Verso: Landscape with castellated town wall at left, country villa, hills beyond and poplar grove at right, in pen and brown ink and brown wash over black chalk. 16 13/16 × 25 inches (426 × 635 mm.). Watermarks: letters PS; triple crescent (*cf.* Heawood 873); letters BEA.

Inscribed by the artist in pen and brown ink at lower left, *Levego verso il Borgo ci Valsugana, dove la Brenta nazze*; illegible inscription in black chalk at lower right.

Despite the magical effects of light and atmosphere, most of Guardi's later landscapes are studio inventions, composed from real and imaginary elements remembered or borrowed from earlier compositions. This large airy view is one of the rare exceptions. Drawn from nature when Guardi journeyed to his family home northwest of Venice in the Val di Sole in the Trentino in 1778, the artist lingered over the work and annotated the finished drawing with an inscription precisely identifying the site. An infrequent traveller, Guardi must have been especially struck by the fresh beauty of this small village with its attractive architecture so typical of the region. He chose a large sheet for the drawing and his flickering penline delineated the chief landmarks of the village to dazzling effect. These include the main thoroughfare, church, and all viewed at some distance through the baroque village gate. In the background an imposing mountain range rises beyond the village.

Lévico, located at a mid-range altitude in the Dolomites, is a health resort, known today, as it was in Guardi's time, for its mineral springs. This drawing is one of six landscapes of this sort known to exist; two others depicting Borgo di Valsugana must have been made at the same time (Morassi, figs. 416, 417). One, a view of the center of the town, was last recorded in the collection of Jean Dubois in Paris, and the other, a distant view of Borgo, which is identified in an inscription by John Strange, a contemporary English visitor to Venice: *View of Borgo di Valsugana with the Castle Giovanelli, and neighboring mountains between Bassano and Trento*, is in the collection of J. Byam Shaw, the distinguished connoisseur and author of a Guardi monograph.

PROVENANCE: Marius Paulme (Lugt 1910); sale, Paris, Galerie Georges Petit, 13 May 1929, lot 101, pl. 69; Mrs. C. I. Stralem, New York; Mr. and Mrs. Donald S. Stralem, New York.

BIBLIOGRAPHY: Karl Erdmann, "Zwei neue Historien-Bilder von Francesco Guardi," *Pantheon*, 1929, pp. 506–10; Rodolfo Pallucchini, *I disegni del Guardi al Museo Correr di Venezia*, Venice, 1943, p. 49; Otto Benesch, *Venetian Drawings of the Eighteenth Century in America*, New York, 1947, no. 66, repr.; J. Byam Shaw, *The Drawings of Francesco Guardi*, London, 1951, pp. 35, 43, 65–66; Fondazione Giorgio Cini, Venice, *Canaletto e Guardi*, exhibition catalogue by Karl T. Parker and J. Byam Shaw, 1962 (mentioned on p. 78); Terisio Pignatti, *I Disegni veneziani del Settecento*, [Milan], n. d., no. 135; Pignatti, *Disegni dei Guardi*, Florence, 1967, no. xxiv, repr.; Antonio Morassi, *Guardi: Tutti i Disegni di Antonio, Francesco e Giacomo Guardi*, Venice, 1975, no. 418, fig. 419.

EXHIBITIONS: Albright Art Gallery, Buffalo, *Master Drawings Selected from Museums and Private Collections of America*, 1935, no. 72, repr.; Museum of Fine Arts, Springfield, Mass., *Francesco Guardi, 1712–1793*, 1937, in addendum to catalogue, no catalogue number; Museum of Fine Arts, Boston, *A Thousand Years of Landscape East and West*, 1945, p. 9; Palazzo Grassi, Venice, *Mostra dei Guardi*, 1965, no. 46, repr. (recto and verso); Metropolitan Museum of Art, New York, *Drawings from New York Collections III: The Eighteenth Century in Italy*, catalogue by Jacob Bean and Felice Stampfle, 1971, no. 208, repr.

GIOVANNI BATTISTA PIRANESI

MOGLIANO, VENETO 1720 – 1778 ROME

23 *A Seated Man Holding a Drawing Board*

Pen and brown ink, some red and black chalk; extraneous marks in graphite. Verso: Slight sketch of a corner of a pediment in red chalk. 11 9/16 × 8 3/16 inches (293 × 206 mm.). Watermark: none. Illegible inscription [cut off] by the artist at left, in red chalk; computations in black chalk; inscribed at lower right, in graphite, *Guardi*.

This large-scale figure drawing is most probably one of Piranesi's latest figure studies, made on the spot as the architectural sketch on the verso seems to suggest, when he was visiting Pompeii or Herculaneum or some other archaeological site in the mid-1770s.

To date no one has added significantly to Hylton Thomas' perceptive discussion of the purpose and source of these peculiarly effective figure studies (Hylton Thomas, *The Drawings of Piranesi*, New York, 1962, pp. 25ff.). Since the drawings are always rapidly executed, it is often difficult to decipher individual features, and some distortion is evident in the artist's rush to capture the unusual gesture and an overall sense of movement. It is clear from the idiosyncratically broad handling of the chalk or pen in these drawings that Piranesi was not so much interested in figure drawing *per se* as he was in conveying the figure in motion. Like Watteau, he would fill his page with unrelated figure studies, building up a repertory of figural motifs and poses which he could later deploy in large-scale compositions.

The late figure drawings are generally larger and coarser in their outlines. The seated man's cap and cloak suggest that Piranesi sketched him—most probably one of his shop assistants or artist companions—outdoors, while gathering material for another series of prints. This man may be identical with another, similarly attired, in a drawing formerly on the London art market (Thomas, *ibid.*, no. 78, repr.).

PROVENANCE: Unidentified collector, mark RC interfaced; Dr. and Mrs. Francis Springell, Keswick, Cumberland; his sale, London, Sotheby's, 28 June 1962, lot 43, repr.; private collection, London; Artemis Fine Arts Ltd., London.

EXHIBITION: P. & D. Colnaghi, London, *Drawings by Old Masters from the Collection of Dr. and Mrs. Francis Springell*, 1959, no. 34.

GIOVANNI DOMENICO TIEPOLO

VENICE 1727 – 1804 VENICE

24 *Scene of Contemporary Life: The Picture Show*

Pen and brown and black ink, gray wash, over some black chalk. 11 5/16 × 16 5/16 inches (287 × 415 mm.). Watermark: graduated triple crescents and letters SOTO IMPERIAL (*cf.* Heawood 867). Signed and dated by the artist in pen and black ink on titulus affixed to column, *Dom.o Tiepol* [cut off] / [illegible] / [illegible] / *1791*.

In 1757 when he was thirty, Domenico Tiepolo decorated the family villa at Zianigo with frescoed genre scenes revealing a taste for the often amusing details of modern life. It was not, however, until the latter part of his life—when he was able to devote himself almost exclusively to drawing—that he drew the Punchinello series and the Scenes of Contemporary Life. Some of Domenico's most appealing work can be found in these picturesque drawings in which he emerges as an innovator in his own right as distinct from his father, Giambattista, who specialized in grand historical subjects.

Although he drew over a hundred Punchinello subjects, he prepared only around twenty of these genre drawings, all signed and dated 1791. Byam Shaw has distinguished three types of subjects within this group: those depicting country scenes with peasants or gypsies, views of the ordinary but colorful daily life of Venice, as well as representations of the life style of the aristocracy. In these drawings Domenico presents modern life in a witty and often satiric vein.

Here, an itinerant showman or connoisseur of sorts, whose versatility is suggested by the guitar slung over his shoulder, appears to be holding forth while standing on a chair, pointer in hand, to a respectful throng on the subject of a print or drawing mounted on the wall before him. It is not clear what his intention is; the presence of the basket alongside him filled with bits of paper suggests receipts for sales or subscriptions.

As has been noted earlier, Domenico frequently borrowed motifs from his father. For this composition he took the reflective pipe-smoking gentleman from one of his father's volumes of caricature drawings (repr. in *Giovanni Battista Tiepolo: Twenty-Five Caricatures*, Arcade Galleries, Ltd., London [1943], no. 3), adding some fashionable stripes to his otherwise plain coat and placing him at the extreme right of the row of spectators.

At one time most of these drawings were contained in an album owned by Alfred Beurdeley which was purchased *en bloc* by Adrien Fauchier-Magnan in 1920. The album was broken up and the drawings sold in various auctions in Paris and London in 1967. *The Picture Show* and three other contemporary life subjects were in the same sale in Paris. A number of drawings from the Beurdeley album are now in New York collections including *A Visit to the Lawyer* and *At the Dressmaker's* which the Morgan Library acquired in London.

PROVENANCE: Alfred Beurdeley; his sale, Paris, Rahir, 31 May 1920, part of an album of 19; Adrien Fauchier-Magnan, Paris; sale, Paris, Palais Galliera, 12 June 1967, lot 159, repr.; Norton Simon, Pasadena.

BIBLIOGRAPHY: Henry de Chennevières, *Les Tiepolos*, Paris, 1898, p. 133; J. Byam Shaw, *The Drawings of Domenico Tiepolo*, London, 1962, for general discussion of the drawings of contemporary life, pp. 46ff.

ALEXANDER COZENS
RUSSIA ca. 1717 – 1786 LONDON

25 *A River between Hills*

Brush and black ink on paper prepared with an orange-brown wash. 9$\frac{1}{16}$×11$\frac{7}{8}$ inches (230×302 mm.). Watermark: horn within a shield surmounted by a crown, with letters C (?) R below (similar to Heawood 2752–58). Signed beneath lower left edge of drawing presumably on the artist's mount, in the same gray ink as the framing lines, *Alex.r Cozens*, and in graphite at upper center, *10*.

Alexander Cozens was born in Russia of English parents who were in the employ of Czar Peter the Great. Although he spent nearly a year in Rome in 1746, Cozens lived in London almost all of his adult life. He was one of the few English eighteenth-century artists who were also professional teachers, and he taught, among others, Sir George Beaumont and Lord Aylesford, later two of the foremost amateur draughtsmen and collectors of their time, the young princes William and Edward, and his own son, John Robert.

Cozens was one of the principal theorists of the period and developed a series of "systems" to aid in landscape composition, some of which he published. His most important treatise appeared in 1785 and was entitled *A New Method of assisting the Invention in Drawing Original Compositions of Landscape*. The work includes sixteen aquatints of "blots," i.e., rapid and freely-brushed strokes, often done on a piece of crumpled paper, resulting in irregular shapes that could be developed into landscapes. Cozens traced the blots onto other sheets of paper from which he created actual drawings. "The blot is not a drawing, but an assemblage of accidental shapes from which a drawing may be made" (*New Method*, p. 8; republished in Oppé, 1952, p. 170). Blots should not be compared to the spontaneous creations of artists of the twentieth century such as the Dadaists; Cozens always stressed that the artist or student needed to have a concept or idea in mind of what the composition was to be. The building of form by mass and tone, and not by line, eliminated details, though the final work produced from a blot had the added concreteness of line.

This moody drawing of a winding river was developed from blot number 10 published in *New Method*, where it is described as "A track, proceeding forward from the eye, bounded by groups of objects." The sheet is typical of Cozens' work. His interest, as Oppé has said (p. 105), was in "light and shade." Like other theorists of the ideal landscape, such as Thomas Gainsborough, who worked in black and white chalks on blue or gray paper, and William Gilpin who worked in gray or brown wash with pen, Cozens used a characteristically restrictive but warm range of color of black or brown wash on yellow, buff, or light-brown prepared paper.

It is difficult to date Cozens' works, with the exception of some drawings done between 1763 and 1768. He used a basic formula for much of his life, and it is not entirely clear when he evolved the system from which many of his drawings grew. Cozens wrote that he had discovered blots late in life, but at least one modern scholar does not think it plausible (Wilton, p. 8). However, it can be said that the qualities of settlement, balance, and conclusiveness evinced in the Thaw drawing belong to his later years. Similar in feeling are some mountain landscapes in the Paul Mellon Collection, Yale Center for British Art, New Haven (Wilton, p. 30).

Cozens was largely unknown until the early twentieth century, though his son John Robert has continuously enjoyed a high reputation. Both father and son are important in understanding the development of English landscape painting—they are the indispensible forerunners of such painters as Constable, Girtin, and Turner.

PROVENANCE: Herbert Horne; Carfax Gallery, London; acquired by Sir Edward Marsh ca. 1903; Hugh L. Agnew; Thos. Agnew & Sons Ltd., London.

BIBLIOGRAPHY: For general information on Cozens see: A. P. Oppé, *Alexander & John Robert Cozens*, London, 1952; Yale Center for British Art, New Haven, *The Art of Alexander and John Robert Cozens*, exhibition catalogue by Andrew Wilton, 1980.

EXHIBITIONS: Burlington Fine Arts Club, London, *Exhibition of the Herbert Horne Collection of Drawings with special reference to the works of Alexander Cozens*, 1916, no. 38; Graves Art Gallery, Sheffield, and Tate Gallery, London, *Drawings and Paintings by Alexander Cozens*, catalogue by A. P. Oppé, 1946–47, no. 41.

THOMAS GAINSBOROUGH
SUDBURY 1727 – 1788 LONDON

26 *Coastal Scene with Shipping, Figures, and Cows*

Brush and black and gray wash, traces of black chalk and stumping; highlights in wetted white chalk; incidental spottings of brown ink; light brown staining throughout. 11¼ × 14 9/16 inches (282 × 370 mm.). Watermark: Strasbourg bend and lily (*cf.* Churchill 433).

"I am sick of portraits," said Thomas Gainsborough. "I wish very much to take my viol-da-gamba and walk off to some sweet village, where I can paint landskips and enjoy the fag end of life in quietness and ease" (Woodall, p. 1). While Gainsborough is now known both for his portrait paintings and his landscapes, the latter were not popular during his lifetime. Most English landscapes and watercolors of the eighteenth century were connected in some way with topographical views, but Gainsborough's were not. Though he sketched from nature, and never wholly abandoned that practice, he was an interpreter of nature, and his landscapes are, to a large degree, imaginative.

Among his landscape drawings, those of coastal scenes are rare. The Thaw sheet is one of several he made in the early 1780s, in the loose brush work of his later years. In the *Coastal Scene*, the forms of the boats, the rocks, the cows, and the people are suggested rather than described in detail. The white chalk has been applied with seeming haste, but so skilled was Gainsborough that the result are works of shimmering light and atmosphere.

Gainsborough's technical mastery was astonishing, and there is perhaps no other English painter or draughtsman except for Turner who possessed such remarkable natural gifts (John Hayes and Lindsay Stainton, *Gainsborough Drawings*, Washington, D.C., 1983, p. 8). His use of wash is impeccable, his highlights are brilliant, and his line is expressive and can suggest form rather than delineate it. Though Gainsborough drew to relax from the tensions involved in his career as a society portraitist, drawing was also a compulsive activity, so much so that he suffered at times from nervous fatigue and sleeplessness as a result of the teeming images in his brain.

Perhaps a manifestation of this need to draw was that he actually drew most of his landscapes indoors, sometimes with rather fanciful results. It is recorded by more than one person that he would compose landscape "views" in his study, setting up broken stones, dried herbs, coal, cork, pieces of looking-glass, even broccoli, to create his scenes of rocks, bushes and trees, and pools of water (Hayes, 1970, p. 33). In the Thaw coastal scene, the imaginative element is seen in the combination of the various figural elements: the two people on the rock at the left, one throwing a stone; the men in the rowboat, the sailboats in the distance, and an old favorite, the cows. Nonetheless, they all work together to create a mood of peaceful calm. But there is perhaps an element of melancholy. One gets a sense, when studying the *oeuvre* of Gainsborough, that it was only in his drawings that he achieved the peace that was denied him by the pressures of his life and temperament.

Unlike Joshua Reynolds and many other English artists, Gainsborough was not a connoisseur. He did not buy drawings or paintings except as they related to his own painting style at the moment. But his own drawings, of which there must have been many more than the nearly 950 catalogued by John Hayes, have been collected ever since his death.

PROVENANCE: Earl Spencer (Lugt S. 2341a); by descent; Thos. Agnew & Sons Ltd., London; Robert Smith, Washington, D.C.; David Carritt, Ltd., London.

BIBLIOGRAPHY: Mary Woodall, *Gainsborough's Landscape Drawings*, London, 1939, no. 299; John Hayes, *The Drawings of Thomas Gainsborough*, London, 1970, I, p. 221, no. 489, II, pl. 154; *A Dealer's Record, Agnew's 1967–81*, London, 1981, repr. p. 167.

EXHIBITIONS: Arts Club, Oxford, *Drawings by Thomas Gainsborough*, 1935, no. 15; Sir Philip Sassoon, London, *Gainsborough*, 1936, no. 67; Arts Council, York and elsewhere, *Gainsborough Drawings*, 1960–1961, no. 39; Victoria and Albert Museum, London, *Treasures from Althorp*, 1970, no. 19.

HENRY FUSELI
ZURICH 1741 – 1825 LONDON

27 *Britomart Frees Amoret from the Enchanter Busirane*

Pen and brush and brown ink, black chalk, over graphite. Verso: A figure being lowered into a grave (?), in brown and some white oil paint. $16\frac{5}{8} \times 13\frac{15}{16}$ inches (422×354 mm.). Watermark: none.

Born and educated in Switzerland, Fuseli traveled to London in 1764 at the age of twenty-three, where, with the exception of eight important years of study in Rome, he remained for the rest of his career, returning to his native Zurich only once. He already knew the works of Homer, Dante, Milton, and Shakespeare through his studies with the influential Swiss critic Johann Jakob Bodmer, and he later used these writers for inspiration, often searching for unusual subject matter to be interpreted in his own dramatic, highly individual style. It is not certain whether Fuseli knew Spenser's *The Faerie Queene* in Switzerland, although it was inevitable that he would be introduced to the poem in England. Gert Schiff suggests that the passage Fuseli chose to represent in this drawing is probably from Book III, Canto XII, Stanzas XXX ff. of *The Faerie Queene*. In the poem, Lady Britomart, the personification of Chastity, promises Scudamour, the Shield of Love, to rescue his beloved Amoret, who has been captured by Busirane. Entering Busirane's castle, Britomart discovers him in a room with Amoret who is bound to a pillar. Armed with her enchanted lance, Britomart frees Amoret, subdues Busirane, and binds him in chains. The Thaw drawing probably illustrates the moment when Britomart rushes into the room and attacks Busirane.

Fuseli illustrated this passage in two other drawings which Schiff on the basis of style dates 1793; one of these is in the Kunsthaus, Zurich (Schiff, catalogue no. 1008) and the other is in the Staatliche Museen, East Berlin (Schiff, catalogue no. 1009). Schiff dates the Thaw sheet ca. 1790–93, considering it to be an early version of the same subject. In 1793, Fuseli exhibited a painting of *Britomart Freeing Amoret*, now lost, at the Royal Academy in London. Toward the end of his life, he returned to the same theme and illustrated it in a painting of 1824 now in the Goethe Museum, Frankfurt am Main (Schiff, catalogue no. 1494).

PROVENANCE: Private collection, London.

BIBLIOGRAPHY: Gert Schiff, *Johann Heinrich Füssli, 1741–1825*, Zurich, 1973, I, p. 634, no. 1763, II, p. 568, repr.

WILLIAM BLAKE

LONDON 1757 – 1827 LONDON

28 *Christ Nailed to the Cross: The Third Hour*

Pen and black ink, watercolor over preliminary drawing in pencil. 13 1/16 × 13 5/8 inches (332 × 346 mm.). Watermark: none visible through lining. Signed with initials in circle, at lower right corner, in pen and black ink, *inv WB*. Inscribed on back of mount, in pencil, partially cut off, . . . [w]*as the third hour, and they* / [crucified] *him"—Mark ch. 15 - v. 25 -* / *155.ff: Gilchrist's life of Blake.*

In 1800, Blake accepted an invitation from his friend William Hayley to stay with him in Felpham, Sussex, a visit which was to last for three years. Although there were many difficulties with Hayley, it was a time of spiritual growth for the artist. He came to believe that it was possible to break free from the limitations of the material world. "One thing of real consequence I have accomplished by coming to the country," he wrote in a letter of 10 January 1802, "which is to me consolation enough: namely, I have recollected all my scatter'd thoughts on Art . . . which in the confusion of London I had very much lost . . ." (Letter to Thomas Butts, in *The Complete Writings of William Blake*, ed. Sir Geoffrey Keynes, London, 1957, p. 812).

This change is reflected in his art of 1800–05 which moves away from the earlier, more dramatic style. The Thaw *Crucifixion*, dated 1800–03, is one of several watercolors Blake made on the theme of the Passion. They were part of a large project initially undertaken by Blake in 1799 when he was commissioned by Thomas Butts (1757–1845), a minor civil servant and Blake's most important patron, to paint fifty illustrations for the Bible. The project grew to over 135 illustrations, with the first fifty or so done in tempera and the rest in watercolor.

These Biblical watercolors lack the overall coherence of the tempera paintings, which were perhaps to have been hung together in a room. The watercolors show a considerable variation in style and size, due in part to their being produced over the course of at least five years. They range from the earlier rather bold compositions, often intensified with chiaroscuro effects, to more symmetrical compositions with bright colors and a soft stipple technique, to the later drawings which are more linear and flatly colored. It may be that Butts did not commission a set number of watercolors, but paid Blake a stipend upon their receipt, intending to have them bound into a volume or interleaved in a large Bible (David Bindman, *Blake as an Artist*, Oxford, 1977, p. 144).

In the Biblical watercolors, however, the Passion cycle as a whole is distinguished by the profound and moving gravity of the drawings and the cumulative power of repetition from sheet to sheet. In nearly all the drawings Christ is centered, almost hieratically, with figures grouped around him symmetrically. Blake believed that color was subservient to form, and in these drawings the use of color, sometimes extremely delicate, supports the symmetry, or acts as a counterpoint to heighten the spiritual effect.

The Thaw drawing has elements of the older sytle as well as the new. Fuseli's influence is still visible in the two figures crouched above the arms of the cross with their grimacing expressions, their elongated arms, and their emphatic gestures. In contrast the huddled mourners crouch below, grouped around the gentle, ethereally floating Christ.

The scene does not exist in real space; it is not clear whether the cross is upright, as the vertical axis would show, or resting on the rocky mound, as the position of the arms indicates. Here Blake has developed an aesthetic of timeless reality in which entities are no longer separated, because spatial and temporal configurations have disappeared. ("The Blakean Aesthetic," by Hazard Williams, in *The Visionary Hand, Essays for the Study of William Blake*, ed. Robert N. Essick, Los Angeles, 1973, p. 190.) In Blake's visionary art, time and space cease to exist, and in this drawing, it is the redemption and love of Christ that is all important.

PROVENANCE: Thomas Butts; Thomas Butts, Jr.; sale, London, Foster and Sons, 29 June 1853, lot 138 as "The Crucifixion"; bought H.G. Bohn; presumably Col. Gould Weston; Alexander Anderdon Weston; his widow; sale, London, Christie's, 28 June 1904, lot 6; bought E. Parsons; sold 1904 to W. Graham Robertson; sale, London, Christie's, 22 July 1949, lot 32; bought Francis Neale for Lord Glentanar; his daughter, the Hon. Mrs. Jean Bruce; sale, London, Christie's, 4 June 1974, lot 134, repr.; Justin G. Schiller, New York; Barry Friedman, Ltd., New York; sold through the Fine Art Society to M. Koike, Tokyo; private collection, Tokyo; Thos. Agnew & Sons Ltd., London.

BIBLIOGRAPHY: Alexander Gilchrist, *The Life of William Blake*, London and Cambridge, 1863, under W.M. Rossetti, "Descriptive Catalogue," II, p. 227, no. 155 (as "The King of the Jews"); and 1880, p. 240, no. 179; Helen Richter, *William Blake*, 1906, Strassburg, no. 4, repr.; Kerrison Preston, *The Blake Collection of W. Graham Robertson Described by the Author*, 1952, pp. 152–53, no. 57; Geoffrey Keynes, *William Blake's Illustrations to the Bible*, 1957, p. 42, no. 138, repr.; Martin Butlin, *The Paintings and Drawings of William Blake*, New Haven and London, 1981, I, p. 360, no. 496, II, pl. 599.

FRANCISCO JOSÉ DE GOYA Y LUCIENTES
ARAGON 1746 – 1828 BORDEAUX

29 *A Young Man with Two Majas. Verso: Majo Watching a Gallant Bowing to a Maja*

Brush and brown and gray wash, over traces of black chalk. 9⅛ × 5$^{11}/_{16}$ inches (232 × 145 mm.). Watermark: fragment of a coat of arms. Numbered by the artist at upper right, in brush and gray wash, *39*; on verso, at upper left, *40*.

This sheet was originally page 39, with the verso as page 40, of the now-dismembered album called by Sánchez Cantón the Large Sanlúcar album to distinguish it from Goya's earlier and smaller Sanlúcar album. It comprised Goya's second book of drawings and was executed between 1796–97. During these years, Goya stayed with the Duchess of Alba in Sanlúcar and later, during an illness, spent a period of convalescence in Cadiz, returning to Madrid in 1797. Valentín Carderera conjectured that this second album was executed in Madrid although he was uncertain where Goya began the album because of the presence at the beginning of the book of scenes inspired in Andalusia (see Carderera, "François Goya—Sa Vie, ses Dessins, et ses Eaux-Fortes," *Gazette des Beaux-Arts*, VII, 1860 pp. 215–27). For this reason, it has been referred to by several names. José López-Rey, following Carderera's text, called it the Madrid album while Elizabeth du Gué Trapier referred to it as the Sanlúcar-Madrid album, implying that Goya began this series of drawings at Sanlúcar. Pierre Gassier catalogued it as the Madrid album (and Album B) although he believes that it was probably begun at Cadiz.

In the Large Sanlúcar album, Goya used both sides of each sheet, numbering the pages in brush and gray ink at the upper right corner of the recto and at the upper left corner of the verso. Like the Sanlúcar album, this volume also focuses on the theme of woman but, as Gassier points out, each woman is now surrounded by other figures and escorted by young men (Gassier, *The Complete Albums*, p. 46). The recto of the Thaw sheet depicts a young man and a *maja* with the head of a second *maja* visible behind the two figures. Goya presents a somewhat detailed rendering of the two foreground figures and, by freely applying a background of gray wash, creates a secondary plane occupied by the figure of the second *maja*. The drawing on the verso of the sheet also depicts three figures: a gallant bowing to a young woman, and a *majo* wrapped in a cloak. Gassier notes that this young woman seems to be the same as the one who appears on pages five and six (now in the Biblioteca Nacional, Madrid). More recently, Eleanor Sayre has observed that this flirtation scene may have been one source of inspiration for print *Tal para qual* (Sayre, *The Changing Image*, p. 67).

PROVENANCE: Paul Lebas, Paris(?); sale, Paris, Hôtel Drouot, 3 April 1877, lot 67; Paul Meurice, Galerie les Tourettes, Basel; Benjamin Sonnenberg, New York; his sale, New York, Sotheby's, 5–9 June 1979, lot 66, repr.

BIBLIOGRAPHY: Eleanor Sayre, "Eight Books of Drawings by Goya," *Burlington Magazine*, CVI, 1964, nos. 39 and 40, figs. 19 and 20; Pierre Gassier, *Francisco Goya Drawings, the Complete Albums*, New York, 1973, nos. B. 39 and B. 40, repr.; Gassier, *The Life and Complete Works of Francisco Goya*, New York, 1981, 2nd ed., p. 174, nos. 407 and 408, repr.

EXHIBITION: Museum of Fine Arts, Boston, *The Changing Image: Prints by Francisco Goya*, catalogue by Eleanor A. Sayre, 1974, pp. 67–68, no. 39, repr. (verso only).

WILHELM VON KOBELL

MANNHEIM 1766 – 1853 MUNICH

30 *A Boy Asking Alms from a Man on Horseback*

Watercolor over a sketch in graphite. $10\frac{1}{4} \times 11\frac{1}{8}$ inches (260×282 mm.). Watermark: none visible through lining. Signed and dated at lower right, in graphite, *Wilhelm v Kobell / 1831*.

Kobell was the outstanding landscapist working in Munich during the first half of the nineteenth century. He practiced a succession of styles from the rococo to Biedermeier, adapting each to his own innovative vision. In addition to pure landscapes, he specialized in battle scenes and cattle pieces, but he is best known for watercolors and paintings that depict encounters between gentlemen on horseback and rural people on foot, set against an extensive view of the Bavarian countryside. Kobell developed the basic compositional arrangement of these works shortly after 1800: the figures and animals dominate the scene from a stage-like rise in the foreground, while the Munich skyline or a glimpse of the Alps appears on the horizon. Over the next fifty years, he introduced innumerable variations into this scheme, drawing upon the careful studies of peasant costumes, horses, cattle, and landscapes that fill his sketchbooks, and making subtle adjustments in the handling of space and light.

The Thaw watercolor epitomizes Kobell's mature Biedermeier style. The silvery light that clarifies the contours and models the precisely described forms, the transparent atmosphere, the restrained action, and the painstakingly observed details of country life all contribute to the harmonious Sunday mood that characterizes the finest of these works. Even the boy begging alms, who hardly seems a sinister reminder of rural poverty, does not strike a discordant note in this image of pastoral serenity.

Siegfried Wichmann, who published an exhaustive monograph on Kobell (*Wilhelm von Kobell. Monographie und kritisches Verzeichnis der Werke*, Munich, 1970), did not know the Thaw sheet until it came to light recently on the Munich art market. In correspondence with the last owner of the drawing, Wichmann compared it to a watercolor datable around 1827 that represents two women buying flowers from a boy (*ibid.*, no. 1434). Both works include a nearly identical view of Munich from the right bank of the Isar River with the village of Bogenhausen at the left. The disposition of the foreground figures in the Thaw work recalls another composition, known in three versions dated or datable to 1823, that also represents a youth asking alms from a rider accompanied by a second, riderless horse (*ibid.*, nos. 1303–05). Despite their similar design, these three works differ from the Thaw watercolor in the details, and especially in the landscape background.

PROVENANCE: Galerie Biedermann, Munich.

CASPAR DAVID FRIEDRICH

GREIFSWALD 1774 – 1840 DRESDEN

31 *The Jacobikirche in Greifswald as a Ruin*

Graphite, pen and gray ink, and light brown wash on wove paper. $10\frac{1}{4} \times 7\frac{11}{16}$ inches (260×195 mm.). Inscribed on verso at lower left, in graphite, *5* and at upper left, ... [illegible] *4*.

Friedrich based this drawing, which is in his late style, on the Gothic nave and choir of the Jacobikirche in his native town of Greifswald on the Baltic. Although the church remains intact, he depicted it as a desolate ruin, and added the pulpit, the crucifix, and probably also the altar. A watercolor that shows the same view, but with differences in detail, was formerly in a private collection in Hannover (Börsch-Supan and Jähnig, no. 489). However, the discrepancies between the two versions make it unlikely that the Thaw work served as a study for the watercolor. Rather, as von Einem observed, the drawing probably relates to a lost oil painting that was exhibited in Dresden in 1829 (*ibid.*, no. 379). A tracing in the Dresden Print Room very likely reproduces the staffage from the lost painting, which differed from the figures in the Thaw sheet (*Caspar David Friedrich. Der Graphiker. Handzeichnungen und Radierungen*, Dresden, Kupferstichkabinett, 1928, no. 84). The painting is otherwise known only from verbal descriptions, so it is impossible to characterize precisely its relationship to the work exhibited here. According to Börsch-Supan and Jähnig, comparison of the dimensions of the staffage in the Dresden tracing with the measurements of the lost canvas suggests that Friedrich exaggerated the height of the dilapidated choir in the picture, just as he did in his lost *Monastery Graveyard*, which also depicted the Greifswald Jacobikirche as a ruin (Börsch-Supan and Jähnig, no. 254).

Friedrich constructed the space according to a perspective system centered on the altar, where the vanishing point is marked by an X. Using a compass, he measured equal intervals along the bottom and sides of the sheet establishing the points from which orthogonals and transversals could have been drawn. The marks made by the compass are still visible on the edges of the sheet.

Many of Friedrich's landscapes, seascapes, and architectural scenes communicate Christian ideas about the inevitability of death and the expectation of eternal life. However realistically he depicted details of light and texture, Friedrich's programmatic compositions and the prominence of symbols that evoke transience, mortality, and resurrection convey the transcendental conception of man and nature that informs much of his work. The watercolor formerly in Hannover includes, among other differences from the Thaw drawing, a view into a vaulted crypt in the immediate foreground and no staffage. It appears to represent man's victory through Christ's sacrifice (the crucifix) over death (the crypt). The Thaw drawing and the related painting, on the other hand, may allude to the transient glory of the Church. In 1829, the year it was exhibited, the lost oil was described by the critic E.H. Toelken as "a kind of picturesque critique or satire on the present condition of the Christian Church, represented symbolically" (*ibid.*, no. 379 and pp. 114–15). Toelken noted that the three meditative staffage figures wore blue, "the color of faith," and that they appeared "to contemplate the former grandeur of the building, but they are strangers from distant lands and a different time" (*ibid.*, p. 115).

PROVENANCE: August Grahl, Dresden(?); Prof. Paul Arndt, Munich; his sale, Leipzig, C.G. Boerner, 16 May 1934, lot 74; private collection, Wittingshausen; sale, Munich, Karl & Faber, 28 November 1979, lot 35.

BIBLIOGRAPHY: Otto Schmitt, "Zum Problem: Dichtung und Wahrheit bei Caspar David Friedrich," *Monatsblätter der Gesellschaft für Pommersche Geschichte und Altertumskunde*, XLIX, 1935, pp. 33–37; Herbert von Einem, *Caspar David Friedrich*, Berlin, 1938, p. 110, note 23; Schmitt, *Die Ruine Eldena im Werk von Caspar David Friedrich. Kunstbrief Nr. 25*, Berlin, 1944, pp. 28–30; Von Einem, *Caspar David Friedrich*, 3rd ed., Berlin, 1950, p. 124, note 23; Gerhard Eimer, *Caspar David Friedrich und die Gotik. Analysen und Deutungsversuche. Aus Stockholmer Vorlesungen*, Hamburg, 1963, pp. 27–28; Sigrid Hinz, *Caspar David Friedrich als Zeichner. Ein Beitrag zur stilistischen Entwicklung und ihrer Bedeutung für die Datierung der Gemälde*, dissertation, Greifswald, 1966, no. 663; Helmut Börsch-Supan and Karl Wilhelm Jähnig, *Caspar David Friedrich. Gemälde, Druckgraphik und bildmässige Zeichnungen*, Munich, 1973, no. 488; *Caspar David Friedrich. Das gesamte graphische Werk*, Nachwort von Hans H. Hofstätter, Munich, 1974, no. 630.

JOSEPH MALLORD WILLIAM TURNER

LONDON 1775 – 1851 CHELSEA

32 *The Pass at Faido, St. Gotthard*

Watercolor, point of brush, scratching out, over traces of pencil on cream-colored wove paper. $11\frac{15}{16} \times 18\frac{1}{2}$ inches (303×469 mm.). Watermark: none.

Turner, one of the greatest of English artists, received much of his inspiration from his many travels. Between 1817 and 1845 alone he made eighteen Continental journeys. He toured extensively throughout England and Wales, through Italy and France, and as far east as Prague. From these trips came some of the most beautiful works of art in European history.

In the 1840s, Turner began a series of yearly trips to Switzerland which ended only because of a serious illness in 1845. On each of these trips, he made numerous pencil sketches on notepads that he always carried with him which served as the basis for many of his oil paintings, watercolors, and engravings.

It was his habit to bring his watercolors to a state of elaborate completion and, beginning in 1842, he undertook this method again. From his many Swiss sketches, some of them only a few lines on a page perhaps with a color notation, he worked up "sample" drawings, color studies that were sometimes as large as the finished watercolors. These free and schematic color "samples" were then shown to his friends and patrons. In order that they should understand what they were being asked to commission, Turner made four finished watercolors from the samples. After receiving the commissions, he then painted the remainder of the finished watercolors, and repeated this process in 1843 and 1845. Typically a final sheet has added details of figures and scenery applied with a fine brush, or rubbed-out areas of damp color, or highlights scratched out by a fingernail or brush end.

From his 1842 trip, Turner received six commissions, including one by the young critic and artist John Ruskin for *The Pass at Faido*, based on the sample study now in the British Museum

(Turner Bequest no. ccclxiv–209; repr. in Wilton, 1976, no. 107). The solid strength and grandeur of the rocky mountainside through which the water cascades are conveyed by the swirling lines and colors that give form to the natural shapes, and by the very texture of the drawing, roughened throughout with scratches. Wilton (1979, p. 238) calls this drawing a "monothematic" work. Indeed, Turner was here concerned with the single dramatic image of the rocks and water bound in a turbulent frenzy that seems to threaten the very existence of the travelers, dwarfed by the mountains, who are attempting to cross the Pass in their carriage. Here is no open vista of light and space, as is more usual in his works. Rather, the viewer, like the travelers, is confronted by the immensity of the towering rocks and rushing water. As Wilton commented in 1980 (p. 179), Turner was perhaps paying a last tribute to the sublime, that eighteenth-century aesthetic of the awful solemnity and wonder of nature.

PROVENANCE: John Ruskin; George Coats (1901); by descent; private collection, United Kingdom; Thos. Agnew & Sons Ltd., London.

EXHIBITIONS: Tate Gallery, London, and Royal Academy, London, *Turner 1775–1851*, catalogue by Andrew Wilton, 1974–75, no. 612; Art Gallery of Ontario, Toronto and elsewhere, *Turner and the Sublime*, catalogue by Andrew Wilton, 1980–81, p. 179, no. 104, pl. 24 (color).

BIBLIOGRAPHY: *Notes by Mr. Ruskin on his Drawings by the Late J. M. W. Turner*, London, The Fine Art Society, 1878, p. 54, no. 66, p. 77, no. 5; John Russell and Andrew Wilton, *Turner in Switzerland*, Zurich, 1976, pp. 110, 139, checklist no. 82, p. 139, repr. p. 161; Wilton, *J. M. W. Turner, His Art and Life*, New York, 1979, p. 243, fig. 253, p. 484, cat. no. 1538; *A Dealer's Record, Agnew's 1967–81*, London, 1981, p. 176, repr.; "Comings and Goings: Private Collections," *Turner Studies*, II, no. 2, Winter 1983, p. 64.

33 *Lucerne from the Lake*

Watercolor over preliminary traces of pencil on cream-colored wove paper. 11⅝×18⅝ inches (295×473 mm.). Watermark: none.

Commissioned by John Ruskin, this drawing was executed by Turner in 1845, in the artist's seventieth year, and is a fully rendered watercolor based on the sample drawing now in the British Museum (Turner Bequest no. ccclxiv–386). The view is of the Lake of Lucerne at sunset, the golden glow of the light shimmering across the distant mountains, with the blue of the water and coast and the red of the figures' clothes gleaming like jewels.

Lucerne from the Lake is one of the many works created in the last and perhaps greatest phase of Turner's art, generally thought to be after 1830. His brushwork is free, as is his use of color. His technical mastery, his willingness to try to capture the intangible through the use of color, enabled him to achieve effects in watercolor that were dazzling, and indeed, revolutionary.

Though Turner's primary concerns were with atmosphere, light, and color, he cannot be considered an Impressionist or proto-Impressionist. There is a timeless quality to his views, even his most contemporary, as well as a feeling that his compositions have been very carefully composed, unlike the aims of the French artists. Malcolm Cormack (Fitzwilliam Museum, Cambridge, *J. M. W. Turner, R.A. 1775–1851*, 1975, p. 16) offers an interesting contrast between Constable, who considered landscape painting a "pursuit, legitimate, scientific, and mechanical," and who was thus a forerunner of the Impressionists, to Turner, who with his grand manner, his sense of drama and ambiguity, was essentially a Romantic and the heir of Claude and Poussin.

As is well known, Turner's later drawings and oils were not understood and much criticized for their lack of form, despite the words of praise by John Ruskin in his *Modern Painters*, the first volume of which appeared in 1843. Ruskin was an avid admirer and champion of the artist and hung this drawing, along with several other views of lakes by Turner, in his dining room. He sold this particular sheet in 1865, because he could not bear to think of how Lucerne had changed over the years.

Despite the public's lack of enthusiasm for these late works, Turner died a wealthy man, though he lived with little regard for his own comfort, or for the condition of his paintings. When he died the contents of his studio became the property of the English nation. More than three hundred oil paintings are now in the Tate Gallery and over 19,000 watercolors and pencil sketches in the British Museum, the prodigious outpourings of a long and productive life.

PROVENANCE: John Ruskin; sold in 1865 to Mrs. Newall; by descent in Newall family until 1978; Thos. Agnew & Sons Ltd., London; private collection, Germany; Rudolph Zwirner, Cologne.

BIBLIOGRAPHY: Walter Thornbury, *The Life of J. M. W. Turner, R.A.*, London, 1862, II, p. 395; "Private Collections in the Tynemouth-Gateshead," *Athenaeum*, 1873, p. 408; Sir Walter Armstrong, *Turner*, London and New York, 1902, p. 263; E.T. Cook and Alexander Wedderburn, *The Works of John Ruskin*, London and New York, 1903–12 (39 vols.), III, p. 552, VI, pp. 277, 361–62, figs. 72, 106, 107, XIII, pp. 201, 476n., 556, 602, XXXV, p. 380n., XXXVIII, p. 363; John Russell and Andrew Wilton, *Turner in Switzerland*, Zurich, 1976, p. 139, no. 88; Wilton, *J. M. W. Turner His Art and Life*, New York, 1979; cat. no. 1544, repr. p. 485; Wilton, *J. M. W. Turner, France, Italy, Germany, Switzerland*, New York, 1982, under no. 115.

EXHIBITIONS: Guildhall Art Gallery, London, *Catalogue of the Loan Collection of Pictures and Drawings of J. M. W. Turner*, 1899, no. 161; Thos. Agnew & Sons Ltd., London, *Annual Exhibition of Watercolor Drawings*, 1929, no. 7; Thos. Agnew & Sons Ltd., London, *Centenary Loan Exhibition of Turner Watercolours*, 1951, no. 120; Thos. Agnew & Sons Ltd., London, *Loan Exhibition of Paintings and Watercolours by J. M. W. Turner, R.A.*, 1967, no. 94; Thos Agnew & Sons Ltd., London, *106th Annual Exhibition of Watercolors and Drawings*, 1975, no. 97, repr.

JOHN CONSTABLE

EAST BERGHOLT 1776 – 1837 LONDON

34 *A View of the Canal, Newbury*

Pencil, gray wash. 6 11/16 × 10 inches (171×255 mm.). Watermark: fragment of J. WHATMAN TURKEY MILLS 1819. Inscribed at lower left, in pen and brown ink, *Newbury Berks / June 5. 1821.*

In June 1821, John Constable visited his good friend the Archdeacon John Fisher and accompanied him on a journey to his rural deaneries in Berkshire. During their travels, Constable made drawings in a sketchbook of the scenery in the neighborhood of Reading, Newbury, Abingdon, and Oxford. It is possible to reconstruct much of the contents of this now dismembered sketchbook as Constable inscribed many, though not all of the sheets, with place and date. The Thaw drawing is one of those sheets, made during the second day. There are eleven dated sheets from the sketchbook in the Victoria and Albert Museum, London, several others in various collections, as well as two or perhaps three undated sheets possibly from this sketchbook in the British Museum, and four sheets of similar subjects dated 1823. From the evidence, Constable evidently used this same sketchbook on at least two different occasions (see Reynolds, 1984, pp. 75–76 for discussion).

Constable seems to have made about seven drawings of Newbury during this visit, with at least four done on the fifth of June. Besides the Thaw sketch, on which Constable changed the "4" to "5" (he misdated at least one other drawing on this trip, that of the Abbey Gate at Reading, which he originally dated the fifth of June and then changed to the sixth; see Reynolds, 1984, no. 21.25), there are four of Newbury in the Victoria and Albert Museum, two dated 5 June, one of the canal, one of St. Nicholas' Church. The Huntington drawing is inscribed as being near Newbury on the fifth, and the drawing in private hands is of the lock, and is dated either the fourth or the fifth as well.

A View of the Canal is a fresh and intimate observation of a rural scene, made domestic by the presence of the house on the right bank and the ducks on the left. Constable's use of the pencil, easier to handle than watercolors when outdoors, has the same effect as he might have obtained from a brush in that forms are not simply delineated, but areas of tone are created. His depiction of light and shade, and the contrast with the balanced masses formed by the trees and building put him squarely in the tradition of his predecessors whom he so admired: Claude, Jacob van Ruisdael, and Thomas Gainsborough.

PROVENANCE: W. W. Winkworth; G. A. W. Lawrence; Baskett & Day, London.

BIBLIOGRAPHY: Graham Reynolds, *Catalogue of the Constable Drawings in the Victoria and Albert Museum*, London, 1973, p. 140; Reynolds, *The Later Paintings and Drawings of John Constable*, New Haven and London, 1984, pp. 75–78, no. 21.22, pl. 231.

EXHIBITION: Wildenstein and Co., Ltd., London, *The Catalogue of a Centenary Memorial Exhibition of John Constable, R.A., his Origins and Influence*, organized by Percy Moore Turner, 1937, no. 136.

35 *View of Cathanger near Petworth*

Pencil, on two sheets of paper pasted together. 8 1/16 × 13 5/8 inches (205 × 347 mm.). Watermark: none visible through lining. Inscribed by the artist, in upper left corner, in graphite, *Petworth Sepr. 12 / 1834 Cat Hanger.*

Constable first set eyes on the Petworth estate in Sussex in July 1834. After considerable prodding from his portrait-painter friend Thomas Phillips, Constable accepted an invitation from Lord

Egremont to return to Petworth House for an extended visit in September of the same year. The artist was provided with a carriage every day to tour the neighboring countryside and the two-thousand-acre park surrounding the mansion that had been landscaped by Capability Brown. Of almost equal inspiration to Constable would have been the family collection of paintings that included the work of Titian, Van Dyck, Claude, Reynolds, Gainsborough, as well as Turner, who enjoyed the patronage of the third Earl of Egremont and had a studio there.

The view from the south side of Petworth House encompasses the farm on the estate known as the "Cat Hanger," which is situated on the far side of the Rother, a tributary of the Arun. The drawing is especially effective when seen at a distance due to the power of suggestion in the dots and dashes of Constable's soft pencil applied with the exactness of an expert draughtsman. It was the artist's custom to use a fixative on drawings executed in soft pencil; the occasional "bare" spot at the lower and middle left as well as the faded year in the inscribed date at the top are areas where the fixative did not take. The artist probably executed this drawing on the spot in his sketchbook, with the drawing extending onto the left-hand page. Later he cut both sheets and pasted them together before applying the fixative.

PROVENANCE: Edward Seago; Baskett & Day, London.

EXHIBITIONS: The Tate Gallery, London, *Constable*, catalogue by Leslie Parris, Jan Fleming-Williams, and Conal Shields, 1976, no. 315, repr., and under no. 316; The Pierpont Morgan Library, New York, *European Drawings, 1375–1825*, catalogue compiled by Cara D. Denison and Helen Mules with the assistance of Jane V. Shoaf, 1981, no. 124, repr.; Graham Reynolds, *The Later Paintings and Drawings of John Constable*, New Haven and London, 1984, I, p. 262, no. 34.31, II, pl. 938.

JEAN-AUGUSTE-DOMINIQUE INGRES
MONTAUBAN 1780 – 1867 PARIS

36 *Portrait of Hippolyte-François Devillers (1767–1837)*

Pencil on wove paper. 9×6$\frac{9}{16}$ inches (228×166 mm.). Watermark: none. Signed, inscribed, and dated at lower right, *Ingres. a rome / 1812.*

Ingres, who studied under Jacques-Louis David, was the winner of the Prix de Rome in 1801, a prize he was unable to take advantage of until 1806 when the school was rebuilt after its destruction in the Revolution. He remained in Rome until 1820, where he earned his livelihood chiefly by making portrait drawings. Fortunately, a large number of these drawings have survived, most of them preserved at the Musée Ingres, Montauban, and the Louvre.

In the years before Waterloo, Ingres developed a clientele among the French officers of the Napoleonic administration in Rome. His work proved popular in Rome but was not initially well received in Paris, and it was not until 1824, with *The Vow of Louis XIII*, that it received critical acclaim from France. Only then did he choose to return to Paris, being at last more confident of success.

His first client in Rome was the Director of Waterworks and Forestry, Charles Marcotte d'Argenteuil, who became friends with the artist while he sat to him, and introduced him to other officials, including Hippolyte-François Devillers. Devillers, the *Directeur de l'Enregistrement*, in charge of transportation tariffs, was a man whom Ingres, in later years, would praise for his helpfulness and solicitude toward him in Rome. Ingres painted Devillers' portrait in 1811. In addition to the painting now in the Bührle collection in Zurich, there are two drawings of Devillers, one dated 1811 which, as of 1977, was in the collection of Mme Jacques Dubourg, Paris, and the present sheet, dated 1812, in the Thaw collection. In the earlier drawing, Devillers is seated, leaning back, relaxed, elbow crooked, his sword in hand. In the painting and the later drawing, Devillers is portrayed standing, his right hand inserted in his breast coat. In the painting he holds his sword while in the drawing his left hand is inserted in his pocket.

Not much is known about Devillers. He left Rome before 1820 to assume a position in Vesoul for the Haute-Saône similar to what he had held in Rome. In Vesoul, he was also a member of the municipal council and was to assume the mayoral duties of the town as well. He seems to have lived a very comfortable life, and his family remained in Vesoul until the middle of the nineteenth century. We know that he married Anne Chaton, who was thirty years younger than he. The couple had four children prior to the marriage and they had two more afterwards.

The Thaw sheet is the more substantial of the two drawings. Devillers was forty-five when he sat for this portrait. The artist's pencil captures not only his physiognomical likeness, but something of his character as well. Devillers is seen as a man of position, though his uniform lacks the badges of office which can be seen in the painting, such as the ear of wheat on his collar, and the sword at his side. His eyes reveal the kindness which Ingres mentioned, though there is also a certain rigidity of character as well.

Typical of Ingres' work is the solidity of Devillers' form in the picture space, and the unerring rhythmic flow of lines. Ingres sustained a level of abstract linear purity that is unequaled in the nineteenth century save in the art of Degas.

PROVENANCE: Mme de Gorsse; Alfred-Louis Lebeuf de Montgermont by 1913; his sale, Paris, Galerie Georges Petit, 16–19 June 1919, no. 121, repr.; Comtesse Bernard de Laguiche (the Princess Clotilde de Broglie); Armand de Laguiche (son of the Comtesse); art market; Robert H. Smith, Washington, D.C.; Feilchenfeldt, Zurich.

BIBLIOGRAPHY: Hans Naef and Ch.-H. Lerch, "Ingres et M. Devillers," *Bulletin du Musée Ingres*, 15, Montauban, September, 1964, pp. 5–16; Naef, *Die Bildniszeichnungen von J.-A.-D. Ingres*, Bern, 1977, I, ch. 29, pp. 255–61, fig. 3, and IV, p. 144, no. 78 (repr.), and under no. 77.

EXHIBITIONS: Palais des Beaux-Arts de la Ville de Paris, *David et ses élèves*, 1913, no. 335; Villa Medici, Rome, *Ingres in Italia*, 1968, no. 36, repr.

JEAN-LOUIS-ANDRÉ-THÉODORE GERICAULT

ROUEN 1791 – 1824 PARIS

37 *Head of a Negro*

Black chalk, stumped, on wove paper. 9 13/16×6 7/8 inches (248×175 mm.). Watermark: illegible fragment.

This impressive head joins four other Gericault drawings in the collection of Mr. and Mrs. Thaw (see Morgan Library, Thaw exhibition, 1975–76, nos. 72–75, repr.), and adds another dimension to their holdings in that it is a study for a figure in Gericault's famous *Raft of the Medusa*, painted in 1819.

The history of the *Medusa* and Gericault's painting has been fully told elsewhere by Lorenz Eitner (1972). In what was a clear case of ineptitude, the *Medusa* foundered in the seas off of Senegal in 1816, and those who were unable to fit into the lifeboats were forced to build a makeshift raft, which was to be towed by the boats. The cable broke and, adrift for thirteen days, only fifteen out of the original 140 people were rescued by the *Argo* (the painting shows the moment when the survivors have sighted the ship). In 1817, two of the survivors, Alexandre Corréard and Henri Savigny, published *Naufrage de la Frégate la Méduse*. It detailed the horrors of their travails, from cannibalism to murder, from thirst to famine and death. The French public was shocked and opinion ran high against the monarchy whose ship it was.

It is not known exactly when Gericault made the decision to paint the incident, but it was to occupy him fully for one and a half years, the longest period he had ever worked on a single project. As the son of wealthy and rather indulgent parents, he had previously followed a highly personal course of studies, characterized by its irregularity and interrupted by distractions, such as his passionate fondness of horses, and sportsmanship, and an involvement with a married woman who was a distant relative.

He threw himself into his new work, researching the disaster and making studies of cadavers and severed limbs, along with many figural and portrait studies, including those of Corréard and Savigny. The Thaw drawing, probably of the famous model Joseph, whom Gericault used several times (L. Eitner, *Géricault, His Life and Work*, London, 1983, p. 176), is a study for the black man recorded as being on the infamous raft and who appears in the painting by the mast, next to Corréard and Savigny.

Historically, the rise of abolitionism was just beginning in France, and Gericault was sympathetic to that struggle. There had been no recognition of the role blacks had played in the *Medusa* incident, and Gericault wanted to rectify that, though in typical Romantic fashion, he exaggerated the truth by portraying three on the raft, including the figure waving to the *Argo* who forms the dramatic apex of the painting. As was natural for the time, Gericault saw blacks, like Turks and other non-Europeans, as exotic, and romanticized them in costume and pose.

Although Eitner suggested that the drawing resembles a tracing worked up with rubbed chalk, no other head like it seems to exist. The Thaw drawing is very sculptural in its execution. There is an evident sympathy between artist and sitter, and Gericault has given us an almost loving portrait of this now unknown man.

PROVENANCE: Pierre Dubaut (Lugt S. 2103b); James Lord, Paris.

BIBLIOGRAPHY: Klaus Berger, *Géricault und sein Werk*, Vienna, 1950, p. 72, pl. 50; D. Aimé-Azam, *Mazeppa-Géricault et son temps*, Paris, 1956, facing p. 208, repr.; F. H. Lem, "Le thème du nègre dans l'oeuvre de Géricault," *L'Arte*, XXXVII, 1962, p. 19ff., pl. 2; Lorenz Eitner, *Géricault's Raft of the Medusa*, London, 1972, p. 172, no. 107, pl. 106.

EXHIBITIONS: Galerie Bignou, Paris, *Géricault cet inconnu*, 1950, no. 52, repr.; Galerie Bernheim-Jeune, Paris, *Cent cinquante ans de dessin*, 1952, no. 69; Marlborough Fine Art Ltd., London, *Théodore Géricault*, 1953, p. 172, no. 55; Kunstmuseum, Winterthur, *Théodore Géricault*, 1953, p. 46, no. 171; Galerie Bernheim-Jeune, Paris, *Gros, Géricault, Delacroix*, 1954, no. 59; Walters Art Gallery, Baltimore, *African Image—Representation of Blacks throughout History*, 1980, no. 6, repr.

FERDINAND-VICTOR-EUGÈNE DELACROIX

CHARENTON-ST. MAURICE 1798 – 1863 PARIS

38 *Compositional Study with Figures in Mediaeval Costume*

Watercolor, brown and gray wash, touches of gum arabic, over graphite. Verso: Slight sketch of the upper torso of the woman stretching out her hand, in graphite. $7\frac{1}{4} \times 10\frac{1}{4}$ inches (183×262 mm.). Watermark: none. Inscribed on verso, in graphite, *l'atelier ingre* (?) and an illegible date.

Delacroix advocated copying as an instructive method of studying the great masters and made copies after works by Raphael, Titian, Rubens, and Rembrandt among others. As Rubens was one of Delacroix's favorite painters, he frequently referred to the Flemish master's technique and specific works in his *Journal*, and kept many of his painted copies after Rubens in his studio (Barbara Ehrlich White, "Delacroix's Painted Copies after Rubens," *The Art Bulletin*, XLIX, no. 1, 1967, pp. 37–51). In addition to oil replicas, Delacroix produced numerous drawings after the Flemish master, and, in his catalogue of Delacroix's *oeuvre*, Alfred Robaut cites ninety-seven pen-and-chalk drawings and eight sepia-and-watercolor sheets after Rubens (lot nos. 635, 636, and 637 of the Delacroix sale).

In the 1820s, Delacroix copied Rubens' *Henri IV Entrusts the Regency to Marie de' Medici* (Louvre, Paris) and his oil copy is today in the Los Angeles County Museum of Art (Lee Johnson, *The Paintings of Eugène Delacroix*, Oxford, 1982, II, pl. 14). It has been noted that the Thaw watercolor is a free copy of the subject, and, in this sheet, Delacroix significantly reduced the space of the composition by almost eliminating the architectural setting, retaining only the central arch which opens out onto a blue sky. The focus is thereby placed on the figures, whose positioning is very close to both the Rubens original and Delacroix's oil copy. In the Thaw study, however, the two central figures, each flanked by an attendant, appear to be clasping hands above the head of a nude putto while a woman holding an orb looks on. In this variant, the figures are dressed in mediaeval costume, altering both the mood and historical context of this composition from those of Delacroix's oil copy and the Rubens original.

PROVENANCE: Riesener, Paris (nephew of the artist); Léouzon le Duc, Paris.

EXHIBITION: Galerie Schmit, Paris, *Aspects de la peinture française, XIXe–XXe siècles*, 1978, no. 79, repr.

39 *Head of a Woman*

Watercolor, over graphite, heightened with white, on wove paper. 7 9/16 × 5 13/16 inches (192 × 148 mm.). Watermark: none.

Although this watercolor study of an old woman has been traditionally connected with the *Massacre of Chios* of 1824, in the most recent catalogue raisonné of Delacroix, it is no longer accepted as a study for that painting and no alternative identification is offered. Delacroix's famous picture, exhibited at the salon of 1824, presents a generalized impression of this episode of the Greek wars of independence which greatly fascinated Delacroix as a subject being both contemporary and exotic. One month after the Chios massacres began, a plague broke out on the island, and it has been pointed out that in the painting Delacroix may have also intended to show the effects of terrible disease along with the destruction of war (Johnson, p. 104). The strongly expressive quality and coloring of the old woman whom Delacroix depicts in middle-Eastern costume explains why the drawing was once connected, by Raymond Escholier and Alfred Robaut, with the artist's preparation for the painting; her red-rimmed eyes and sunken cheeks suggest that she has been ravaged by time and disaster. This woman, however, cannot be connected with any particular figure in the *Massacre of Chios*, nor has she been connected with any other work by Delacroix.

PROVENANCE: Delacroix sale (atelier stamp E.D. in red ink at lower left; Lugt S. 838a), 22–27 February 1864; Alfred Robaut, Paris; Moreau-Nélaton (no mark; see Lugt 1900); Acquavella Galleries, New York.

BIBLIOGRAPHY: Raymond Escholier, *Delacroix, Peintre, Graveur, Écrivain*, Paris, 1926, I, p. 121, repr.; Alfred Robaut, *L'Oeuvre complet de Eugène Delacroix*, New York, 1969, no. 94, repr.; Lee Johnson, *The Paintings of Eugène Delacroix*, Oxford, 1981, I, p. 91.

EXHIBITION: Acquavella Galleries, New York, *XIX & XX Century Master Drawings and Watercolors*, 1985, no. 1, repr. in color.

40 *Studies of a Cat*

Pen and brown ink with some brush. Verso: One cat traced through by another hand, in pencil. 7 9/16 × 11 inches (192 × 279 mm.). Watermark: none. Inscribed by the artist at upper right, *Patte dedevant. gauche.*

Delacroix's fascination with animals is evident in his atelier sale of 1864 which included many drawings of horses, tigers, lions, and, on a more domestic level, cats. Although the Thaw collection already contains two impressive watercolors of exotic animals by Delacroix, the *Head of a Lion* and the *Royal Tiger* (Morgan Library, Thaw exhibition, 1975–76, nos. 79 and 81), this appealing sheet of cat studies presents another facet of the artist's preoccupation with animals.

Delacroix's economic pen line caught the essence of the cat, showing him in one study crouched, with his neck extended, while the most complete rendering appears at the lower left of the sheet where Delacroix depicted the cat stretched out comfortably on a cushion. The pose of this cat is almost identical to one in another drawing by the artist (Raymond Escholier, *Delacroix, Peintre, Graveur, Écrivain*, Paris, 1927, II, p. 184).

PROVENANCE: Delacroix sale (atelier stamp E.D. in red ink at lower left; Lugt S. 838a), 22–27 February 1864, probably part of lot 509; National Arts Club, New York.

JOHAN CHRISTIAN CLAUSSEN DAHL

BERGEN 1778 – 1857 DRESDEN

41 *A View of the Elbe Valley*

Brush and gray wash. 8¼×13⅞ inches (209×352 mm.). Signed, lower right, in pen and brown ink, *JD*(in ligature)*ahl f.*, and verso, lower right, in graphite, *JD*(in ligature)*ahl f.* Watermark: shield with a posthorn, ADUNC below.

A native of Norway, Dahl spent most of his career in Dresden, where he settled in 1818 and where, from 1823 until 1840, he shared a house with Caspar David Friedrich. Despite his close association with Friedrich, Dahl followed an independent course in his work, which is characterized by a more realistic approach to the representation of nature than Friedrich's and seldom embodies the kind of spiritual meaning that often informs the German master's pictures. Although he played an important role in German Romantic art and his painting influenced Friedrich's development as a colorist, Dahl has been little studied outside Norway, in part because much of his work is preserved there. He remains best known for his Scandinavian landscapes and stormy coastal scenes, which were inspired by several visits to his native country between 1826 and 1850.

Judging from the handling of the wash and from the organization of the vista into large, broadly described forms, we can conclude that the Thaw study dates from the 1820s. During those years Dahl drew numerous panoramic views of the Elbe River valley that convey the soft atmosphere and gentle topography of the countryside around Dresden (*Johan Christian Dahl, Tegninger og Akvareller, Nasjonalgalleriet og Bergens Bildgalleri*, introduction by Leif Østby, Oslo, 1957, pls. 122–24; Royal Museum of Fine Arts, Copenhagen, inv. no. TU 130a/9; National Gallery, Oslo, inv. no. B1779). Like several of these studies, the Thaw work is executed with the brush in washes ranging in tone from the light, transparent gray of the river to the dense, charcoal shadows of the hillside. Dahl seems to have developed the free brushwork used in the Thaw study during his Italian sojourn of 1820–21: the handling of the wash here resembles the technique of drawings of the Bay of Naples executed in 1820 (*ibid.*, pl. 116; *Deutsche Romantik Handzeichnungen*, Marianne Bernhard, ed., Munich, I [1973], pl. 159).

PROVENANCE: sale, London, Sotheby's, 27 November 1980, no. 111, repr.

SAMUEL PALMER

NEWINGTON 1805 – 1881 REDHILL

42 *The Haunted Stream*

Pen and brown ink, brown wash, over traces of pencil. 3⅝×4¾ inches (92×120 mm.). Watermark: none visible through lining.

Traditionally it has been thought that Samuel Palmer had his most creative and fertile period in his twenties, during the seven years when he lived and worked in the tiny village of Shoreham in Kent. He exhibited and sold his first work when he was fourteen, and by the time he was seventeen he had already become acquainted with the leading English artists Thomas Stothard, John Linnell, John Varley, and William Mulready. It was to Linnell that he owed what was undoubtedly the most important artistic event in his early life, his meeting with William Blake.

Palmer moved to Shoreham with his father in the 1820s for his health. Gathered around him was a group of young artists including Edward Calvert, George Richmond, Francis Oliver Finch, Frederick Tatham, Henry Walter, and Welby Sherman. They were united by their respect and admiration for Blake, who was their spiritual leader, by their interest in the classics, and by a philosophy that was essentially neoplatonic in outlook. They called themselves The Ancients, to identify themselves with what they believed to be the superiority of pre-modern man.

Perhaps The Ancients' primary concern was the role of nature in man's life, epitomized in their enthusiasm for Blake's woodcuts for Thornton's Virgil, which Palmer described as "visions of little dells, and nooks, and corners of Paradise; models of the exquisitest pitch of intense poetry . . . . in all such a mystic and dreamy glimmer as penetrates and kindles the inmost soul, and gives complete and unreserved delight, unlike the gaudy daylight of this world" (Pressly, 1969, p. 27). Palmer continually studied the effects of clouds, of sunsets and moonlight, as well as the trees, shrubs, and orchards, transforming natural phenomena by his inward vision into "the veil of Heaven, through which her features are dimly smiling . . ." (Letter to Linnell, 1828, quoted in William L. Pressly, Jr., "Samuel Palmer and the Pastoral Convention," *Record of the Art Museum*, Princeton University, Princeton, 28, no. 2, 1969, p. 24). Particularly during his years in Shoreham, Palmer seemed to have a nearly ecstatic sense of the bounty and glory of the natural world, though there was always an element of orthodox Christianity in his thought and art. His works were little gems redolent of nature which represented a world of pastoral purity.

Palmer's words in praise of Blake's work seem to apply as well to the Thaw drawing, which has been dated about 1826. Here is a corner of nature, a gently winding river illuminated by a light more strong than the crescent moon and stars seem capable of providing. The young poet, a favorite Miltonian subject ("Such sights as youthful poets dream / On summer eves by haunted stream," *Allegro*, II, 129–30), sits moodily on the bank of the glimmering river, while the Gothic chapel with its white, almost unearthly glow, on the opposite bank reminds both poet and the viewer of the foundations of Christianity in the natural order of the world. It is a scene both tranquil and charged, both everyday and yet extraordinary, an example of Palmer's use of the visionary in his art. It is no wonder that Alfred Barr long cherished this sheet.

In the early 1830s, Shoreham began to experience the agrarian unrest that preceded the Reform Bill of 1832. Palmer, conservative by nature, became politically active for a time, supporting the most conservative elements in the area, perhaps in an attempt to reconcile his inner vision with the real world. It may have been for this reason as well as a difference in artistic temperament from Blake that Palmer could not sustain the visionary quality of his work, and there was a lessening in its intensity in the 1830s. He seems to have needed a change in his life, which occurred with his marriage in 1837 to Linnell's daughter Hannah, and a subsequent trip through Italy. Thereafter his art took on a softer, more romantic quality.

PROVENANCE: Mrs. George A. Martin, Cleveland, Ohio; Mr. and Mrs. Alfred Barr, Jr., New York.

BIBLIOGRAPHY: Geoffrey Grigson, *Samuel Palmer, The Visionary Years*, London, 1949, p. 165, no. 44, pl. 17.

EXHIBITIONS: Cotswold Gallery, London, *101 Drawings by English Artists*, 1934, no. 67, pl. IV; Durlacher Brothers, New York, *A Loan Exhibition; The Work of Samuel Palmer 1805–1881*, 1949, no. 3; The Arts Council of Great Britain, London, *Samuel Palmer & his circle*, 1957, p. 11, no. 9.

MORITZ VON SCHWIND
VIENNA 1804 – 1871 MUNICH

43 *Jesus Blessing Little Children*

Pen and black ink, watercolor and graphite on *chine appliqué*, laid down. 16⅞×9¼ inches (428×236 mm.). Inscribed at lower right, in graphite, *MS* (in ligature) and dated, *1859*, and, lower center, *5 10 100*, and in watercolor, lower center, *Sinite parvulos venire ad me, et ne probibu- / eritis eos. talium enim est regnum Dei. Am- / en dico vobis: Quisquis non receperit regn- / um Dei. velut parvulus, non intrabit in illud: / Et complexans eos et impenens manus sup- / er illos benedicebat eos.*

The prolific painter, draughtsman, and designer Moritz von Schwind ranked among the most prominent artists of his generation in Germany and Austria. Best known for his pictures, prints, and book illustrations that depict scenes from folklore and mediaeval history, Schwind also painted murals in the Munich Residenz, the Vienna Opera, and, among other important buildings, the castles of Wartburg in Thuringia and Hohenschwangau in Bavaria.

Although the Thaw watercolor is clearly a project for stained glass, none of the windows known to have been executed from Schwind's designs represented Jesus Blessing Little Children (see Alois Trost, "Moritz von Schwinds Entwürfe für Kirchenfenster," *Mitteilungen der Gesellschaft für vervielfältigende Kunst*, in *Die Graphischen Künste*, 40, 1917, pp. 41–48). The drawing perhaps records an unexecuted project for a window in Glasgow Cathedral or the Protestant church at Sonneberg, Thuringia. Both of these commissions were completed in 1859, the date on the Thaw sheet. However, as Keith Andrews pointed out in correspondence, the drawings associable with Schwind's compositions for stained glass differ in style and character from the Thaw work. The coats-of-arms in the lower corners of the sheet, which might provide information about the church for which this design was intended or the patron who commissioned it, remain unidentified.

The story of Jesus Blessing Little Children is told in the Gospels of St. Matthew (19: 13–15), St. Luke (18: 15–17), and St. Mark (10: 13–16). While Jesus was teaching, children were brought to him for his benediction. When the apostles tried to send them away, Jesus became displeased and spoke the words inscribed on Schwind's design, "Permit the little children to come unto me, and forbid them not; for of such is the kingdom of God. / Verily I say unto you, Whoseover shall not receive the kingdom of God as a little child, he shall not enter into it." The inscription on the watercolor concludes with the verse that appears only in the Gospel of St. Mark, "And he took them up in his arms, put his hands upon them, and blessed them."

PROVENANCE: In the same family collection since the end of the nineteenth century (according to Kurt Meissner); Kurt Meissner, Zurich.

HILAIRE-GERMAIN-EDGAR DEGAS

PARIS 1834 – 1917 PARIS

44 *Two Studies of Dancers*

Black chalk, heightened with white on green prepared paper. 17½×11 5/16 inches (445×286 mm.). Watermark: none visible through lining.

Shortly after the end of the Franco-Prussian War in 1871, Degas began his first pictorial essays on the ballet, a subject which was to interest him to one degree or another until the end of his life. The artist's preoccupation, however, was never so great as it was in the decade of the 1870s when he filled his sketchbooks and portfolios with a repertory of poses and studies from life, many of which he employed in his paintings. Probably through the influence of such friends as the composer Bizet, the librettist Halévy, as well as musicians in the Opéra orchestra, Degas was able to gain access to the dance classes in the Opéra school in the rue Peletier with windows looking out at the gardens of the former Choiseul mansion. The artist, who loved accidental rather than posed compositions, found a perfect subject in these dancers so absorbed in their strenuous work as to be unconscious of his presence.

Not satisfied with pure linear notation, he often resorted to more painterly means as in this study on green paper executed in black chalk with touches of white to indicate the dramatic effects of light on the dancers' figures and costumes. Since the larger and more complete study, with the page in vertical orientation, appears in two of Degas' finished paintings of *The Rehearsal* (Lillian Browse, *Degas Dancers*, London, 1949, figs. 36, 37), the Thaw drawing must predate both versions of the picture, the one in the collection of Mr. and Mrs. J. Watson Webb in New York and the other version, which for many years also was in New York, and which is now part of the Wertheim Bequest to the Harvard University Art Museums.

The girl in the Thaw drawing can be identified with the dancer between two of the large windows in the version in the Webb Collection who stands, even in repose, in second position, watching a group of dancers rehearsing with a violinist, partially cut off by the edge of the picture, but visible at the extreme left of the composition. Degas used this study as well as the other study in the opposite direction in the Wertheim picture. The girl represented in the lower part of the drawing can be seen in a group engaged in conversation to the immediate right of the girl watching the rehearsal. While the artist's interest in the contrast between the brilliant sunlight streaming into the room from the windows and the areas of shade is evident in both studies, the play of light and shadow is more developed in the study of the girl watching the other dancers.

Among Degas' other studies for *The Rehearsal* are two on pink paper, one of which is in the Museum Boymans-van Beuningen in Rotterdam (Browse, fig. 37a), and a sheet, formerly in the Marie Harrison Gallery in New York. Another drawing for this picture, in the collection of

Mr. and Mrs. Edwin C. Vogel, New York, closely parallels the Thaw drawing in that Degas again employed green paper and turned the page both vertically and horizontally to get two studies in the place of one ("Drawings of Seven Centuries at Knoedler's New York," *Burlington Magazine*, CI, 1959, p. 351, fig. 54).

PROVENANCE: Third Degas atelier sale (Lugt 657–58), 9 April 1919, lot 343 (in a lot of two), repr.; Paul Rosenberg, New York; Irene Mayer Selznick, New York.

45 *Sketchbook (nb. 29)*

21 drawings on 43 leaves. Chiefly pencil with touches of charcoal, and a few leaves executed in blue chalk, on wove paper, mostly white, with some light brown, tan, and gray towards the back of the book. Leaves measuring approximately $9\frac{7}{8} \times 13\frac{3}{8}$ inches (249×339 mm.), in linen-clad boards measuring $10\frac{1}{8} \times 13\frac{1}{2}$ inches (258×345 mm.). Watermark: none. Inscribed by Halévy throughout, notably on first leaf in pen and black ink, *Tous les croquis de cet album / ont été faits chez moi par Degas. / Années 1880 et suivantes.*

Thirty-eight of the sketchbooks (or notebooks as Reff calls them) of Edgar Degas have survived essentially intact. They cover the more than thirty years between 1853 and 1886, and constitute the most significant sustained record of any artist of the Impressionist period. The full publication of these sketchbooks involved the comprehensive study of approximately 2,000 sketches (and 500 pages of notes) concerning the chronological order of their use; it was the subject of more than fourteen years of study by Theodore Reff. The majority of the notebooks are the twenty-nine in the Bibliothèque Nationale in Paris which were donated in 1920 by the artist's brother René shortly after Degas' death. Of the nine remaining, two were purchased by the Cabinet des Dessins of the Louvre in 1922 and another was acquired by the Metropolitan Museum of Art, New York in 1973. The other six are in private collections or on the art market.

The book, which is the subject of this discussion, is one of two large sketchbooks bound in linen-clad covers, both of which were in the possession of the playwright and librettist Ludovic Halévy (1834–1908) and his family until quite recently. Although most of the Degas notebooks are small enough to be portable, it is obvious from their relatively large size that the Halévy notebooks were not meant to be carried about.

According to Mme Halévy's written reminiscence in 1924, when these notebooks (Reff notebooks 28 and 29) were first exhibited (Galerie Georges Petit, Paris, *Degas*, 1924, no. 188), she and her husband had a few of their closest friends to dinner every Thursday evening. The group included Halévy's fellow playwright Henri Meilhac, the composer Ernest Reyer, Jules Lemaître, Anatole France, and Degas. These dinners were either in the Halévys' apartment in Paris on rue de Douai or at their summer residence at St. Germain-en-Laye. After dinner Degas, who infrequently participated in the conversation, often sketched on little scraps of paper. Halévy finally decided to buy the two albums for his friend's use on these occasions. Halévy later inscribed many of the leaves and, at the beginning of the book now in the Thaw collection, noted that all of the sketches were made in his home by Degas in the years 1880 and following. It was Mme Halévy's recollection also that while the first album (notebook 28) was begun in Paris in 1877, the second was started, but never completely used up because of Degas' steadily failing eyesight, at St. Germain-en-Laye in 1880. This account is confirmed by their son, Daniel Halévy, in his preface to the facsimile of both notebooks in 1949. He remarks that because of his eyesight Degas never drew in the evening after 1881 or 1882. The date assigned by the Halévy family to the Thaw sketchbook is supported by Ronald Pickvance.

Writing in 1983 after Reff's monumental catalogue, Pickvance differs with him as to the chronology of the sketchbook. Reff dated the book between 1877 and 1880, based on the evidence of what he plausibly took to be preparatory sketches for some of the key works which engaged Degas during those years, such as *Les Deux Danseuses* (Lemoisne 599), painted ca. 1878–80, *Miss Lala at the Cirque Fernando* (Lemoisne 522), now in London, on which Degas was working between January and April of 1879, as well as *Scènes de Ballet* (Lemoisne 610), of ca. 1880. He reasoned that since one page illustrates the scene in which a model poses as a laundress for an artist in *La Cigale*, Halévy and Meilhac's play which was first produced on 6 October 1877, the book must also date from that time.

Pickvance, on the other hand, feels that the book must postdate July 1879, when the first of what were to become weekly dinners took place at the Pavillon Henri IV; an identified view of the restaurant is on the first drawn leaf in notebook 29. He argues that the evidence put forth by Reff for an earlier dating is not so much a record of works in progress as a recollection of these paintings which may have been elicited by the artist's friends during the course of their after-dinner conversations. Looked at this way, the leaf with the sketch of Miss Lala, for instance, with the detail of the metal bit, onto which she held with her teeth, might be regarded as the answer to a question from one of Degas' friends as to how she had managed such a feat of strength. The book also includes a number of sketches of friends and acquaintances, often satirical in character, many of whom are identified in Ludovic Halévy's inscriptions.

Among the satiric drawings, one of an Oriental lounging in a seraglio-like setting may be recognized as William Busnach, a man who always claimed to be of Arabian origin. Pickvance goes further than Reff in identifying the *café-concert* singer, whose slim figure appears a number of times in the book, as Mlle Émélie Bécat, the subject of *Aux Ambassadeurs* (No. 46). If the book may be said to have a theme, Pickvance feels it is self-indulgence and pleasure, that it essentially represents "an all-male view of the world, with its broad robust humor and mocking in-jokes." The view that Degas drew for the benefit of his male companions is further corroborated by the opening which shows a prostitute and her pimp, inscribed "*une grue*" (a French slang expression meaning a woman of easy virtue) at the upper left.

PROVENANCE: Ludovic Halévy, Paris; by descent to Daniel Halévy, Paris.

BIBLIOGRAPHY: *Edgar Degas, Album de dessins*, ed. Daniel Halévy, Paris, 1949, published in facsimile with another sketchbook (nb. 28) with the same provenance; Theodore Reff, *The Notebooks of Edgar Degas, a Catalogue of the Thirty-Eight Notebooks in the Bibliothèque Nationale and other Collections*, Oxford, 1976, 2 vols., I, pp. 2f., 10f., 17, 30, 31, 131ff., II, repr., n.p., under nb. 29.

EXHIBITIONS: Galerie Georges Petit, Paris, *Degas*, 1924, no. 188 (with nb. 28), not repr.; David Carritt Limited, London, *Edgar Degas, 1834–1917*, catalogue by Ronald Pickvance, 1983, no. 21 (lent by Mr. and Mrs. Thaw), six leaves repr.

46 *Aux Ambassadeurs: Mlle Bécat*

Pastel over lithograph. $9\frac{1}{16} \times 7\frac{7}{8}$ inches (230×200 mm.). Signed and dated at lower right in pastel, *Degas/85*. Watermark: none.

In retrospect Degas is recognized as one of the greatest printmakers of the nineteenth century. The artist, however, regarded the process essentially as a private means to explore new techniques and create different kinds of images. Because not many of his prints were published, few beside his friends and fellow artists knew this aspect of his art.

The present work is based on a lithograph Degas made around 1877, which he enlarged in 1885, adding two strips of paper to the side and lower edge. He then worked up the image in pastel and continued on the additional paper, drawing the three women spectators and the framing column at the right. This effectively changed the perspective of the original print, moving Mlle Bécat from the immediate foreground to the middle of the composition.

Although in the original lithograph, Degas was interested in the tonal values of black and white, here he added color to striking effect, especially in the sharply contrasting representation of the same colors to indicate the effect of different kinds of light. The performer is illuminated by pink gaslight, the pale but warm color of which is repeated in her gown. A bright fresh green is used for the wooden framing elements as well as the bits of foliage in the background while clear pinks and blues are used for the fireworks lighting up the summer night. In marked contrast to the vivid theatrical light and the fireworks, the three women spectators are cast in shadow, illuminated only by an unflattering half-light which tinges their skin blue. For these figures, the artist chose a muted palette of blue-greens, purples, and ochers, using color in a way that suggests the difference between the mundane and the magical world of the theatre.

The artist frequented the theatre, the ballet, and also this informal open-air concert, the Café des Ambassadeurs in the Champs-Elysées, where Mlle Émélie Bécat was the star. She was the subject of another three lithographs executed by Degas, as well as a number of other works (*Edgar Degas: The Painter as Printmaker*, 1984–85, nos. 26, 30, and 31). He made numerous sketches of her in his notebooks, including several in the sketchbook illustrated here (see No. 45).

In 1891 Lucien Pissarro wrote to his father that he had again seen the little lithograph retouched with pastel—which they had admired some years earlier in Degas' studio—in the collection of "a young man who knows Degas." The young man was Walter Sickert, the English artist who, like Degas, was fascinated by theatrical themes. Sickert apparently gave it to his wife's sister, Mrs. Fisher Unwin, who lent it to the first exhibition of the International Society of Sculptors, Painters and Gravers, held in London in 1898.

PROVENANCE: Mr. and Mrs. Walter Sickert (by May 1891); Mrs. Fisher Unwin (1898); M. Knoedler & Co., New York; Mrs. Ralph King, Cleveland, Ohio; David Tunick, Inc., New York.

BIBLIOGRAPHY: John Rewald, *Camille Pissarro, Lettres à son fils Lucien*, 1950, p. 239.

EXHIBITIONS: International Society of Sculptors, Painters and Gravers, London, 1898, no. 119 (as *Café Chantant*); Cleveland Museum of Art, Cleveland, *Works by Edgar Degas*, 1947, no. 44 (as *At the Music Hall*); David Carritt Limited, London, *Edgar Degas, 1834–1917*, 1983, no. 26, repr. in color; Museum of Fine Arts, Boston, and elsewhere, *Edgar Degas: The Painter as Printmaker*, catalogue by Sue Welsh Reed and Barbara Stern Shapiro, with contributions by Clifford S. Ackley, Roy L. Perkinson, Douglas Druick, and Peter Zegers, 1984–85, no. 31b (exhibited in Boston); repr. in color.

PAUL CÉZANNE

AIX-EN-PROVENCE 1839 – 1906 AIX-EN-PROVENCE

47 *Sketchbook*

73 drawings on 48 leaves, bound in linen-clad boards. Pencil, with watercolor on one leaf only, on wove paper, four sheets of blue interleaved. Leaves measuring approximately $4\frac{15}{16} \times 8\frac{1}{2}$ inches (126×216 mm.), in binding measuring $5\frac{5}{16} \times 8\frac{5}{8}$ inches (134×221 mm.). Watermark: MONTGOLFIER S A.

As compared with Degas, Cézanne drew relatively little. Chappuis lists eighteen sketchbooks in his *catalogue raisonné*, many of which are represented only fragmentarily (Chappuis, 1973, p. 20ff.). Five sketchbooks, including the one now in the Thaw collection, remained in the possession of the artist's son until the 1930s at which time they were sold as a group, through the Parisian dealer Maurice Renou, to a collector in Lyons. In 1950 all five of these books were acquired by Sam Salz, a dealer in New York, who presented one to the Louvre and sold the others to American collections, including one to the Art Institute in Chicago, and two to Mr. and Mrs. Ira S. Haupt of New York. The Thaw sketchbook was sold at that time to Mr. and Mrs. Leigh Block of Chicago. The entire group was published by John Rewald in 1951.

It is generally acknowledged by scholars that they were executed between 1870 and 1885 and date to a period in Cézanne's life when he was most concerned with drawing. Like many of his Impressionist contemporaries, Cézanne was primarily a colorist and did not need to draw in the usual sense to realize his artistic conceptions, which he visualized in terms of color, light, and volume. Nevertheless, at a stage of his development dating from around 1870, he wanted to find out more about light and the representation of space in terms of black and white, rather than color, and concentrated on drawing in an attempt to sort out the relationship between the structural qualities of line and the naturalistic properties of color. While in the early sketchbooks Cézanne's notations are sometimes awkward, he gradually developed into an assured draughtsman. Eventually—having worked out his problems in the process of drawing—he almost abandoned pencil drawing and continued in color alone.

To be regarded essentially as technical exercises, the sketchbooks contain a variety of images, not usually connected with works in progress. In several Cézanne made copies of the works of earlier masters, such as his studies after Rubens and Delacroix, which occur in the earliest book (now in Mrs. Haupt's collection), or of sculpture in the Louvre (now in the Cabinet des Dessins).

Most Cézanne authorities agree that the artist used the Thaw sketchbook between 1875 and 1885. Worked on during a ten-year period, this book offers an especially broad range of subject matter, including sketches of the Provençal landscape, and concentrated drawings of an assortment of items, often domestic in origin, and occasionally extraordinary, such as the suit of armor (probably seen at Émile Zola's house). Most often, however, it is the back of a chair, a vase of flowers, or the clock on the mantel which is studied. Cézanne put so much energy into these that they may almost be considered as small still-lifes in their own right.

The book also contains a number of informal portrait studies, including one of Camille Pissarro at work before his easel, two of Émile Zola, a self-portrait, several studies of his wife, and one of a sleeping child, possibly their son, drawn on one of the blue leaves. It is believed that, besides the suit of armor, Cézanne also sketched a number of other items in Zola's house. An early sketch for the *Bathers* (which Rewald dates to 1875) is of particular interest for the study of the development of that work. Occasionally, the juxtaposition of images on a leaf can be startling. This is the case in several instances where one or more portrait sketches occur on a page or where a head appears on a page otherwise occupied by a piece of furniture with a vase on top of it.

Although most of Cézanne's essays in pure draughtsmanship are confined to the relatively small size of sketchbook leaves, there are a few large-scale pencil drawings, notably *The Card-Player*, which Mr. and Mrs. Thaw presented to the Morgan Library in 1975 (Morgan Library, Thaw exhibition, 1975–76, no. 98, repr.). Usually, however, "once the artist began to draw on a good-sized piece of paper, he seems to have felt the urge to animate these lines with touches of color" (Rewald, 1983, p. 20).

PROVENANCE: The artist's son, Paul Cézanne, Paris; Maurice Renou, Paris; Poyet collection, Lyons; Maurice Renou, Paris; Sam Salz, New York; Mr. and Mrs. Leigh Block, Chicago.

BIBLIOGRAPHY: John Rewald, *Carnets de dessins*, Paris, 1951, 2 vols., for general discussion of all five, repr.; Gertrude Berthold, *Cézanne und die alten Meister*, Stuttgart, 1958, no. 333 (f. 13), repr.; Adrien Chappuis, *The Drawings of Paul Cézanne*, Greenwich, Conn., 1973, p. 9f., 16, 20f., 22 (no. 16), nos. 550, 551; John Rewald, *Paul Cézanne Sketchbook, 1875–1885*, New York, 1982, discussion of the Thaw sketchbook and facsimile.

48 *The Terrace of the Garden at Les Lauves*

Watercolor over pencil, on white wove paper. 17×21 1/16 inches (432×534 mm.). Watermark: none. Numbered in blue pencil on verso at upper right, *39*. Mostly effaced inscription in French in pencil at lower left of verso, directions for a frame, *gros cadre feuille* / [*C*]*arte* [*gris*] *ou bleu.*

In some respects Cézanne's watercolors develop in a way that is parallel to his pencil drawings. The earlier watercolors rely more heavily on clear outlines and recognizable forms than do the later ones. As the artist matured, the contours tend to disappear and modelling and the concretion of form are accomplished in the layering of color.

It is clear that Cézanne found in watercolor an expressive medium which filled a different set of esthetic needs than did oil. The oil paintings are massive in effect, whereas the watercolors are light and vibrant. In watercolor the artist could apply successive layers of color, allowing each to dry before painting another. Since each layer was diluted so extensively that it left only a sheer tint of color, it created a "splendid variety of nuances" which is "accompanied by a delicate contrast of textures" (Rewald, 1983, p. 31). There is, moreover, an almost wistful, poetic quality to the watercolors which, as Meyer Schapiro has observed, "permits us to dwell on the intimacy of Cézanne's sensing of a pictorial aptness in things; we experience . . . his attentiveness, his fine hesitations and scruples, his delicacy of touch . . ." (Meyer Schapiro, "Cézanne as a Watercolorist," in *Cézanne Watercolors*, 1963, p. 12).

Although it is often difficult to fix precisely the chronology of Cézanne's watercolors, Rewald dates this work to the four years between 1902 and 1906 (Rewald, 1983, no. 621). It is one of several views from the terrace of Cézanne's studio at Les Lauves near Aix where he worked from 1902 until his death in 1906. The mood is especially poetic here and the artist's use of pale color suggests that he painted it in the spring when greens are at their freshest. Greens and blues predominate and are complemented by the pale washes of rose madder and ocher used to indicate the flowerpots and the play of sunlight on the stone terrace. Although he had a remarkable view from his terrace of the range of mountains known as the Châine de l'Étoile—indicated here in summary fashion with a curving blue line—he gave his full attention to the terrace itself (Rewald, 1983, no. 621).

PROVENANCE: Ambroise Vollard, Paris; Georges Bernheim, Paris; Knoedler Galleries, Paris and New York; Mrs. Thalia Malcolm; Knoedler Galleries, New York; Sam Salz, New York; Erich Maria Remarque, Ascona; Feilchenfeldt, Zurich.

BIBLIOGRAPHY: Lionello Venturi, *Cézanne, son art, son oeuvre*, Paris, 1936, no. 1072; Edward Alden Jewell, *Paul Cézanne*, New York, 1944, p. 21, repr.; John Rewald, *The Watercolors of Paul Cézanne*, Boston, 1983, no. 621, repr. in color, pl. 36.

EXHIBITIONS: Columbus Gallery of Fine Arts, Columbus, Ohio, 1939–40, no. 14; Knoedler Galleries, New York, *Remarque Collection*, 1943, no. 33; Wildenstein Galleries, New York, *Cézanne*, 1947, no. 86; Art Institute, Chicago, and Metropolitan Museum, New York, *Cézanne*, 1952, no. 103, repr.; Gemeentemuseum, The Hague, *Cézanne*, 1956, no. 89, repr.; Kunsthaus, Zurich, *Paul Cézanne*, 1956, no. 142, repr.; Haus der Kunst, Munich, *Französische Malerei des 19. Jahrhunderts, von David bis Cézanne*, 1956, no. 110, repr.; Museum Boymans, Rotterdam, *Van Clouet tot Matisse*, 1958, no. 155, pl. 159; Musée de l'Orangerie, Paris, *De Clouet à Matisse*, 1958–59, no. 155, pl. 172; Metropolitan Museum of Art, New York, *French Drawings from American Collections*, 1959, no. 153, pl. 170; Knoedler Galleries, New York, *Cézanne Watercolors*, 1963, no. 63, repr. pl. LXI; Museum of Modern Art, New York, and Museum of Fine Arts, Houston, *Cézanne, The Late Work*, 1977–78, no. 108, pl. 104; Grand Palais, Paris, *Cézanne, Les dernières années*, 1978, no. 74, repr.

49 *Still-Life with Pears and Apples, Covered Blue Jar, and a Bottle of Wine*

Watercolor over black chalk. Verso: Landscape sketch with Mont Sainte-Victoire and trees in black chalk with touches of watercolor. $18\frac{3}{4} \times 24\frac{5}{16}$ inches (476×617 mm.). Paper embossed: MONTGOLFIER S A. Numbered on verso in black chalk, *69.* and *1984.*

It was often remarked by those who knew him that Cézanne cared little for his watercolors. Nevertheless, he spent a good deal of time working in the medium, and at least 651 watercolors have survived (Rewald, 1983, p. 10). During his lifetime they were admired and collected by a significant minority including such artists as Degas and Renoir. While a few were exhibited in Cézanne's first retrospective in 1895, the watercolors were not given a separate exhibition until 1905 (by Ambroise Vollard) by which time Cézanne's reputation had grown significantly. It was not, however, until 1907, the year after Cézanne's death, when Bernheim-Jeune held a large memorial exhibition devoted to the artist's work which included a number of the watercolors, that they began to attract the wider audience that they have continued to command ever since. They had an immediate impact on the Cubists, who admired them for their abstract volumetric qualities. One of the most prominent figures in the movement, Delaunay, declared: "The watercolors of Cézanne announce Cubism . . . the colored, or rather luminous planes destroy the object." (Theodore Reff, "Cézanne's Watercolors and Modern Taste," in *Cézanne Watercolors*, 1963, p. 15.)

Here the artist began with a tentative sketch of his favorite landscape motif, Mont Sainte-Victoire, before turning the sheet over and starting *Still-Life with Pears and Apples*. This still-life is a perfect example of Cézanne's late watercolor manner which John Rewald has characterized as "bold, superbly fluent, and self-assured" (Rewald, 1983, p. 37). Although the subject matter as well as the close viewpoint and stronger color values differ from the *Jardin des Lauves* watercolor, the artist's handling of the brushwork is similar in both drawings and Rewald dates them to the same period, 1902–06. While a faint pencil sketch is visible, the artist has addressed the white paper directly with his brush, using patterns of bright color to mold forms which are almost abstract, and retracing many of the contours with a broken blue brushline.

In contrast to the soft coloring of the *Jardin des Lauves* (No. 48), Cézanne here employed a palette that is dominated by bright, cool blues and reds, using gold and pink tones to model the pears at the left while the piles of apples are indicated in yellow and green. The process of ripening is suggested here by a faint bluish-pink apparent in some of the apples. The blue pot at the left is similar to the blue enamel coffee pot that appears in a number of Cézanne's watercolors (Rewald, nos. 554, 571, 572), but (as Rewald notes) it is so much smaller here it may be wondered if it is in fact the same object.

PROVENANCE: Ambroise Vollard, Paris; Henri Manguin, Paris; Lucile Manguin-Martinais, Paris; Galerie de Paris, Paris; Norton Simon, Los Angeles; Norton Simon Inc. Museum of Art, Pasadena.

BIBLIOGRAPHY: Richard W. Murphy, *The World of Cézanne*, New York, 1968 (detail used as front endpaper); François Daulte, *French Watercolors of the 20th Century*, New York, 1968, no. 8, repr.; John Rewald, 1983, no. 567, repr. in color.

EXHIBITIONS: Tate Gallery, London; Museum and Art Gallery, Leicester; Graves Art Gallery, Sheffield, *Paul Cézanne, An Exhibition of Watercolors*, 1946, no. 43; Musée d'Art Moderne, Paris, *De l'Impressionnisme à nos jours*, 1958, no. 31; Musée Jenisch, Vevey, *De Cézanne à Picasso, Maîtres de l'Aquarelle au XXe Siècle*, 1962, no. 33, repr.; Knoedler Galleries, New York, *Cézanne Watercolors*, 1963, no. 68, pl. LXIII; Los Angeles County Museum, Los Angeles, *Special Exhibition for College Art Associates*, 1965.

ODILON REDON

BORDEAUX 1840 – 1916 PARIS

50 *The Fool (or Intuition)*

Charcoal on light brown wove paper. $15\frac{1}{2} \times 13\frac{1}{2}$ inches (394×343 mm.). Watermark: none. Signed at lower right, *Odilon Redon*; inscribed on verso at upper left, *Mephistophélès*; at lower left center, *91*.

For nearly thirty years from the late 1860s through the 1890s Redon worked almost exclusively in black. Probably through the influence of Corot, he discovered charcoal, "that powder which is volatile, impalpable, and fugitive. It expressed me best and I kept to it." Redon loved his black pictures, "mes noirs," as he called them. "One must respect black . . . It does not please the eye and it conveys no sensuality. It is the agent of the mind far more than the most beautiful colors of the palette or the prism . . ." (*A.S.M.*, p. 125).

It is estimated that he produced between four and five hundred charcoal pictures and worked in lithography as well. In the 1870s Redon began what was to be the most intensely creative period of his life. From rather conventional beginnings he gradually evolved an idiosyncratic canon of symbolic motifs and he achieved the most intense blacks. He developed a series of imaginary portraits often characterized by a weird, secret imagery known only to himself.

The key to the interpretation of the imaginary portraits may be found in this passage from one of Redon's letters: "The sense of mystery consists in existing always under some aspect of ambiguity. This may be a double or triple aspect or even suspicions of such aspects; for example: images within images, forms which are becoming or will become in accord with the viewer's state of mind" (*A.S.M.*, p. 97).

The Fool (*or Intuition*) illustrates the sort of ambiguity Redon sought. It is interesting to contrast it with another imaginary portrait of the same date (repr. in Claude Roger-Marx, "Odilon Redon, peintre et mystique," *L'Oeil*, no. 17, May 1956, opp. p. 21 [Collection Claude Roger-Marx, Paris]) which was also meant to be interpreted on various levels of meaning and to evoke a "sense of mystery" in the mind of the viewer. It is entitled *Mephistopheles* (*Foolishness*) (*Madness*). Both heads are similar in type: emaciated, mask-like, and dressed in mediaeval fashion. The one is dressed in cap and bells, while the subject of the Thaw portrait wears a cap trimmed with a feather, the angle of which complements his eloquently crooked finger. The look in the eyes is also quite different. The eyes of the Roger-Marx portrait are huge, vacuous, melancholic, and unfocused. The eyes of the fool in the Thaw portrait, on the other hand, are knowing and perceptive, perhaps reflecting that aspect of the title, *Intuition*.

Redon was familiar with and admired the works of Poe and Baudelaire, as witness his lithographic suites inspired by their works (*À Edgar Poe*, 1882, and *Les Fleurs du Mal*, 1890). Both of these writers found aesthetic meaning in distortion and the unnatural, the concept that there is beauty in evil. Here, Redon invests these portraits with several seemingly contradictory aspects. It would seem from his inscriptions that the artist had Mephistopheles in mind, the elegant, smiling devil introduced in Goethe's *Faust*.

PROVENANCE: Jacques Dubourg, Paris; René Malamoud, Zurich; Hazlitt, Gooden, & Fox, London.

BIBLIOGRAPHY: Klaus Berger, *French Master Drawings of the Nineteenth Century*, New York, 1950, no. 51, repr.; Claude Roger-Marx, *Redon: Fusains*, Paris, 1950, no. 2, repr.; Klaus Berger, *Odilon Redon*, London, 1964, no. 578, pl. 43; Jean Selz, *Odilon Redon*, Lugano, 1971, p. 33, repr.

EXHIBITIONS: Kunsthalle, Bern, *Odilon Redon*, 1958, no. 19, repr.; Matthiesen Gallery, London, *Odilon Redon*, 1959, no. 6, repr.; Venice, *Biennale XXXI*, 1962, no. 19, repr.; Hazlitt, Gooden, & Fox, London, *Exhibition of Nineteenth Century French Drawings*, 1977, no. 66, pl. 64.

51 *Cavalier*

Charcoal pencil on light brown wove paper. $21\frac{1}{8} \times 14\frac{3}{4}$ inches (535×375 mm.). Watermark: none. Signed at lower left, ODILON REDON.

Between 1865 and 1866 Redon prepared at least nine etchings of *cavaliers* or riders. These demonstrate both his admiration of Delacroix and his debt to his master, Rodolphe Bresdin. Although they are conventional works, they reflect the strong influence of the Romantic movement. An exact contemporary of Monet, Redon did not aspire to the naturalistic goals of his Impressionist contemporaries. He was more interested in the mysterious than in the actual. He read extensively and his imagination was stirred by many literary sources, including classical myths and mediaeval legends. Horses recur in his art, whether the winged Pegasus of Greek mythology, or those of the chivalric legends. He also executed a number of Oriental subjects which were inspired by Delacroix's numerous studies of Arabian horsemen. About twenty years later, Redon returned to the thematic material of the earlier etchings and produced a series of drawings and lithographs suggestive of the Middle Ages. The subject of the Thaw drawing resembles one of the earlier etchings, *Porte-étendard franchissant un gué* (as noted by Agnes Mongan in *French Drawings in American Collections*, 1959, no. 177).

The *Cavalier* is one of Redon's best-known charcoal pictures and was exhibited in the retrospective exhibition of his works in Paris in 1926, ten years after his death. As in all his works, its content is enigmatic. Even though it is related to the mediaeval etchings of the 1860s, it is not really clear from the unspecific nature of his costume whether the rider carrying a standard is mediaeval at all. Redon delighted in this sort of unconventional dream-like imagery which challenged his viewers' imagination.

Introduced to a greater public in J. K. Huysmans' controversial and widely-read novel of decadence, *A Rebours*, published in 1884, Redon aroused much interest in those who wished to identify with the literary *avant-garde*. Before this he was appreciated only by the very small circle of Symbolist artists and writers, including Stéphane Mallarmé and Huysmans himself. The Symbolists saw in Redon's art a visualization of their ideas. Mallarmé wrote in appreciation of Redon: "In your silences you ruffle the plumage of reverie and night . . . What is personal in you issues from your dreams . . . your inventions are as profound as are certain of your blacks . . . ."

PROVENANCE: Gustave Fayet, Béziers; Alexander M. Bing, New York; sale, New York, Christie's, 17 May 1984, lot 110, repr.

BIBLIOGRAPHY: Klaus Berger, *Odilon Redon: Fantasy and Colour*, New York, 1966, p. 228, no. 623 (called *Rider*).

EXHIBITIONS: Musée des arts décoratifs, Paris, *Odilon Redon, Exposition rétrospective de son oeuvre*, 1926, no. 208; C. M. de Hauke & Co., New York, *Exhibition of Odilon Redon*, 1928, no. 60; Museum of Modern Art, New York, *Picasso, his graphic art, Redon, drawings and lithographs*, 1952, no. 8; Museum Boymans, Rotterdam, *Van Clouet tot Matisse*, 1958, no. 177, pl. 169; Musée de l'Orangerie, Paris, *De Clouet à Matisse*, 1958, no. 177, pl. 183; Metropolitan Museum of Art, New York, *French Drawings from American Collections*, 1959, no. 177, pl. 169.

52 *Two Pears*

Charcoal, with touches of pen and white gouache on faded pink paper. $5\frac{1}{8} \times 4\frac{1}{4}$ inches (130 × 108 mm.). Watermark: none. Signed at lower left in charcoal pencil, *Od. R.*

Redon wrote, "For practice and for my own edification I have many times labored over the object right down to the most trivial details of its visual appearance; but the day would leave me sad and frustrated. And the next day I would turn to that other source (that of the imagination) in order to recall the form, and then I would be reassured and satisfied" (*A.S.M.*, p. 115).

This exquisite little drawing shows how astonishingly effective his work could be even on a small scale. Here, using only charcoal on a toned paper, Redon achieved an effect of magic realism peculiar to him alone. At the same time that the artist rendered exactly the form of the pears, he imbued the work with an intangible, surrealistic quality. It is as if the artist wished to suggest something of the impermanence of nature. His vibrant drawing transcends the reality of the pears, suggesting the recollection of the fruit rather than the study of it.

Fruit seems to have been more rare as a subject for Redon than flowers. Although he loved flowers and always worked with a bouquet near him in the studio, it was not until the beginning of the century and his subsequent change to works in color, that he turned to flowers as subjects and executed numerous flower-pieces in glowing, unearthly tones. This study of two pears, however, belongs to that earlier period when he worked almost exclusively in black. Stylistically, it seems close to several drawings of spherical objects which he executed in the 1880s. These, too, are charged with symbolic power.

PROVENANCE: Robert Schmit, Paris.

VINCENT VAN GOGH

GROOT-ZUNDERT 1853 – 1890 AUVERS-SUR-OISE

53 *Two Cottages at Saintes-Maries-de-la-Mer*

Reed pen and brown ink over graphite on white laid paper. $12\frac{3}{8} \times 18\frac{3}{4}$ inches (315×474 mm.). Watermark: PL BAS.

Van Gogh's fifteen-month sojourn in Arles (20 February 1888 to 8 May 1889) was recently the subject of a comprehensive exhibition at the Metropolitan Museum, which examined his motives for moving to the South of France as well as the extraordinary development of his art during his stay there. Apart from seeking the warmer climate after a desperate winter in Paris, Van Gogh went to Provence, "Wishing to see a different light, thinking that looking at nature under a bright sky might give us a better idea of the Japanese way of feeling and drawing. Wishing also to see this stronger sun . . . because one feels that the colors of the prism are veiled in the mists of the North" (Letter to Theo, Sept. 1889. See *Van Gogh in Arles*, p. 12).

Eagerly anticipating his first glimpse of the Mediterranean, Van Gogh left Arles on 30 May 1888 for a brief excursion to the small fishing village of Saintes-Maries-de-la-Mer. Before returning to Arles on 3 June he painted two marines and a view of the village, and completed nine drawings, including the Thaw *Two Cottages* (*ibid.*, pp. 69, 83–92, 261).

The visit to Saintes-Maries precipitated a significant change in Van Gogh's style. On the eve of his departure he wrote to his brother Theo, "I want to get my drawing more spontaneous, more exaggerated" (29 May 1888; *ibid.*, p. 83). In the studies of cottages and village streets executed in Saintes-Maries he fulfilled this intention, working with a new boldness that he ascribed in part to the liberating influence of the Mediterranean sunlight and the purity of color and atmosphere at the coast (*ibid.*, p. 89). Unusually long or broad strokes of the reed pen, laid down with astonishing freedom over a vigorous pencil sketch, animate several of these sheets with an expressionist energy unprecedented in his *oeuvre*. Vincent characterized the style of this group as "harsh," adding, "but I also have some carefully drawn ones" (Letter to Theo, ca. 4 June 1888; *ibid.*, p. 85). With its serene mood and relatively restrained touch, the Thaw work must be one of the latter. It brilliantly captures the strong contrasts of shimmering reflections and mobile shadows caused by the Mediterranean sun as it beats down on the thatched cottages and abundant, wind-driven vegetation. The intimate view of the farmhouses, the sensitive rendering of nuances of light and atmosphere, and the use of the reed pen and a warm brown ink recall, more than most drawings of the Arles period, the landscape studies of Rembrandt, which Van Gogh knew and admired.

Of the nine drawings he produced in Saintes-Maries, Vincent sent five to Theo immediately upon returning to Arles. He kept a study of beached fishing boats and three drawings of cottages, including the Thaw work, which he intended to execute in oils (*ibid.*, p. 84). One of these studies of farmhouses, drawn with the jagged, slashing strokes he described as "harsh," may represent the same pair of cottages as the sheet exhibited here (*ibid.*, no. 36). In the end, the Thaw drawing was the only one of the four which he retained that Van Gogh did not work up into a painting.

PROVENANCE: Mrs. J. van Gogh-Bonger, Amsterdam; Miss E. Bonger, Amsterdam; Willem Mengelberg, Amsterdam; Mr. and Mrs. Louis Ritter, Scarsdale, New York; private collection; Acquavella Galleries, New York.

BIBLIOGRAPHY: Johan Bart de la Faille, *L'oeuvre de Vincent van Gogh*, IV, Paris, 1928, no. 1440, pl. CLV, repr.; De la Faille, *The Works of Vincent van Gogh*, Amsterdam, 1970, no. 1440, repr.; Jan Hulsker, *The Complete Van Gogh*, New York, 1980, p. 331, fig. 1451.

EXHIBITIONS: Stedelijk Museum, Amsterdam, *Vincent van Gogh*, 1905, no. 380; Wildenstein & Co., New York, *Vincent van Gogh, A Loan Exhibition*, 1955, no. 100; Municipal Art Gallery, Los Angeles, *Vincent van Gogh, A Loan Exhibition of Paintings and Drawings*, 1957, no. 33; Fine Arts Associates, New York, *Paintings from the Ritter Foundation*, New York, 1959, no. 15; Metropolitan Museum of Art, New York, *Summer Loan Exhibition, Paintings, Drawings and Sculpture from Private Collections*, 1966, no. 9; Acquavella Galleries, New York, *XIX and XX Century Master Drawings and Watercolors*, 1984, no. 5, repr.; Metropolitan Museum of Art, New York, *Van Gogh in Arles*, catalogue by Ronald Pickvance, 1984, no. 35, repr.

EDOUARD VUILLARD

CUISEAUX, SAÔNE-ET-LOIRE 1868 – 1940 LA BAULE

54 *Les Chapeaux*

Watercolor over pencil on wove paper. 8 3/16 × 11 5/8 inches (207 × 295 mm.). Watermark: none visible through lining. Stamped at lower right, *EV*.

In 1888 at the Académie Julien, Vuillard became friends with a group of important artists, including Paul Sérusier (1863–1927), Pierre Bonnard (1867–1947), and Maurice Denis (1870–1943). These men, whom Paul Sérusier introduced to Paul Gauguin's expressive use of color and rhythmic pattern, formed a loosely organized artistic fraternity in 1892, calling themselves the Nabis. The term Nabi was derived from a Hebrew word meaning prophet, and it was adopted by this group who formed a society rooted in symbolism, mysticism, and Catholicism. The movement was a highly intellectual one which rejected the realism of the Impressionists in favor of art as a means of expression.

Vuillard's style developed from the work of Degas, Gauguin, Redon, and from Japanese prints. Since much of his subject matter was domestic, Vuillard, along with Bonnard, was often referred to as an "intimist." Vuillard's depictions of interiors usually include people, often women, who were a favorite subject of his. He rarely made fully worked-up finished drawings; rather the artist executed numerous rapid preliminary sketches which he would later use as ideas for his paintings. The Thaw sheet has been dated ca. 1893 and here Vuillard's quick brush strokes have captured a moment of conversation among three women. The dappled areas of green watercolor lend a cohesiveness to the composition and serve as a background creating an intimacy in the grouping of the women.

PROVENANCE: Estate of the artist; Alfred Ayrton, Switzerland; J.P.L. Fine Arts, London.

EXHIBITION: J.P.L. Fine Arts, London, *Edouard Vuillard*, 1985, p. 13, no. 10, repr. in color.

HENRI MATISSE
CATEAU CAMBRÉSIS 1869 – 1954 NICE

55 *Still-Life with a Chocolatière*

Brush and black ink. 9×11$^3/_4$ inches (228×299 mm.). Watermark: none. Signed at lower right, *Henri. Matisse.*

The boldly executed Thaw drawing is a study for Matisse's painting *Still-Life with a Chocolatière* of 1900 in the Hermitage Museum, Leningrad (Izerghina, 1978, no. 7). The format of the Leningrad canvas is vertical, and there are significant changes in composition between the drawing and the painting. In the picture, the table is set deeper in the space, so that nearly all of its top is visible and the objects that comprise the still-life are not presented so immediately to the viewer. The interior is more extensive in the painting, the walls are more legible, and Matisse placed the back of the chair behind the covered dish, which further enhances the impression of depth in the room.

Matisse used the same chocolate pot in different contexts in other paintings dated 1900, including *Flowers in a Chocolatière* in the Pablo Picasso Collection in the Louvre; and *Still-Life with a Chocolatière* in the Maguy Collection, Paris (*ibid.*, p. 122, both repr.).

Shortly before 1900 Matisse's drawing style changed radically from its naturalistic origins to the expressive manner of the Thaw study, which is based on powerful contrasts between the white paper and impetuously applied patches of ink. In these drawings the conventional functions of line and modeling are denied: contours are obliterated and volumes characterized by reserved white areas embedded in the surrounding shadows, an approach Matisse himself likened to the photographic negative (see Elderfield in *The Drawings of Henri Matisse*, pp. 31–32). Here, he drew inspiration from the procedure followed by Paul Cézanne, who declared, "Line and modeling do not exist" (*ibid.*, p. 31). At about the same time Matisse took an interest in the drawings of Vincent van Gogh, two of which he acquired around 1899. In the Thaw work the broad, energetically brushed marks of ink that form a nervous pattern on the table top and the wall at the left suggest the influence of the reed pen drawings Van Gogh made in Arles (see No. 53).

PROVENANCE: Edward Bragaline, New York.

BIBLIOGRAPHY: Antonina Izerghina, *Henri Matisse: Paintings and Sculpture in Soviet Museums*, Leningrad, 1978, under no. 7, repr.

EXHIBITIONS: Musée National d'Art Moderne, Centre Georges Pompidou, Paris, *Matisse. Dessins, sculpture*, 1975, no. 4; Hayward Gallery and Arts Council of Great Britain, London, and Museum of Modern Art, New York, *The Drawings of Henri Matisse*, catalogue by John Elderfield and Magdalena Dabrowski, 1984–85, no. 4.

56 *Portrait of a Girl (Cocoly Agelasto)*

Graphite. $13\frac{3}{4} \times 10$ inches (350×254 mm.). Watermark: none. Signed at lower right, in graphite, *Henri Matisse.*

Study of the human figure, Matisse wrote in his *Notes of a Painter* of 1908, "permits me to express my almost religious awe towards life . . . I penetrate amid the lines of the face those which suggest the deep gravity which persists in every human being" (*The Drawings of Henri Matisse*, 1984–85, p. 70).

Portraiture dominated Matisse's activity as a draughtsman from 1912 through 1916. The portrait drawings of these years rank among his most fascinating works, not only because of their penetrating characterizations, but also because he used them to help him negotiate fundamental formal problems during a period of intense artistic development.

Although most of the sitters portrayed in drawings of ca. 1915 were the artist's friends, patrons, or members of his family, they seldom appear in an intimate or sympathetic light. Always remote and frequently gloomy, they are often depicted frontally and so close to the picture plane that the top of the head exceeds the limits of the sheet, as in the Thaw *Portrait of a Girl.*

The Thaw work is surely one of the most arresting of these studies, in part because the innocent age of the sitter makes such a striking contrast with her disturbing expression and the hieratic *mise-en-page*. Looming above the rigid, harshly drawn vertical folds of the collar, the disembodied face engages the viewer intently through impenetrable, almond-shaped eyes. Compounding the psychological complexity of the portrait are the appropriately dainty lips and chin (firmly redrawn over erasures), the sensuously evoked textures of the hair, and the coquettish curls that fall in graceful serpentine curves from the ribbon above her ear.

Near the end of his life, Matisse selected this study for inclusion in *Portraits*, a publication of 1954 devoted to his portrait drawings of all periods. There, the sitter was identified as Cocoly Agelasto, and the sheet dated 1915. Not surprisingly, Matisse must have regarded the Thaw drawing as an outstanding example of his work.

PROVENANCE: Jean Matisse, Paris; Harold Diamond & Co., New York.

BIBLIOGRAPHY: Henri Matisse and André Sauret, *Portraits*, Monte Carlo, 1954, p. 30.

EXHIBITIONS: Hayward Gallery and The Arts Council of Great Britain, London, and Museum of Modern Art, New York, *The Drawings of Henri Matisse*, catalogue by John Elderfield and Magdalena Dabrowski, 1984–85, no. 35, repr.

57 *Portrait of Eva Mudocci*

Charcoal and pencil on wove paper. $14\frac{13}{16} \times 11\frac{1}{16}$ inches (375×282 mm.). Watermark: none. Signed at lower right, in pencil, *Henri-Matisse.*

Matisse's portrait drawings of 1915 and 1916 attest to his recent interest in the Cubist works of Picasso, Georges Braque, and Juan Gris. His response to their innovations took the form of a struggle to reduce the figure to its essential structure, epitomized in an armature of angular lines and geometric shapes. In the Thaw sheet, as in other portrait studies of these years, he worked from the relatively detailed toward the abstract, without sacrificing the impression of personal "gravity" that he discovered "amid the lines of the face" (see No. 56). The features are condensed into dark, decisively drawn strokes that summarize the more elaborate drawing underneath, which he erased.

The Thaw work and another in a Parisian private collection (André Sauret, *Portraits*, Monte Carlo, 1954, p. 27, repr.) are relatively naturalistic representations that preceded the large ($36\frac{1}{2} \times 27\frac{3}{4}$ inches) and highly abstract portrait of the same sitter in the collection of Pierre Matisse (Hayward Gallery, London, and Museum of Modern Art, New York, *The Drawings of Henri Matisse*, 1984–85, no. 41). There, she is depicted half-length, seated, her head turned three-quarters to the left and her right hand resting on her cheek.

Eva Mudocci, whose real name was Evangeline Muddock, was a celebrated English concert violinist. She specialized in performances of Scandinavian music which she played dressed in antique peasant costumes. She was the mistress and longtime companion of Edvard Munch, whom she met in Paris in 1903. Eva's beautiful face and wavy hair were immortalized in the Norwegian master's lithograph *Madonna: The Brooch* (Reinhold Heller, *Munch: His Life and Work*, London, 1984, pp. 180–81). Matisse must have taken an interest in her not only because of her handsome features, but also because he was an enthusiastic amateur violinist.

PROVENANCE: Pierre Matisse, New York; John Berggruen Gallery, San Francisco.

BIBLIOGRAPHY: "Hommage to Henri Matisse," *XXe Siècle*, New York, 1970, p. 100.

EXHIBITIONS: Philadelphia Museum of Art, Philadelphia, *Henri Matisse. Retrospective Exhibition of Paintings, Drawings, and Sculpture Organized in Collaboration with the Artist*, 1948, no. 115; John Berggruen Gallery, San Francisco, *Henri Matisse. An Exhibition of Drawings*, 1982, no. 5, repr.

PIET MONDRIAN
AMERSFOORT 1872 – 1944 NEW YORK CITY

58 *Dunes at Domburg*

Black chalk on light brown paper; extraneous mark of blue-green crayon. $17\frac{15}{16} \times 26\frac{15}{16}$ inches (457×685 mm.). Watermark: none visible through lining. Signed at lower left, *PM* (in ligature).

Although famous for works such as *Broadway Boogie-Woogie*, now in the Museum of Modern Art, New York, with its abstract pattern of red and yellow squares reminiscent of marquee lighting, Mondrian grew up in the tradition of northern naturalism. In his early years, predating his turn to Cubism in 1912, Mondrian (who gallicized the spelling of his name from Mondriaan before he moved to Paris) predominately studied trees, church façades, dunes, and the sea. In 1908 he made his first visit to Domburg, on the island of Walcheren, and was to return there for the next few summers in order to paint and study, spending his winters in Amsterdam.

Mondrian scrutinized the natural world not for its sensuous surfaces but as a way to transcend everyday reality. Like Van Gogh he was of an intensely religious temperament, and his early art reflects his romantic nature with its sense of drama, seen in the persistent motif of the bleak and uninhabited landscape. In the Thaw sheet, the long flowing lines that form the dune landscape, which are strangely reminiscent of a geological survey map, reinforce the sense of stability and permanence of the earth. Mondrian theorized that the feminine essence in nature was evoked in horizontality, and thus the undulating dunes as well as the horizon add to the sense of awe and mystery, which he carried over into his studies of the female nude itself.

The Thaw landscape is dated 1911, and was done in what was probably his final summer at Domburg. It was evidently exhibited there as well (according to a label on the back of the sheet in Mondrian's hand). The year 1911 was an important one for the artist. Not only did he send his work to the spring *Indépendents* exhibition in Paris, but in the autumn he attended the first *Moderne Kunstkring* exhibition in Amsterdam and there saw, probably for the first time, works by Braque and Picasso done in the Cubist style. Within a few months, he moved to Paris to begin his own revolutionary studies.

PROVENANCE: W. de Sitter; by descent; L.U. de Sitter; Rolf Weinberg, Zurich.

BIBLIOGRAPHY: J. M. Joosten, "Documentatie over Mondriaan (1)," *Museumsjournaal*, 13, Amsterdam, 1968, p. 210, 9; Hans L. C. Jaffé, *Piet Mondrian*, New York and Cologne, 1970–71, p. 22, pl. 34.

EXHIBITIONS: Art Gallery of Ontario, Toronto and elsewhere, *Piet Mondrian 1872–1944*, catalogue by Robert Walsh, 1966, no. 60, repr.; Staatsgalerie, Stuttgart and elsewhere, *Mondrian. Drawings, Watercolors, New York Paintings*, catalogue arranged by Ulrike Gauss, 1980–81, p. 83, no. 59, repr.

PAUL KLEE

BERN 1879 – 1940 MURALLO-LOCARNO

59 *Red, Green Gradation*

Point of brush and watercolor; borders of the drawing extended 6 mm. onto the mount, in pen and black ink. $9\frac{1}{4} \times 12\frac{1}{16}$ inches (235×305 mm.). Watermark: none visible through lining. Inscribed on mount at lower left, in pen and black ink, *1921 / 102* and in graphite, *Stufung rot / grün. (roter Zinnober)*.

Paul Klee began his career as a draughtsman and an etcher and in 1914 went to Tunisia where he undertook his experiments with color, considering himself to be a painter from that time onward. Immediately following his return from Tunisia, he began to use color extensively which resulted in his Kairouan watercolors.

Like many twentieth-century artists, Klee left a record of his work in several publications. In 1918 the artist wrote an essay on the elements of graphic art which was published in 1920 as part of his theoretical text *Creative Credo*. His two essays *Ways of Nature Study* (1923) and *Exact*

Experiments in the Realm of Art (1928), published during his Bauhaus period, are concerned with questions of teaching method.

Klee taught at the Bauhaus from January 1921 through April 1931 and his career as a teacher brought him into close contact with Wassily Kandinsky and Lyonel Feininger. Teaching required him to develop a theoretical system, and there was a close interrelationship between his theoretical ideas and his artistic output during this period. Klee's group of watercolors *Color Gradations*, to which the Thaw sheet belongs, were the result of these experiments in color movement in which the artist explored the color theories of Goethe, Philip Otto Runge, Delacroix, and Kandinsky (Christian Geelhaar, *Paul Klee and the Bauhaus*, Bath, 1973, p. 35). In this series of drawings, the artist began with abstract elements of form and measured the gradation of color by glazing or applying transparent layers of watercolor over a ground. Klee kept exact records in his catalogue of the color he used as a starting point for each gradation (*ibid.*, p. 36). In the Thaw sheet, Klee makes use of the complementary colors red and green, specifying the red as red vermilion. The Thaw watercolor is very similar to the succeeding one in the series, entitled *Rot/Grüne Stufung, 1921/103* in the Yale University Art Gallery which makes use of the same complementary colors (Kunsthalle Köln, *Paul Klee, Das Werk der Jahre 1919–1933, Gemälde, Handzeichnungen, Druckgraphik*, 1979, no. 44, repr.).

PROVENANCE: Dr. William R. Valentiner, Detroit; Heinz Berggruen, Paris; Helen Serger (Galerie La Boetie), New York; Acquavella Galleries, New York.

EXHIBITION: Fuji Television Gallery, Tokyo, *Paul Klee*, 1981, p. 67, no. 9, repr.

PABLO PICASSO
MALAGA 1881 – 1973 MOUGINS

60 *Portrait of Marie Derval*

Pen and brush in black ink over graphite on wove paper. $19\frac{3}{4} \times 12\frac{5}{8}$ inches (500×321 mm.). Watermark: A. LEPAGE AINÉ TOCHON LEPAGE. Signed at lower right, in black ink, *RUIZ*, and in graphite, *Picasso / 1901*.

This drawing is one of four studies of entertainers by Picasso that were reproduced under the title *Beuglant et Chahut* (*Bellowing and Horseplay*) on a single page of *Le Frou-Frou* on 14 September 1901. The others represented the singer Polaire and the dancers Jeanne Avril and Grille d'Egout (see *Master Drawings by Picasso*, p. 237, fig. 5). Marie Derval, the subject of the Thaw portrait, was a celebrated actress around the turn of the century.

The artist was identified beneath one of these illustrations as Ruiz, the name with which he originally signed the Thaw sheet. Although he often incorporated his father's surname Ruiz into his signature through 1900, the present drawing and the illustration in *Le Frou-Frou* are the only documented examples after that year. The signature and date *Picasso / 1901*, inscribed in pencil beneath *Ruiz*, are genuine but were probably added later (*ibid.*, p. 44).

Picasso worked up this large portrait from a smaller preliminary sketch, also in black ink (Christian Zervos, *Pablo Picasso*, 21, Paris, 1969, no. 299). The figure in the sketch is relatively loosely defined with looping strokes and open contours, and lacks the firm structure imposed by the thick, decisive outlines of the Thaw work. In addition, there are differences in detail between the sketch and the finished portrait: Picasso reversed the angle of the hat, changed the sitter's hairstyle, and elaborated her jewelry and the patterns of her dress.

The energetic contours of the figure, her frightening stare, and the flat, aggressively brushed marks of black ink boldly juxtaposed with the white paper, lend the portrait an expressionist vigor that is typical of Picasso's art from the middle of 1900 to the end of 1901. The scenes and characters from Parisian nightlife that he often depicted during this period were familiar from the works of Henri de Toulouse-Lautrec. Elements of Picasso's short-lived expressionist style were also inspired by Toulouse-Lautrec, but it has been noted that the Thaw drawing—with its stark contrasts of black and white, imposingly frontal figure, and psychological intensity—recalls the prints of Edvard Munch, which Picasso could have seen either in Paris or Barcelona (*Master Drawings by Picasso*, p. 49).

PROVENANCE: Gertrude Stein, Paris (?); Pierre Loeb, Paris; James Pendleton, California.

BIBLIOGRAPHY: *Le Frou-Frou*, 14 September 1901, p. 820, repr.

EXHIBITIONS: Museum of Modern Art, New York, *Pablo Picasso: A Retrospective*, catalogue by William Rubin, 1980, p. 33, repr.; The Fogg Art Museum, Harvard University, Cambridge, Mass., *Master Drawings by Picasso*, catalogue by Gary Tinterow, 1981, no. 8.

61 *Head of a Man*

Black chalk on white laid paper. $25\frac{5}{8} \times 18\frac{3}{4}$ inches (628×476 mm.). Signed at upper left, in graphite, *Picasso* and on verso, at upper right, *Picasso 1909*. Watermarks: Ingres 1871; and shield with a caduceus and letters CF, FRANCE below.

Datable to the spring of 1909, the Thaw drawing is one of the earliest examples of a head study in the Cubist idiom developed by Picasso and Georges Braque in 1908 and 1909. Here, the primitive masks of the *Demoiselles d'Avignon* yield to a radically new approach to portraiture: the volumes of the head are fractured into flat planes that intersect in sharp ridges, giving the face a faceted, crystalline appearance. At this stage, the figure is still conceived as a discrete, intact sculptural mass. In 1910, Picasso will introduce a more drastic fragmentation of the body and an ambiguous interplay between the human form and its inanimate surroundings.

The tentative modeling and contours of the jaws and chin reflect the experimental nature of this early attempt to apply the new style to the analysis of a head. Moreover, the Thaw work is probably a rapidly executed preliminary study for a more finished drawing of the same subject in gouache (Daix and Rosselet, no. 250). In both works Picasso concentrated on the face and forehead, while the rest of the head, the neck, and the shoulders were summarily sketched. The face is marginally longer in the gouache, which is drawn on a sheet of nearly the same dimensions, and the disposition of light and dark planes differs slightly from one work to the other. Finally, the gouache is more vigorously and resolutely modeled and has a psychological animation in the eyes that is not yet present in the study.

After completing these two drawings on paper, Picasso executed an even more finished version of the same head in gouache on panel (*ibid.*, no. 251).

PROVENANCE: Beyeler Gallery, Basel; Berggruen & Cie, Paris.

BIBLIOGRAPHY: Maurice Jardot, *Los Dibujos de Pablo Picasso*, Barcelona, 1959, no. 27, repr.; Christian Zervos, *Pablo Picasso*, Paris, 26, 1973, no. 398, repr.; Pierre Daix and Joan Rosselet, *Picasso, The Cubist Years, A Catalogue Raisonné of the Paintings and Related Works*, Boston, 1979, under no. 250.

EXHIBITIONS: Musée National d'Art Moderne, Paris, *Le Cubisme*, 1953, no. 16; Berggruen & Cie., Paris, *Picasso: dessins d'un demi-siècle*, 1956, n.p., repr.

62 *Pipe and Wineglass*

Pasted papers and pencil on white laid paper. 7 1/16 × 9 7/16 inches (179 × 240 mm.). Watermark: none visible through lining. Signed at lower right, in pencil, *Picasso*.

The invention in 1912 of collage—the combination of pieces of pasted paper with conventional drawing media—precipitated the stylistic transition from Analytical to Synthetic Cubism. In Analytical Cubist works, such as the Thaw *Head of a Man* (No. 61), objects are broken down into their abstract components through intense scrutiny of light, line, and plane, while the picture surface retains its traditional meaning as an imaginary window into space. In the synthetic phase, objects are no longer analyzed by means of line and modeling, but fabricated from flat patches of color, outlined geometric shapes, or pasted papers. This preference for flat pictorial components, which deny the illusion of depth, led to one of the fundamental innovations of twentieth-century painting and drawing, namely, "that the pictorial illusion takes place upon the physical reality of an opaque surface rather than behind the illusion of a transparent plane" (Robert Rosenblum, *Cubism and Twentieth-Century Art*, revised edition, New York, 1966, p. 72).

The clarity of pictorial elements as well as the visual and intellectual complexity of the Synthetic Cubist collage are evident in the Thaw work, which dates from early in 1914. Although simply constructed from cut and pasted paper and a few strokes of the pencil, this still-life exhibits a witty interplay between media, surfaces, objects, and spatial planes. The tabletop is defined sparely with three contours buttressed by scattered areas of hatched shadow. We seem to view the goblet at once from above and from the side, and it appears both to lie flat and to stand securely on its foot, which is composed of a half circle drawn on the white paper and reflected in a reserve area cut out of the brown sheet. The irregular shape removed from the body of the glass stands for the volume and contents of its bowl, an illusion supported by several passages of shading with the pencil. In his "open" sculpture *Glass of Absinthe*, also of 1914 (Daix and Rosselet, 1979, nos. 753–58), Picasso will again punch an opening in the bowl, this time of a three-dimensional glass, to create an analogous effect of depth and spatial ambiguity. The cut and pasted pipe is so brilliantly worked up with *trompe-l'oeil* modeling that we seem to glimpse it not only in the round, but also simultaneously from above, from the left side, and end-on. Finally, a pattern that evokes the molding of the table's edge has been drawn on the lateral strips of brown paper, introducing yet another angle of vision to the daring conjunction of planes at the center of the sheet and obliterating any vestige of traditional spatial logic.

PROVENANCE: Galerie Kahnweiler, Paris; probably sale, Paris, Hôtel Drouot, 17–18 November 1921, lot 165; Galerie Georges Petit, Paris(?); Marcel C. Coard, Paris; Sidney Janis Gallery, New York.

BIBLIOGRAPHY: Christian Zervos, *Pablo Picasso*, II, part 2, Paris, 1942, no. 455; Pierre Daix and Joan Rosselet, *Picasso, The Cubist Years 1907–1916. A Catalogue Raisonné of the Paintings and Related Works*, Boston, 1979, no. 665.

EXHIBITIONS: Probably Galerie Georges Petit, Paris, *Picasso*, catalogue by Charles Vranken, 1932, no. 90; probably Kunsthaus, Zurich, *Picasso*, catalogue by Charles Vranken and W. Wartman, 1932, no. 80.

63 *Portrait of Marie-Thérèse Walter*

Pen and black ink and gray wash. $20\frac{3}{16} \times 13\frac{3}{8}$ inches (510×339 mm.). Watermark: ARCHES A LA MAIN. Inscribed at upper left, in black ink, *28 juillet / XXXVI.*

Picasso's compelling study of his companion Marie-Thérèse Walter, dated 28 July 1936, is at once a moving portrait and a poignant record of the artist's emotional life. Marie-Thérèse, whom Picasso had known since 1927, had given birth to their daughter Maia in October 1935, but during the summer of 1936 the artist's affair with another woman caused a crisis in their relationship. Within a few days after making this drawing Picasso departed for Mougins to enjoy a week-long clandestine assignation with the young photographer Dora Maar, who had begun to replace Marie-Thérèse in his affections. The cold stare and unsympathetic, tight-lipped expression Marie-Thérèse wears in the Thaw study undoubtedly reflects these circumstances. Although Picasso executed this large drawing with great bravado, combining vitally charged penwork with broad but sensitively harmonized washes, and working in a naturalistic mode uncommon at this period, the portrayal of his lover's resentful countenance must have been emotionally painful for him. It is no wonder that this highly personal document remained in the artist's possession until his death.

During the 1930s Picasso's work was anything but homogeneous, and he practiced several styles at the same time. His naturalistic portrait of Marie-Thérèse Walter dates within a year of the completion of *Guernica* (June 1937) and belongs to a decade in which much of his work, influenced by Surrealism, was populated with imaginary and often grotesquely distorted figures.

PROVENANCE: Estate of the artist; Marina Picasso.

EXHIBITIONS: Haus der Kunst, Munich, *Pablo Picasso. Eine Ausstellung zum hundertsten Geburtstag. Werke aus der Sammlung Marina Picasso*, 1981, no. 185, repr.; Centro di Cultura di Palazzo Grassi, Venice, *Picasso: opera dal 1895 al 1971 dalla Collezione Marina Picasso*, 1981, no. 243, repr.; Museo Tamayo, Mexico City, *Los Picassos de Picasso en Mexico*, catalogue by William S. Lieberman, 1982–83, no. 73.

GIORGIO DE CHIRICO

VOLO, TESSAGLIA 1888 – 1978 ROME

64 *The Poet and the Philosopher*

Pencil on buff-colored paper. 12 11/16×9½ inches (322×241 mm.). Watermark: none visible through lining. Signed, dated, and inscribed, at lower center, in pencil, *G. de Chirico / 1913* and *le poète et le philosophe*.

Born in Greece of Italian parents, Giorgio de Chirico began his studies in Athens where he was introduced to the work of two of the most important nineteenth-century German Romantic artists, Caspar David Friedrich and Karl Blechen. After his father's death, de Chirico moved to Munich where he became acquainted with the philosophy of Schopenhauer, Weininger, and Nietzsche, and the art of Arnold Böcklin and Max Klinger. In July of 1911 de Chirico moved to Paris where he developed his metaphysical style, and it is to this period that the Thaw drawing belongs.

During his metaphysical period, which spanned the years 1911–17, de Chirico produced approximately 130 works. The artist himself recorded his discovery of a new style when he wrote of his painting the *Enigma of an Autumn Afternoon*. While sitting one day in the middle of the Piazza Santa Croce in Florence, he had "the strange impression that I was looking at those things for the first time, and the composition of the painting revealed itself to my mind's eye. Now every time I look at this picture, I see that moment once again. Nevertheless the moment is an enigma for me, in that it is inexplicable. I like also to call the work derived from it an enigma" (Museum of Modern Art, 1982: Maurizio Fagiolo dell'Arco, "De Chirico in Paris, 1911–15," p. 11).

In a painting from his metaphysical period entitled the *Dream of the Poet*, de Chirico first introduces the use of a mannequin, a motif that will appear repeatedly in his later works. In the Thaw sheet, the figure of an armless mannequin, the philosopher, sits with his head bent pensively as he gazes into a painting composed entirely of stars in the sky. The poet sits at a desk. His face is entirely blank with the exception of two interlocking ovals which approximate the placement of eyes, and his hand rests on the table in front of him as if he were engaged in creative work rather than mere contemplation. Although in this drawing de Chirico does not use any readily identifiable method of perspective, his intention is nevertheless to present these objects in a deep space. This is indicated by the lines on the floor, the painting on the easel, and the building and clouds viewed through an open window opposite the philosopher.

The Thaw drawing is preparatory for the painting *The Philosopher and the Poet* dated 1914, done a year later (Museum of Modern Art, 1982, pl. 46). De Chirico also returned to the theme of a philosopher and a poet in a pencil drawing of 1915–16, now in the Galleria Nazionale d'Arte Moderna e Contemporanea, Rome (Museum of Modern Art, 1982, pl. 103).

PROVENANCE: André Breton; Paul Éluard, Paris; Sir Roland Penrose; E.V. Thaw and Co., New York; Rolf Weinberg, Zurich.

EXHIBITIONS: Museum of Modern Art, New York, *De Chirico*, catalogue ed. by William Rubin, 1982, no. 102, repr.; Haus der Kunst, Munich and Centre Georges Pompidou, Paris,

Giorgio de Chirico der Metaphysiker, catalogue by William Rubin, Wieland Schmied, and Jean Clair, 1982–83, no. 97, repr.

MAX ERNST

BRÜHL 1891 – 1976 PARIS

65 *Je remarque avec ettonnement* [sic] *que le cheval . . .*

Collage consisting of hand-colored print made in ten parts, with additional pen and black ink in central tail; framing line in pen and black ink over pencil. 5 3/16 × 4 inches (131 × 102 mm.). Watermark: none visible through lining. Inscribed at lower right, *Max Ernst.*

Max Ernst was one of the most important painters of the Dada and Surrealist movements. His art always retained an air of intellectuality, no doubt due to his background as a philosophy student. He was greatly attracted to the art of Giorgio de Chirico, with its mannequins placed in dream-like settings, and to Dada. This literary and artistic movement began in Switzerland mainly to express disillusionment with war and the political and cultural situation that spawned it, and hoped to destroy art as it had previously existed. Ernst and some of his friends celebrated international Dada in Cologne with an exhibition which became famous in part because it was located in a public urinal. With the advent of Surrealism in the early 1920s, Ernst joined the new movement, one to which he long remained faithful.

Surrealism was based on the liberation of the unconscious mind, a liberation which led to increased spontaneity and experimentation, especially in the juxtaposition of unrelated visual and verbal images. In Ernst's *oeuvre* the results are often weird, even malevolent. His invention of *frottage*, a use of rubbings to create form, as well as his advanced use of collage, contributed to his sometimes mischievous, sometimes unsettling vision.

His interest in collage derived from the technique of *papier collé* used by the Cubist painters Braque and Picasso, wherein such everyday items as newspapers, stamps, and matchboxes were incorporated into the picture surface to become the actual subject. In Ernst's work, however, the drawn elements remained primary, and his collages are less a display of objects than a creation of an illusionary world made from various unrelated objects—mainly taken from nineteenth-century engravings in magazines.

The Thaw sheet is such a collage. Executed for the 1938 book by Leonora Carrington entitled *La Maison de la peur* (Paris, p. 7), it is one of several illustrations of horse people. This type of figure derives from the nineteenth-century tradition of Grandville, whose fame rested on his portrayals of animals dressed in human costume involved in human activities. Ernst has taken this type and given it a sinister turn—they are now humans with animal heads, figures in a world that is and is not ours. In the Thaw illustration, the horse-headed beings march up and down the stairs, and the contrast between them and the man hesitating at the top of the stairs (where do the stairs lead?) is slightly unnerving, especially in relation to the two strongly foreshortened bodies seen resting on a large block, suggesting death. Ernst has created a whole world, coherent in itself, but distorted from reality.

PROVENANCE: Peggy Guggenheim; Marius Bewley.

BIBLIOGRAPHY: Werner Spies, *Max Ernst Collagen: Inventar u. Widerspruch*, Cologne, 1974, no. 475, repr.; Spies, *Max Ernst, les collages: inventaire et contradictions* (tr. by Eliane Kaufholz), Paris, 1984, no. 475, repr.

JACKSON POLLOCK

CODY, WYOMING 1912 – 1956 EAST HAMPTON, NEW YORK

66 *Sketchbook*

Contains 38 drawings on 40 sheets of cream-colored Japanese mulberry paper, most of which are folded to form double-sided pages, with several missing or torn (probably by the artist), bound between heavier paper covers with twine and stamped in red ink on the spine, MADE IN CHINA, and with Chinese characters surrounded by an oval. Chiefly executed in felt pen, blue-ink pen, brush and gray-black ink, and pencil; approximately one-third is in brush and gray-black ink. Binding: 5⅝ × 12⅞ inches (143 × 327 mm.). Leaves approximately: 5⅝ × 11 13/16 inches (143 × 301 mm.). Watermark: none.

Jackson Pollock is perhaps best known for his "drip paintings," those works done primarily in the later 1940s, in which he was creating a new sense of space and surface, and a new way of relating to the canvas and paint. However, those very large, non-figurative, and colorful works were, in a sense, less typical than his figurative (though in no sense naturalistic) work done before and after. In about 1951 Pollock turned away from non-figurative art as well as from color to begin a period in which he reintroduced the figure, using only black paint. It was during these years of the black paintings that the Thaw sketchbook was used.

Although it is not known exactly when or by whom the pad was acquired, it became Pollock's evidently early in 1950 for use by the telephone, for memoranda, and for drawing. His wife Lee Krasner also used it occasionally for notes, and there are messages left by others as well. Among the items recorded are telephone numbers, three dreams Pollock jotted down and illustrated (probably made in conjunction with a telephone conversation held with his psychoanalyst), and a list made in May 1950 of vanguard artists involved in a protest against a proposed competition of contemporary art to be held by the Metropolitan Museum of Art the following December (see Lieberman, pp. 5–10 for information). But as William Lieberman has written, it is the last fourteen drawn pages, which he dates no earlier than 1952 and no later than 1953, that are the most interesting from an artistic viewpoint. Executed in brush and gray-black ink, these pages form a continuous whole, an outpouring of shapes and images that are marvelous in their intimacy and form.

The early 1950s was a difficult time for the artist. He was working incessantly, and though he was gaining a measure of success in this last decade of his life, his work was still derided by art critics. In January of 1951 he wrote a letter to a friend in Europe and revealed that "I really hit an all time low—with depression and drinking. . . ." Further on he adds, "I hope this letter doesn't seem so damned down and out—because I have been making some drawings on Japanese paper and feel good about them" (*Jackson Pollock*, Museum of Modern Art, New York, exhibition catalogue by Francis V. O'Connor, p. 58).

The drawings referred to were not those of the sketchbook itself, but several made on large sheets of Japanese paper. No doubt Pollock had been intrigued by what he had created almost unthinkingly in his small sketchbook, mixed among the doodles and telephone numbers, and wished to continue exploring the combination of ink and paper, and the spontaneous imagery created therefrom. If Lieberman is correct, Pollock returned to his sketchbook to produce the last fourteen drawings after ending his experimentation with the large sheets of Japanese paper. Perhaps he used the privacy of the sketchbook to search for something revealed in the gentle, almost lyrical configurations. As Lieberman has noted, Pollock never again used this particular technique of applying first a wash and then drawing in brush and ink.

Pollock's figurative art was made up of images invented and found in the act of creation itself. The image was created by the interaction of the flatness of the picture plane, be it canvas or paper, with the paint. Thus, in Pollock's art, there can be no separation between subject matter and medium. The organic quality of these small drawings, with their vaguely plant- or animal-like forms floating gracefully in an unearthly atmosphere, is also reminiscent of paintings that Pollock was doing in the early 1950s. Compare the images found, for instance, in folio 25 of the sketchbook with those in the paintings *Number 3, 1951 (Image of Man)*, (O'Connor and Thaw, no. 321, repr.) or *Number 2, 1951* (O'Connor and Thaw, no. 342, repr.).

Pollock used several other sketchbooks during the course of his life. There are three known from the 1930s, at least one from the forties, and only one, the Thaw sketchbook, from the fifties. One must, however, heed Pollock's words about his working method: "I don't work from drawings," he said in a taped interview in 1950. "I don't make sketches and drawings and color sketches into a final painting" (O'Connor, p. 79). "The source of my painting is the unconscious," he said elsewhere. "I approach paintings the same way I approach drawing. That is direct—no preliminary studies. The drawings I do are relative to my painting but not for it" (O'Connor, p. 40). It is perhaps best, therefore, to see the images in the Thaw sketchbook as a complete series that sheds further light on the thoughts and working habits of an artist counted among the greatest of the twentieth century.

PROVENANCE: Lee Krasner Pollock, New York.

BIBLIOGRAPHY: Francis Valentine O'Connor and Eugene Victor Thaw, *Jackson Pollock: A Catalogue Raisonné of Paintings, Drawings, and Other Works*, New Haven and London, 1978, III, pp. 338–63, nos. 879–915, repr.; Grace Glueck, "Pollock Telephone Pad Moves to Coffee Table," *The New York Times*, 2 December 1982; *Jackson Pollock, The Last Sketchbook*, introduction by William S. Lieberman, New York, 1982.

WATERCOLORS OF EUROPEAN DOMESTIC INTERIORS

FRANZ XAVER NACHTMANN

OBERMAIS 1799 – 1846 MUNICH

67 *The Dressing Room of King Ludwig I at the Munich Residence Palace*

Pen and black ink and gouache, heightened with gold, over graphite on wove paper. $8\frac{3}{4} \times 11\frac{1}{4}$ inches (222×286 mm.). Watermark: none. Signed and dated at lower right, in pen and black ink, *Nachtmañ 1836.*

This sheet and the following ten works (Nos. 67–77) belong to a distinctive type of watercolor that represents an actual domestic interior in minute detail. Although the taste for such views originated in the family of the Emperor Napoleon I, it eventually spread throughout nineteenth-century Europe and in bourgeois as well as aristocratic circles. Thanks to the popularity of these works, which reached its zenith in Germany and Austria during the middle of the century, we have a comprehensive record of the architecture, decoration, and furnishings of countless palaces and middle-class houses, many of which have since been altered or destroyed.

Domestic scenes and architectural views had been depicted in European art for centuries, but this kind of precisely rendered watercolor of an existing interior was a characteristic product of the designers and patrons who created the Empire style of decoration. The earliest examples are the watercolors of 1812 by the French painter Auguste Garneray of the interiors of Napoleon's château Malmaison, the first Empire-style building. Completed in 1800, Malmaison was the masterpiece of the architect Charles Percier, whose practice of making detailed watercolors of his projects for interior decoration probably inspired Garneray to represent the completed rooms in the same medium and in the same sober, descriptive style.

Garneray's works were made for the Empress Eugénie or for her children Eugène and Hortense. Eugène, who was Viceroy of Italy, married Auguste Amalia, a daughter of King Max I Joseph of Bavaria. Following the collapse of Napoleon's empire, Eugène was created Duke of Leuchtenberg and the couple resided in Munich. His sister Hortense spent a period in exile in Augsburg, where Garneray depicted her salon in 1816. Eugène, who commissioned watercolors of the interiors of his residences in Milan and Munich before 1820, undoubtedly sparked an interest in works of this type at the Bavarian Court. From there, the fashion spread throughout Central Europe.

In 1820 Caroline von Baden, Queen of Bavaria, commissioned a group of artists to paint watercolors depicting interiors in the royal family's city residence in Munich and summer palace at Nymphenburg. These were assembled in an album, which she presented to her husband, King Max I Joseph, as a birthday gift. Following his death in 1825, some sheets were removed from the volume and others rearranged, but several more were added during the reign of his successor Ludwig I. Today, the Wittelsbach Album, as it is known, contains thirty watercolors painted between 1820 and about 1850 that represent interiors created between 1799 and 1848. Apart from its value as an architectural record, the volume documents the taste and lifestyle of the Bavarian Court during the first half of the nineteenth century. In each of the watercolors, the viewpoint and vanishing point are pushed to the left, which permits the most complete view of the interior and its furnishings. (See Hans Ottomeyer, *Das Wittelsbacher Album*, Munich, 1974.)

Other series of watercolors of interiors of Bavarian residences, most of them by the same artists who contributed to the Wittelsbach Album, are preserved in the Stockholm Palace; in the Palace of Sansouci, Potsdam; in the Schlossmuseum, Darmstadt; and in the collection of Princess Margaret of Hesse. These works belonged to Bavarian princesses who, when they married and went to live at foreign courts, took them along as mementos of the rooms where they spent their childhood (*ibid.*, pp. 134 and 153–56).

Franz Xaver Nachtmann, a painter of floral still-lifes on Nymphenburg porcelain as well as of easel pictures of landscape and architecture, contributed several superbly executed watercolors between the early 1820s and 1844 to the Wittelsbach Album and to the related series of interiors. The pristine Thaw sheet of 1836 represents the dressing room of Ludwig I in the new Renaissance-style wing of the Munich Residence, which was completed in 1835 to the designs of Leo von Klenze. The idealistic king had the walls of his palace decorated with murals of literary subjects rather than with expensive fabrics, paneling, and mirrors. His dressing room is painted with Pompeian-style ornamental motifs that frame circular and lozenge-shaped panels with scenes from ancient literature. The heavy, austere Empire furniture was designed by Von Klenze to conform to the classicizing taste of the architecture and painted decoration.

The Thaw watercolor relates closely to another work of 1836 by Nachtmann that also depicts a room in the new wing of the Residence, the writing cabinet of Ludwig's wife Queen Therese, which was decorated with murals representing scenes from German poetry (*ibid.*, pl. 25). While the latter sheet is preserved in the Wittelsbach Album, we know nothing about the commission or the early history of the Thaw work.

PROVENANCE: Galerie Biedermann, Munich.

SOTIRA

AUSTRIAN active ca. 1830

68 *The Apartment of Princess Alexandra of Russia*

Pen and black ink, watercolor, gouache and gray wash, heightened with white; framing line in pen and black ink on wove paper. 10 13/16 × 16 1/16 inches (275 × 407 mm.). Watermark: J WHATMAN (similar to Heawood 3462). Signed at lower right in white ink, *Sotira / 1835*.

There is little biographical data about the artist who signed and dated this work. Since the entry for him in Thieme-Becker indicates that he was active chiefly in Vienna, it may be assumed that he was Austrian. His first name is not known and it is possible that Sotira was a name that he assumed professionally. From this watercolor rendering as well as six others reproduced in Mario Praz (*An Illustrated History of Interior Decoration*, New York, 1982), we know that he worked in Russia between 1835 and 1838. Although his watercolors are not as meticulous in finish as Nachtmann's (No. 67), it is evident that Sotira was expert in the genre.

Princess Alexandra was a Hohenzollern princess, the daughter of Frederick-William III,

King of Prussia. She was born Frederica-Louisa-Charlotte-Wilhelmina but after her marriage in 1817 to Nicholas I (1796–1855), she changed her name to Alexandra and converted to the Russian Orthodox faith in accordance with Russian imperial custom. In 1825, after his brother Alexander I died, Nicholas became Czar of Russia.

The size of the room and its many fine appointments, including a number of old master paintings, suggest that its location is the Winter Palace in St. Petersburg, the official residence of the czars since the eighteenth century. Since the Winter Palace was completely destroyed by fire two years after Sotira dated his view of the Princess' apartment, this identification cannot be verified.

The room contained at least eighteen paintings including what appears to be a large Rembrandt at the end of the room, a Loutherbourg shipwreck over the mantel, and an early sixteenth-century Netherlandish portrait. Despite its size, it was a comfortable, somewhat informal room with a desk before which the Princess may be seen seated. A candlestand for light is on the desk and nearby there is a brazier for extra warmth when needed. The room seems to be quite long and has a shallow barrel-vaulted ceiling which is coffered and decorated with classicizing reliefs, presumably in stucco. The walls are painted an attractive shade of robin's egg blue and red occurs throughout the general color scheme. Five distinct areas for seating, including a number of chairs and banquettes upholstered in a deep blue cut-velvet, are visible. The floor is wooden parquet, partially covered with an oriental carpet. Five long windows are visible in Sotira's view, each filled with plants. An enormous gilt bronze chandelier suspended from the ceiling opposite the fourth window, is a good indication that there were probably eight windows altogether. Mirrors or pier glasses, used as reflectors for candelabra lighting, alternate with piers filled with statuary.

The other Russian watercolors reproduced by Praz are all in the collection of Don Agostino Chigi, Rome. *The Bathroom of the Princess Barjatinsky at Pavlino, July 1835* (Praz, fig. 9); *The Little Living Room at Pavlino, July 1835* (Praz, fig. 284); *The Princess' Study at Pavlino, August 1838* (Praz, fig. 292); *The New Living Room at Pavlino, August 1838* (Praz, fig. 293); and *The Drawing Room at Pavlino* (Praz, fig. 294).

PROVENANCE: Popoff & Cie, Paris.

RUSSIAN SCHOOL
ca. 1830

69 *Bedroom in a Country Dacha, 1839*

Watercolor, some pen and blue ink, gum arabic highlights, over graphite. 7 3/16 × 9 9/16 inches (182 × 242 mm.). Watermark: none visible through lining. Inscribed on original mount in pen and brown ink, *spal'naya v Kishkovskoi dachi 1839 goda.*

In contrast to the opulent comfort of Princess Alexandra's apartment, this bedroom in a Russian country cottage or *dacha* is spare in its furnishings. The use of the word *dacha* makes it clear that this is no grand country house but a much simpler sort of residence. The artist is not known but he or she identified and dated the drawing as the bedroom in the Kishkovsky *dacha* in the year

1839. It may be that it was rendered by a member of the Kishkovsky family or perhaps by one of their guests as a souvenir of a visit.

The furniture is Biedermeier, the style which dominated continental interior decoration for forty years between 1820 and 1860. In keeping with its country character the curtains, bedclothes, and the screen are dark green. The room is airy and the artist has taken evident delight in showing how the light from the long windows fell on the ingrain carpeting on the floor. Even in its simplicity the decor includes a few bits of clutter which reflect the prevalent fashion, such as the hanging bookcase, the curio cabinet, and an assortment of pieces on the desk. The walls are covered in a yellow and blue damask striped wallpaper and a pier glass hangs between the windows. The ceiling has a stencilled blue design in imitation of elaborate stucco work.

PROVENANCE: Hazlitt, Gooden & Fox, London.

EXHIBITION: Hazlitt, Gooden & Fox, London, *Interiors*, 1981, no. 64, pl. 59.

AUSTRIAN SCHOOL
ca. 1840

70 *Interior*

Watercolor, gouache with touches of gum arabic, over graphite on wove paper. $11\frac{3}{8} \times 8\frac{1}{2}$ inches (289×215 mm.). Watermark: fragment of WHATMAN and number *8*(?).

As noted previously (see No. 67), it was the fashion to draw or paint interiors throughout the nineteenth century. By far the largest number of these drawings were German or Austrian in origin (Peter Thornton, *Authentic Decor, the Domestic Interior 1620–1920*, New York, 1984, p. 217). The comfortable room depicted in the Thaw drawing appears to be a small, hall-bedroom in a city house or apartment. It is rectangular in plan with a high, coved ceiling from which a lantern with a glass dome, probably Venetian, is suspended. Green curtains, which would pull in to cover the bed, hang from a valence or pelmet. These match the window curtains at the far end of the room. The walls are decorated with gray, white, and mauve striped wallpaper; the carpet is heavily patterned, probably floral in motif, with two smaller oriental rugs and several cushions scattered on top of it. Numerous knick-knacks and ornaments cover the tables and fill the curio cases.

The furniture is of the Biedermeier style, the German and Austrian variant of the late Empire. The chairs and couch are upholstered *en suite* in geometric-figured velour. The walls are covered with miniature pictures suspended on wires or cords from the molding; several of the pictures appear to be drawings. An easel, turned toward the window to catch the best light, is placed among the furniture on the left side of the room. The presence of the easel suggests that this may be an artist's or more probably a collector's room.

If the artist who executed this drawing was Austrian, it is possible that this interior was in Vienna. He was obviously a skilled draughtsman and has managed successfully to suggest a narrow interior with high ceilings while at the same time creating a sense of depth within the room. His somewhat impressionistic style, seen most clearly in the treatment of the rug and covering of the furniture, captures the comfortable, informal ambience of the room.

PROVENANCE: Julius Böhler, Munich; Adrian Ward-Jackson, London.

EXHIBITION: Julius Böhler, Munich, *Gemälde Handzeichnungen Plastiken*, 1982, no. 49, pl. xxv.

CHARLOTTE BOSANQUET
LONDON 1790 – 1852 LONDON

71 *The Library at Dingestow*

Pen and black ink, watercolor over graphite. 6 7/16 × 9 7/16 inches (163 × 239 mm.). Watermark: none visible through lining.

Dingestow Court, Monmouthshire, Wales was one of two country houses belonging to the Bosanquets, a distinguished Huguenot family. (The other country residence of the Dingestow branch was Forest House, Essex.) Charles Bosanquet (1764–1856) served as governor of the South Seas Company and was also the author of various short treatises on British economics. Samuel Richard Bosanquet (1800–1882) inherited the family estates in 1843 when he was forty-three. Described as a "miscellaneous writer" in the *Dictionary of National Biography*, he lived at Dingestow and was active in the Monmouthshire quarter sessions. He was "beneficent to the poor" and "a man who promoted local institutions and enterprises."

An old label on the back of the frame identifies the Thaw drawing as the "Library at Dingestow as it was in the time of Samuel Bosanquet and Emily Courthorpe, his wife, whom he married in 1830"; another old label dates the watercolor to "about 1850." Charlotte was their London-bred cousin. She made frequent visits to friends and relations, occasionally portraying the interiors of their houses. There is an album of her watercolors in the Ashmolean Museum, Oxford, dating from the 1840s.

The bouquet of flowers as well as the rose-and-white striped slipcovers on the furniture indicate that Charlotte chose to depict this very pleasant room in the summer. The predominant color scheme of the room is rose and blue and there is also a figured carpet in these tonalities. Although it is apparent from the Elizabethan beamed ceiling and the pedimented window, with vertical mullions at the center, that Dingestow Court is quite old, the furnishings are nineteenth century, an indication that the room has been modernized and made more comfortable. Dingestow Court is said to have been built in 1623 on the site of an earlier mansion. In the eighteenth century its Jacobean front was enclosed by a Georgian façade. An extensive renovation was undertaken in 1843 by the architect Lewis Vulliamy (1791–1871).

PROVENANCE: Art market, London.

BIBLIOGRAPHY: For general discussion see John Cornforth, "Some Early Victorians at Home," *Country Life*, CLVIII, 4 December 1975, pp. 1530ff.; Cornforth, *English Interiors, 1790–1848, The Quest for Comfort*, London, 1978, p. 58, figs. 52–54, 146–50; Susan Lasdun, *Victorians at Home*, London, 1981, pp. 45ff.

L. ROSSI

Active in Germany and France, ca. 1850

72 *The Music Party*

Watercolor, slightly heightened with white, over preliminary drawing in graphite on wove paper. $12\frac{1}{4} \times 9\frac{5}{16}$ inches (310×237 mm.). Watermark: none. Signed at lower right, in pen and black ink, *L. Rossi* and inscribed on an old album leaf, *L. Rossi.*

The Music Party was originally included in a group of 63 drawings in a now-dismembered album compiled for Henri, Duc de Bordeaux, titular King Henri V of France and Navarre who died in 1883. These were presented to him by his friends, family, and in the case of *The Music Party* and six other drawings by Rossi, by the artist himself. Although the signature of the artist L. Rossi appears on the Thaw watercolor and his name is clearly inscribed on the old album leaf to which it is mounted, no information concerning him is available. Another drawing signed by Rossi in the album depicts a Baroque church in a South German town, which therefore indicates that the artist was active in Germany as well. The style of the women's coiffures and gowns and the original placement of the sheet in the album date the drawing to the mid-nineteenth century.

With its gray walls and brown doors, the room is rather plainly decorated. The walls have been embellished, however, with a classical wallpaper frieze and the floor is covered with an ingrain carpet. Three pictures hang over the bookcase while two more are partially visible above the harpsichord. Although the furnishings consist solely of ladderback chairs and a bookcase, the room appears cluttered because the music stands, instruments, and musicians have all been pushed back in space toward the corner of the room. It is evident that perspective was not the artist's main concern, rather he was more interested in the subject of *The Music Party*. The men depicted here are not playing modern instruments but the viola da braccio and the viola da gamba. Rossi is also interested in the representation of light and shadow to suggest tactile values, and this is most evident in the play of light on the richly fringed mantle draped over a chair and the harpist's dress which suggest that the material of these garments is satin. The sentimental mood of *The Music Party* is emphasized by the presence of a spaniel who gazes faithfully up at the harpist.

PROVENANCE: Sale, London, Christie's, 17 July 1979, lot 138, repr.; Thos. Agnew & Sons Ltd., London.

R. PARMINTER CUFF

Active in London between 1860 and 1876

73 *Sitting Room*

Watercolor and gray wash, over graphite on wove paper. Verso: Study of the head of a girl wearing a hat with a green feather; slight sketch in graphite of her face and mouth. $10\frac{15}{16} \times 13\frac{5}{8}$ inches (279×345 mm.). Watermark: none. Signed, dated, and inscribed at lower left, in pen and black ink, *R P Cuff, London 7 Owen's row, Goswell road, Augt 1855*; signed and dated on verso, *R P Cuff Augt 1855*; inscribed at upper right, in graphite, *R CC.*

There is plenty of detail to look at in this loosely-brushed watercolor of a middle-class Victorian parlor. Although the furnishings are nineteenth century, the house was built in the latter part of the eighteenth century. The Owens Row property was part of the estate bequeathed by Mrs. Alice Owens to the Brewers' Company in 1613. It was not, however, until 1773, a hundred and sixty years later, that it was actually developed by Thomas Rawstone, an Islington bricklayer. If it were not for the records which show that the name of the ratepayer at Owens Row in 1855 was Peacock, it might seem logical to suppose that the artist, R. Parminter Cuff, was rendering a view of his own sitting room.

Cuff, an architect, exhibited at the Royal Academy between 1860 and 1876. As it is, he never completed the watercolor, leaving the carpet and—what is even more disconcerting—the woman who stands near the window, unfinished. He had already indicated her cast shadow in gray wash. Gray wash is also used here to suggest the embroidery of the curtains and the photograph over the mantel. The wallpaper is a striped floral pattern and all the furniture, which is Sheraton, belongs to the early part of the nineteenth century. This includes the pair of armchairs, a drop-leaf pedestal table which here served as a library table, and the sewing table in front of the window.

Although the room is modest, it is appealing and looks quite comfortable. There is a fair amount of clutter about, especially on the mantelpiece which has a number of objects, perhaps souvenirs. A needlepoint scatter rug is thrown before the cast iron fender and grate, probably to protect the Aubusson carpet from stray sparks and cinders.

The watercolor portrait on the verso of a young girl wearing a feathered hat has no apparent connection with the occupants of the Owens Row house.

PROVENANCE: Hazlitt, Gooden, & Fox, London.

EXHIBITION: Hazlitt, Gooden, & Fox, London, *Interiors*, 1981, no. 28, repr.

TIELEMAN CATO BRUINING
NIEUWKOOP 1801 – 1877 THE HAGUE

74 *Interior of the Oranjezaal, Huis ten Bosch*

Watercolor, ruling pen over graphite on wove paper. $17\frac{1}{4} \times 17\frac{1}{8}$ inches (438×435 mm.). Watermark: none.

This sheet, one of a series of four large watercolors of the Oranjezaal in the Huis ten Bosch, almost certainly was part of a royal commission given by Queen Sophie of the Netherlands to the artist Tieleman Cato Bruining. Toward the middle of the nineteenth century, Queen Sophie (1818–1877), first wife of King William III, used the Huis ten Bosch as a summer retreat. In accordance with her custom of ordering watercolors of all the residences she had occupied, she commissioned Bruining to produce a series of nine detail studies of the Oranjezaal, and this survives in the Koninklijk Huisarchief in The Hague. The series of four works, which includes the Thaw drawing, is without doubt by the same hand as the nine drawings, and probably was part of the same project. (We are most grateful to Dr. B. Woelderink and Mr. M. Loonstra of the Koninklijk Huisarchief for the above information.)

The series of four interior views record the overall decoration and architecture of the Oranjezaal. The complex plan of the Oranjezaal, a Greek cross with an octagonal crossing, allowed the room to be decorated on sixteen sides, with thirty canvases. Instead of recording the adjacent paintings on each wall of the four arms, the draughtsman has depicted the views he saw from his position in the center of the room. For the Thaw drawing he faced southward, and his views toward the north, east, and west are preserved in the three other studies, now in The Pierpont Morgan Library. The four sheets in New York, together with the nine in The Hague, form a complete record of the grandest of rooms in the Huis ten Bosch, the only surviving residence built by the House of Orange in the seventeenth century.

The Huis ten Bosch, designed by Pieter Post, originally was to be a simple retreat for Frederik Hendrik's wife Amalia van Solms, and building commenced in 1645. When the stadtholder died in 1647, his widow, identifying herself with Artemesia, decided that the Oranjezaal should be made into a monument to her husband's memory. The decorative program which celebrates the *Triumph of Frederik Hendrik* was entrusted to the learned humanist, writer, and former secretary of State, Constantijn Huygens, and to Jacob van Campen, architect of the Amsterdam Town Hall. The project was planned in minute detail, with a great many notes, sketches, and letters to artists, and documents of payment surviving in the Koninklijk Huisarchief in The Hague.

Conceiving the decorative scheme in the Rubensian tradition of the Marie de Medici series of 1621–25 (Hanna Peter-Raupp, *Die Ikonographie des Oranjezaal*, Hildesheim–New York, 1980), Huygens and Van Campen employed Dutch classicists like Cesar van Everdingen, or Flemish painters who had worked in Rubens' circle, including Jacob Jordaens (Jan van Gelder, "De schilders van de Oranjezaal," *Nederlandsch Kunsthistorisch Jaarboek*, 1948–49, pp. 118–64). Jordaens' canvas showing the *Triumph of Frederik Hendrik*, the largest picture in the room, is just visible on the extreme left of the present drawing.

Moving left to right in the Thaw work, we see the lower painting of *Gifts Received from East and West*, which is by Van Campen himself, and is part of a continuous frieze of scenes of triumph that runs across the lowest register of the room. The frieze incorporates the triumphal arch-shaped windows seen in the present drawing, and ultimately leads back to Jordaens' great *Triumph*. The canvas above *Gifts*, possibly also by Van Campen, shows *Frederik Hendrik's Conquest of the Rivers*, or *Brilliance among the Stars* as Beatrijs Brenninkmeyer-de Rooij labels it, identifying the poem by Hooft to which it is related, in her excellent article "Notities betreffende de Decoratie van de Oranjezaal in Huis Ten Bosch," (*Oud Holland*, 1982, pp. 133–85).

Though somewhat indistinctly represented in the present sheet, between the paired pilasters on the decorated planes of the octagonal crossing are ancestors and family members of the House of Orange, surmounted by their armor and heraldry. Nor are the paintings on the walls immediately to the left and right of the windowed-wall legible, but these scenes are carefully delineated in the Morgan Library's views toward the east and west respectively.

Two paintings adorn the central, southernmost wall: above the windows, Gerard van Honthorst's painting shows the *Marriage of Frederik Hendrik and Amalia van Solms*. Brenninckmeyer-de Rooij (*ibid.*, 1982, p. 144) identifies the artist of the top canvas, the *Allegory of the*

Marriage, as Cesar van Everdingen rather than Van Campen as was previously thought. On the next plane to the right of the second set of pilasters, Salomon de Bray's *Triumph with Captured Weapons* continues the triumphal procession at the bottom. And above, Theodoor van Thulden has depicted the *Education of Frederik Hendrik*.

In the Thaw study the hanging of the paintings differs from the original arrangement in the room, which subsequently was restored. In the present work, the position occupied by *Gifts from East and West* (south wall of east arm) originally was hung with the *Triumph of Time* by Jacob Jordaens, as we learn from the first depiction in 1665 of the Oranjezaal by Pieter Post, which was engraved by Daniël Marot in 1686. The decoration remained constant through 1767, from which date we have a description of the room by J. van Dijk. An anonymous report of 1821, however, records nine of the paintings in different positions, and among them, Jordaens' *Time* has been moved. The new arrangement was maintained throughout the nineteenth century, as is reflected in the Thaw work which dates from just after the middle of the century, ca. 1860.

In representing his overall impression of the great hall, rather than faithfully copying each canvas, the draughtsman has considerably exaggerated the height of the room, apparent in the depiction of the central canvases where the figures seem elongated and thin. This tall and refined appearance was indeed intended by the designers of the Oranjezaal, and Van Campen, most notably, used the identical device of slim, fluted pilasters spanning two stories to similar effect in the classicizing interior of the Amsterdam Town Hall.

PROVENANCE: Galerie Biedermann, Munich.

FERDINAND LE FEUBURE
MUNICH 1815 – 1898 MUNICH

75 *The Bedroom of the Emperor Dom Pedro I of Brazil, Palace of Queluz*

Watercolor and gouache, touches of gum arabic, over graphite. $7\frac{15}{16} \times 12\frac{5}{8}$ inches (201 × 320 mm.). Watermark: none. Signed and dated at lower right, in pen and black ink, *Ferd. le Feubure / 1850*. Inscribed on mount, in pen and black ink, *Chambre où mourut mon. père, dans le Palais de Queluz.*

Like Nachtmann (No. 67), Ferdinand Le Feubure was employed in the studios of the Nymphenburg porcelain works, where he painted equestrian scenes and views of Munich on plates and helped decorate a large dessert service for the court in the 1830s and 1840s. A watercolor by him of an interior in the Wittelsbach Palace is preserved in the collection of Princess Margaret of Hesse (Hans Ottomeyer, *Das Wittelsbacher Album*, Munich, 1979, p. 148, fig. 7 and p. 154). The work exhibited here, assuming it was done on the spot, attests to Le Feubure's presence in Portugal in 1850.

The Thaw watercolor represents the bedroom in the Palace of Queluz, near Lisbon, where Emperor Pedro I of Brazil died in 1834. It is inscribed, "Room where my father died in the Palace of Queluz," in the hand of Princess Marie Amélie, daughter of Pedro I and his wife Princess Amélie von Leuchtenberg. In 1851, Marie Amélie, who was only three years old in

1834, revisited the palace for the first time since her father's death. She found the bedroom exactly as it had been seventeen years earlier, and it remains so to this day (Galerie Biedermann, Munich, 1981, no. 1). We do not know when or how she came into possession of Le Feubure's watercolor of 1850.

The Palace of Queluz, built primarily by the architect Mateus Vicente de Oliveira between 1747 and 1760, is the outstanding example of the Rococo style in Portugal. Le Feubure's work conveys the dainty scale and intimate feeling that characterize what is in reality a rather large building (George Kubler and Martin Soria, *Art and Architecture in Spain and Portugal and their American Dominions 1500 to 1800*, Baltimore, 1959, p. 114). The frieze and overdoors of the chamber where Pedro I died are decorated with scenes from Don Quixote, and the room is known also as the Salle Don Quixote.

PROVENANCE: Galerie Biedermann, Munich.

EXHIBITION: Galerie Biedermann, Munich, *Aus einem Album um 1850*, 1981, no. 1, repr.

ALEXANDRE NIKOLAEVICH BENOIS

ST. PETERSBURG 1870 – 1960 PARIS

76 *The Bedroom of Czarina Maria Alexandrovna, Gatchina Palace, St. Petersburg*

Watercolor and gouache, over pencil and some red chalk, slightly heightened with white, on wove paper. $12\frac{3}{8} \times 16\frac{13}{16}$ inches (315×425 mm.). Watermark: none. Signed at lower right, in pen and black ink, *Alexander / Benois* and inscribed, in graphite, *chambre / de / l'Imperatrice Marie / Alexandrovna à / Gatchina.*

Alexandre Benois came from a family distinguished in the arts and theatre. His great-grandfather was Director of La Fenice, Venice, and his grandfather was the architect of the Bolshoi theatre in Moscow. His immediate family was part of the intellectual circle in St. Petersburg, and he himself was interested in all aspects of Russian culture. Above all, he was a noted theatrical designer, but he was also an artist and an art historian and served, during the Revolution and for several years thereafter, as the Director of the Hermitage Museum. He traveled rather frequently to Western Europe, and eventually settled in Paris in 1930, never to return to Russia.

He first gained notice, according to Bénézit, through his series of watercolor sketches of scenes from the time of Catherine II and of Louis XV. The Thaw drawings do not date from the same time as the watercolor series, but are later renderings of the rooms, executed either after the palace became the property of the State, or perhaps from memory.

Gatchina was the summer palace of the imperial family of Russia, built in 1766–81 under the Empress Catherine II by the architect Antonio Rinardi (ca. 1709–1794). It served as a country retreat, and originally was meant for Catherine's lover of twelve years, Grigori Orlov, who is said to have given her the world's fourth largest diamond for her scepter. It still stands in modern-day Leningrad, where its treasures are on view to the public.

Generations of Romanovs left the imprint of their decorative taste in the rooms of the palace. A visitor recording his impressions of the palace a few years after the deposing of the czars and the Revolution, made note of the different styles evident in the various private apartments of the ruling family (Sir Martin Conway, *Art Treasures in Soviet Russia*, London, 1925, pp. 128–34). The rooms in which the family of Alexander II lived were, naturally for their time, Victorian in appearance, with heavy dark furnishings and rich dark colors in the fabrics.

Czar Alexander II ruled until 1881, when he was assassinated in a bomb attack which occurred during the increasingly violent fervor for far-reaching political reforms in Russia. After the Czarina, the former Princess Marie of Hesse-Darmstadt, died in 1880, the Czar married his mistress, the Princess Catherine Dolgoruky, by whom he had previously had three children.

The bedroom of the Empress, feminine in its floral wallpaper and fabrics, and its patterned carpet, is dominated by the large bed with its massive head- and footboards, and its separate frame from which hang curtains to close off the bed from the rest of the room. The furnishings, including the divan at the foot of the bed, the couch, and the armchairs, are Rococo-revival, a style which was popular in the second half of the nineteenth century. The heavily framed picture on the left wall is probably one of the royal children. The overall effect of the room is rich but heavy. The weightiness of the materials and the muted light give the room a kind of muffled magnificence.

PROVENANCE: Bury Street Gallery, London.

EXHIBITION: Palais des Beaux-Arts, Brussels, *Exposition d'Art russe ancien & moderne*, 1928, no. 42.

77 *The Study of Czar Alexander II, Gatchina Palace, St. Petersburg*

Watercolor and gouache over pencil and some red chalk, ruled in pencil. 12$\frac{1}{16}$ × 18$\frac{3}{8}$ inches (307 × 467 mm.). Watermark: letters MBM. Signed at lower left center, in pen and black ink, *Alexander Benois* and inscribed at lower right center, in pencil, in Cyrillic script, which translates as Study of Alexander II.

By contrast, the green study of the Czar is a brighter room than the Czarina's bedroom. This is largely owing to its two light-filled windows covered by sheer curtains and topped by pelmets. The room has been arranged for groupings of people, from the card or gaming table at the right with chairs grouped around it, to the armchairs placed by the three-legged circular table at the left, and the large couch, built in such a way as to fit into the curved wall of the room. A small table stands in the embrasure of the left window, on which flowers may have been sometimes placed. The pictures, mainly landscapes and a few portraits hanging in the room, are just a few of the over 3,000 paintings in the palace; they were originally collected by Catherine II and then housed there. Their arrangement on the wall, seemingly with little regard for their visual impact, is rather haphazard, and reflects contemporary sensibility.

PROVENANCE: See No. 76.

CHECK LIST OF DRAWINGS EXHIBITED IN *DRAWINGS FROM THE COLLECTION OF MR. & MRS. EUGENE V. THAW* (1975–76)

Bartolomeo, Fra (Baccio della Porta). 1472–1517.
Virgin and Child. Cat. no. 5 (now in The Pierpont Morgan Library, Acc. No. 1973.23).

Virgin of the Annunciation. Cat. no. 6 (now in The Pierpont Morgan Library, Acc. No. 1976.44).

Barye, Antoine-Louis. 1796–1875.
Tigress on her Back. Cat. no. 76.

Beccafumi, Domenico. ca. 1486–1551.
Leda and the Swan, Seated Figure, and a Faun. Cat. no. 7 (now in The Pierpont Morgan Library, Acc. No. 1976.45).

Bonington, Richard Parkes. 1802–1828.
Goetz and Elisabeth. Cat. no. 111.

Breu, Jörg, the Younger. after 1510–1547.
Horseman Attacking a Fallen Warrior. Cat. no. 10 (now in The Pierpont Morgan Library, Acc. No. 1978.38).

Brown, John. 1752–1787.
The Dagger Merchant. Cat. no. 69.

Burgkmair, Hans, the Elder, attributed to. 1473–before 1531.
Seven Women's Heads, Elaborately Coifed. Cat. no. 9 (now in The Pierpont Morgan Library, Acc. No. 1976.47).

Callot, Jacques. 1592–1635.
Dancing Dwarfs and Fiddlers. Cat. no. 12 (now in The Pierpont Morgan Library, Acc. No. 1972.14).

Three Dancing Dwarfs. Cat. no. 13 (now in The Pierpont Morgan Library, Acc. No. 1972.15).

Canal, Antonio, called Canaletto. 1697–1768.
Capriccio: Pavilion by the Lagoon. Cat. no. 39.

Castiglione, Giovanni Benedetto. ca. 1600–1665.
Allegory with a Courtier and a River God. Cat. no. 23 (now in The Pierpont Morgan Library, Acc. No. 1981.73).

Cézanne, Paul. 1839–1906.
The Card Player. Cat. no. 98 (now in The Pierpont Morgan Library, Acc. No. 1975.39).

Trees. Cat. no. 99.

Bare Trees by a River. Cat. no. 100.

Mont Sainte-Victoire. Cat. no. 101.

Corot, Jean-Baptiste-Camille. 1796–1875.
Cività Castellana. Cat. no. 77.

Portrait of a Man. Cat. no. 78.

Daumier, Honoré. 1808–1879.
"*L'Accusation.*" Cat. no. 85.

"*La Lecture.*" Cat. no. 86.

"*Un Avocat Lisant.*" Cat. no. 87.

"*Deux Avocats Conversant.*" Cat.no. 88.

Degas, Hilaire-Germain-Edgar. 1834–1917.
Self-Portrait. Cat. no. 90.

Self-Portrait and Details of Hand and Eye. Cat. no. 91.

Rosa, La Duchessa di Morbilli. Cat. no. 92.

Portrait of a Woman (sometimes called Mme Ducros). Cat. no. 93.

M. Gouffé, the String Bass Player. Cat. no. 94.

Race Horse. Cat. no. 95.

Group of Four Jockeys. Cat. no. 96.

Dancer. Cat. no. 97.

Delacroix, Ferdinand-Victor-Eugène. 1798–1863.
Royal Tiger. Cat. no. 79.

A Persian Horseman with a Lance. Cat. no. 80.

Head of a Lion. Cat. no. 81.

Moroccans outside the Walls of Tangier. Cat. no. 82.

A Man of Tangier. Cat. no. 83.

Pauline Villot in Algerian Costume. Cat. no. 84.

Fragonard, Jean-Honoré. 1732–1806.
An Imaginary Italian Garden. Cat. no. 36.

Franco-Flemish School(?). 15th Century.
Drapery Study. Cat. no. 1 (now in The Pierpont Morgan Library, Acc. No. 1970.14).

Friedrich, Caspar David. 1774–1840.
Tree. Cat. no. 106.

Moonlit Landscape. Cat. no. 107 (now in The Pierpont Morgan Library, Acc. No. 1984.2).

Gauguin, Paul. 1848–1903.
Crouching Tahitian Woman Seen from the Back. Cat. no. 103.

Gellée, Claude, called Claude Lorrain. 1600–1682.
Seated Man Looking toward a Distant Town. Cat. no. 14.

Tiber Landscape. Cat. no. 15.

Reclining Cow. Cat. no. 16.

Two Men Tending an Ox. Cat. no. 17.

Rocky Hillside with a Traveler. Cat. no. 18.

Two Cows and a Bull Reclining on a Slope. Cat. no. 19.

Christ on the Road to Emmaus. Cat. no. 20.

Landscape with St. John. Cat. no. 21.

View of Distant Hills with Tree and Plant in the Foreground. Cat. no. 22.

Gericault, Jean-Louis-André Théodore. 1791–1824.
"*Mustapha*." Cat. no. 72.

Saddled Horse. Cat. no. 73.

Groom Holding Four Horses. Cat. no. 74.

The French Farrier. Cat. no. 75.

Gogh, Vincent van. 1853–1890.
Saint-Rémy, Workers in the Field. Cat. no. 115.

Goya y Lucientes, Francisco José de. 1746–1828.
"*Locura*" (*Madness*). Cat. no. 64.

"*Habla con su gato*" (*She talks with her cat*). Cat. no. 65.

"*Dejalo todo a la probidencia*" (*Leave it all to providence*). Cat. no. 66.

"*Muy acordes*" (*They go well together*). Cat. no. 67 (now in The Pierpont Morgan Library, Acc. No. 1984.1).

Hunter in Ambush. Cat. no. 68.

Guardi, Francesco. 1712–1793.
Bust of the Virgin in Prayer. Cat. no 49 (now in The Pierpont Morgan Library, Acc. No. 1969.20).

Venetian Courtyard. Cat. no. 50.

Capriccio with Ruins. Cat. no. 51.

Capriccio with a Squall on the Lagoon. Cat. no. 52.

Group of Three Men and a Woman. Cat. no. 53.

Ingres, Jean-Auguste-Dominique. 1780–1867.
Portrait of M. Marcotte Genlis. Cat. no. 70.

Study for the Figure of Marie de' Medici. Cat. no. 71 (now in The Pierpont Morgan Library, Acc. No. 1981.76).

Jongkind, Johan Barthold. 1819–1891.
La Chapelle de Grâce, Honfleur. Cat. no. 114.

Lear, Edward. 1812–1888.
Panoramic View of Tivoli. Cat. no. 113.

Magnasco, Alessandro. ca. 1667–1749.
Two Shepherds and a Woman Seated by a Tree. Cat. no. 24.

Mantegna, Andrea, school of. 1431–1506.
Hercules and the Lion and Other Studies after the Antique. Cat. no. 2.

Martin, John. 1789–1854.
Caius Marius Mourning over the Ruins of Carthage. Cat. no. 110.

Milanese School. Early 16th Century.
Profile Head of a Young Man. Cat. no. 8 (now in The Pierpont Morgan Library, Acc. No. 1976.46).

Millet, Jean-François. 1814–1875.
The Potato Harvest ("*La Récolte des Pommes de Terre*"). Cat. no. 89.

North Italian School. Late 15th Century.
Profile Head of a Monk. Cat. no. 4 (now in The Pierpont Morgan Library, Acc. No. 1976.43).

Palmer, Samuel. 1805–1881.
Pear Tree in a Walled Garden. Cat. no. 112 (now in The Pierpont Morgan Library, Acc. No. 1980.37).

Perugino, Pietro, after. ca. 1445–1523.
The Prophet Jeremiah. Cat. no. 3 (now in The Pierpont Morgan Library, Acc. No. 1976.42).

Piranesi, Giovanni Battista. 1720–1778.
Assassination Scene. Cat. no. 54 (now in The Pierpont Morgan Library, Acc. No. 1968.13).

A First Idea for Santa Maria del Priorato(?). Cat. no. 55.

The Temple of Isis at Pompeii. Cat. no. 56 (now in The Pierpont Morgan Library, Acc. No. 1979.41).

Prud'hon, Pierre-Paul. 1758–1823.
Female Nude. Cat. no. 38 (now in The Pierpont Morgan Library, Acc. No. 1974.71).

Redon, Odilon. 1840–1916.
Bottom Gazing at his Reflection. Cat. no. 102.

Rembrandt van Rijn. 1606–1669.
St. Peter. Cat. no. 25.

St. John the Baptist Preaching. Cat. no. 26.

Farm Houses and Trees along a Frozen Canal. Cat. no. 27.

Farm Buildings and Trees. Cat. no. 28.

The Finding of Moses. Cat. no. 29.

Three Studies for a Descent from the Cross. Cat. no. 30.

Robert, Hubert. 1733–1808.
Draughtsman in an Italian Church. Cat. no. 37 (now in The Pierpont Morgan Library, Acc. No. 1981.74).

Rubens, Sir Peter Paul. 1577–1640.
Studies for "The Descent from the Cross." Cat. no. 11.

Seurat, Georges. 1859–1891.
Nurse with a Child's Carriage. Cat. no. 104.

Tiepolo, Giovanni Battista. 1696–1770.
Angelica and Medoro. Cat. no. 40.

Bearded Oriental in Turban and Cloak. Cat. no. 41.

Bearded Oriental in Flat Cap and Striped Coat. Cat. no. 42.

Two Orientals. Cat. no. 43.

Oriental Seen from the Back. Cat. no. 44.

Young Man in a Broad-Collared Tunic. Cat. no. 45.

Reclining Woman Seen from Below. Cat. no. 46.

Head of an Old Man. Cat. no. 47.

Drunken Punchinello. Cat. no. 48.

Tiepolo, Giovanni Domenico. 1727–1804.
The Slaying of Zacharias ("Le Meurtre"). Cat. no. 57.

Christ on the Mount of Olives. Cat. no. 58.

A Session of the Magistrates. Cat. no. 59.

The Presentation of the Fiancé. Cat. no. 60.

The Quack Dentist. Cat. no. 61.

The Marriage Feast of Punchinello's Parents. Cat. no. 62.

The Last Illness of Punchinello. Cat. no. 63.

Toulouse-Lautrec, Henri-Marie-Raymond de. 1864–1901.
Mlle Lender. Cat. no. 105.

Turner, Joseph Mallord William. 1775–1851.
Lurleiberg. Cat. no. 108.

Waves Breaking on the Beach. Cat. no. 109.

Watteau, Jean-Antoine. 1684–1721.
Copy of Rubens' Self-Portrait. Cat. no. 31.

Seated Soldier. Cat. no. 32.

A Member of the Persian Embassy. Cat. no. 33.

Head of an Old Bearded Man. Cat. no. 34.

Seated Young Woman. Cat. no. 35.

PLATES

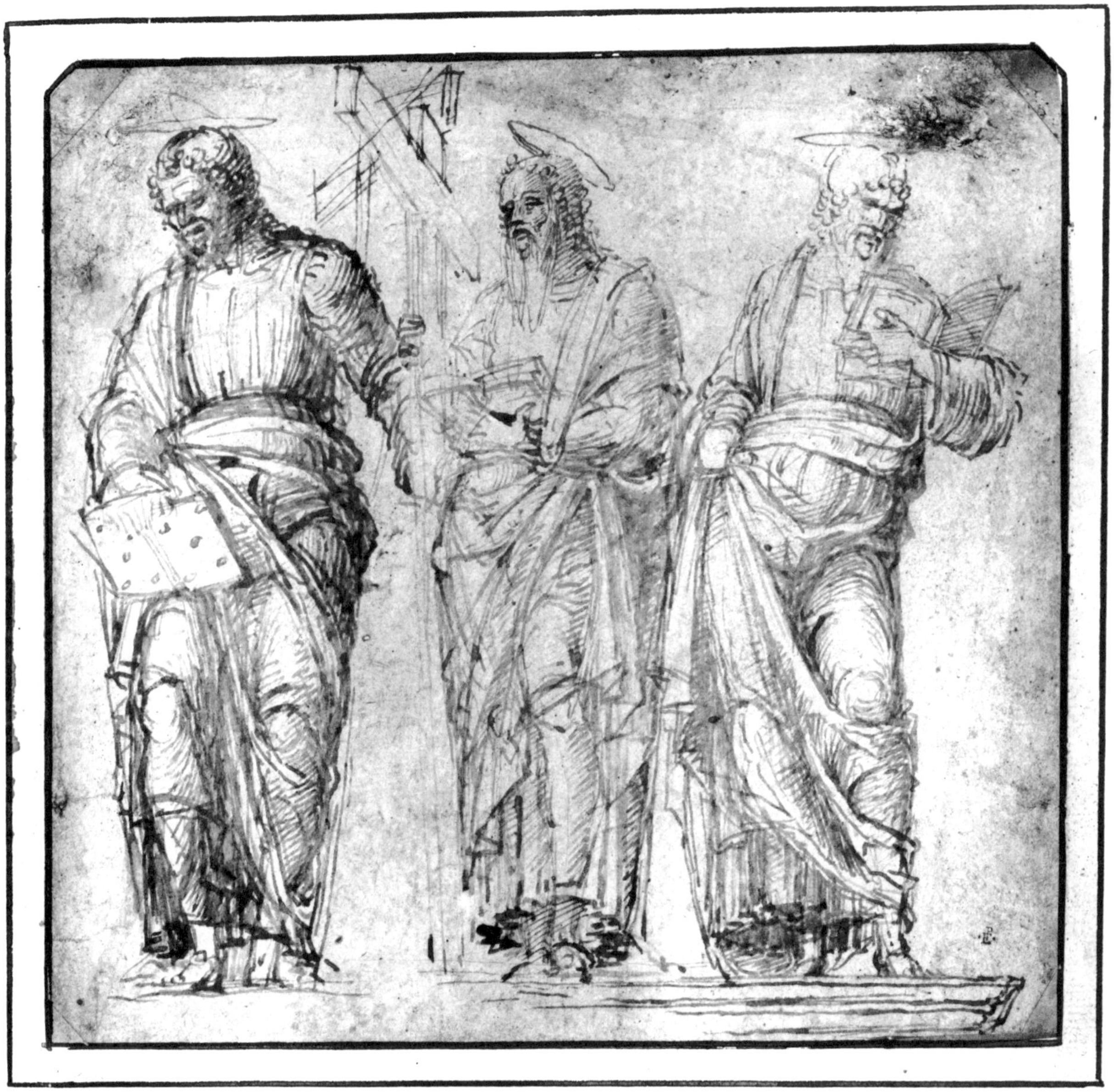

1 Andrea Mantegna *Three Standing Apostles*

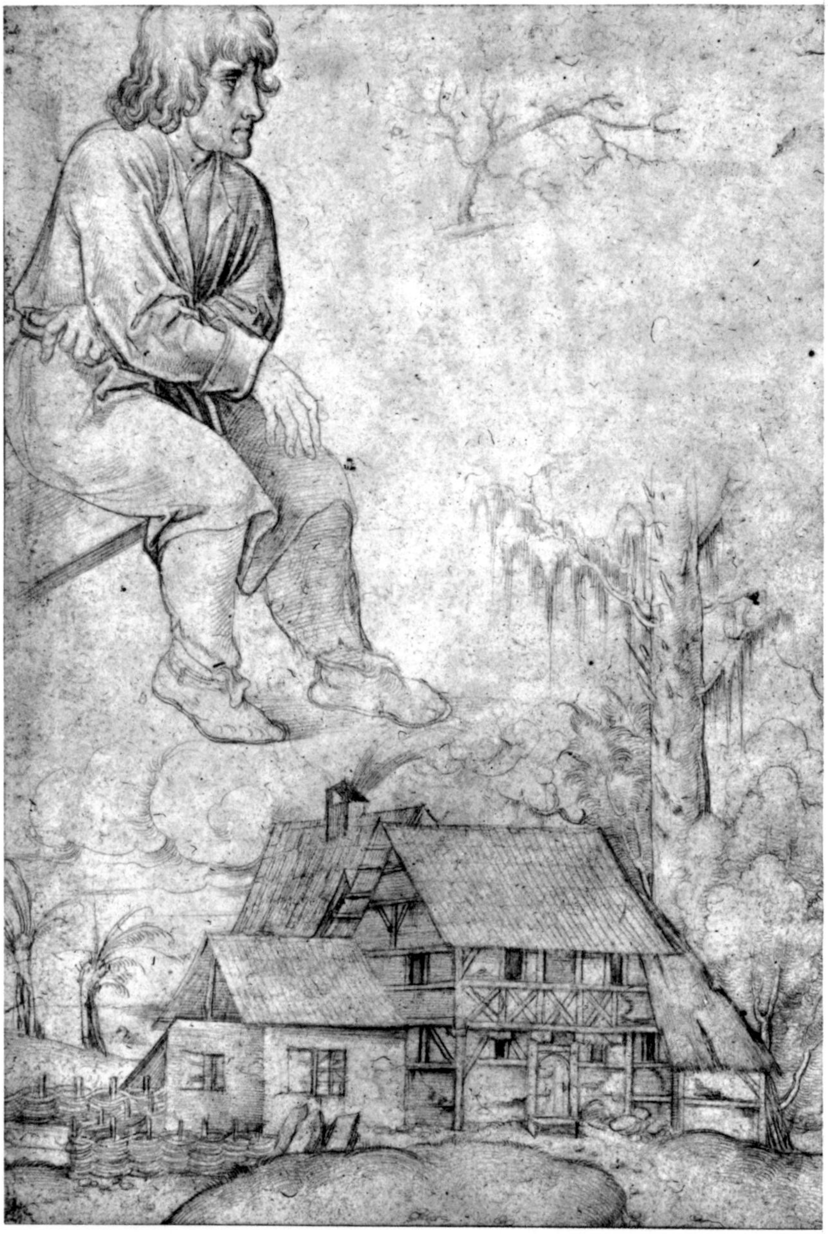

2 German School *Sheet of Studies with a Seated Man and Farmhouses in a Landscape*

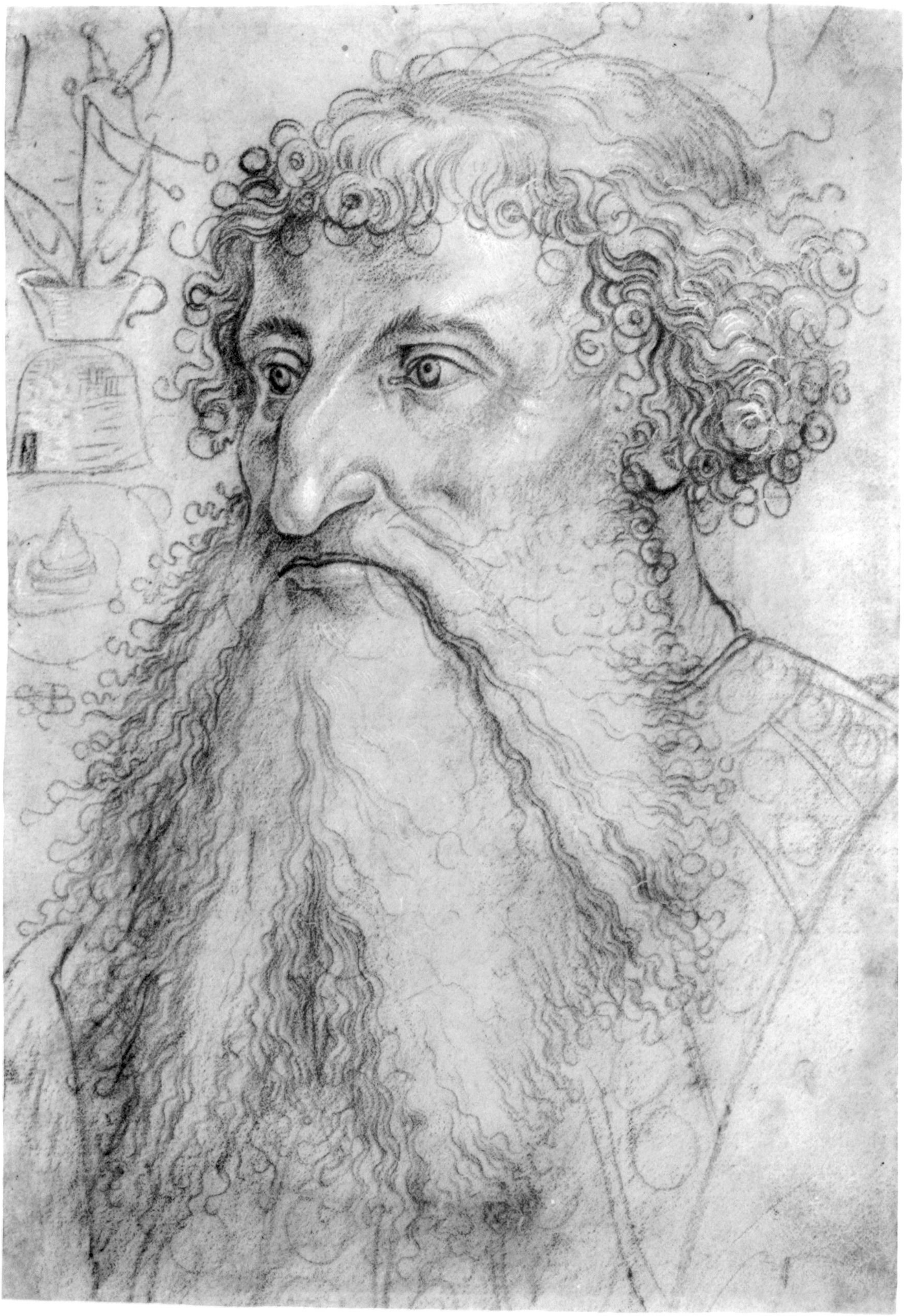

3 Hans Sebald Beham *Portrait of a Man*

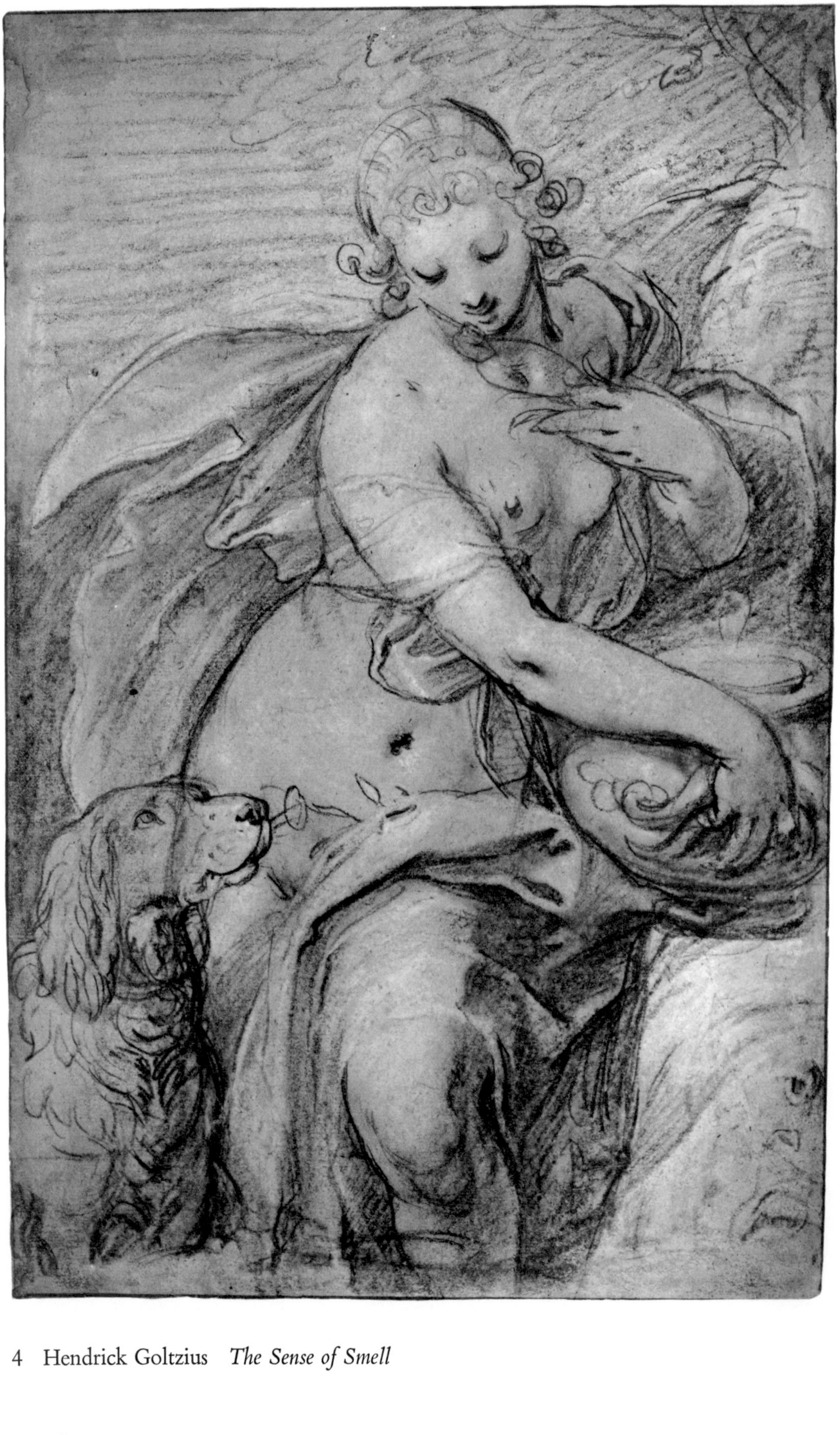

4 Hendrick Goltzius *The Sense of Smell*

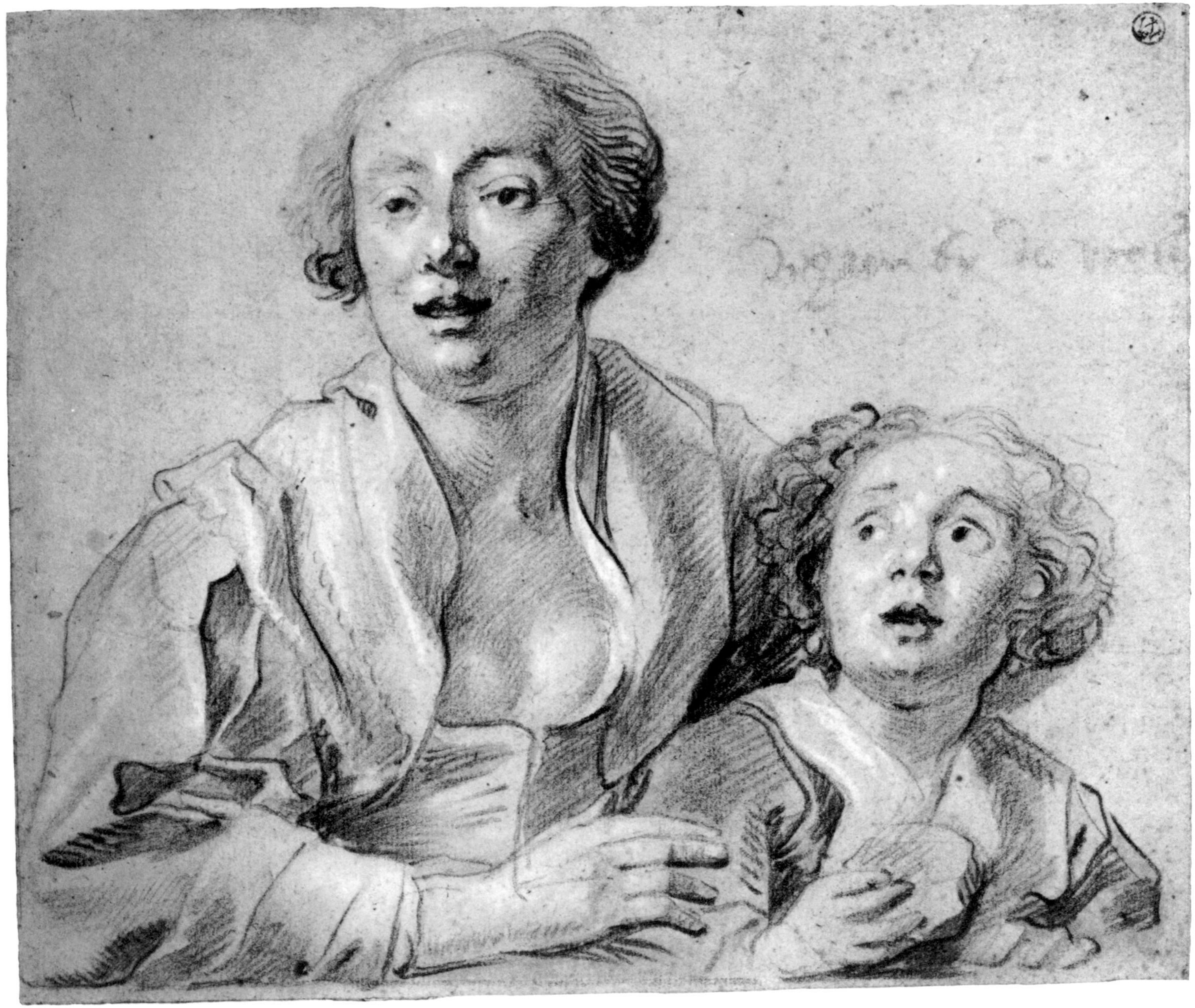

5 Jacob Jordaens *Mother and Child*

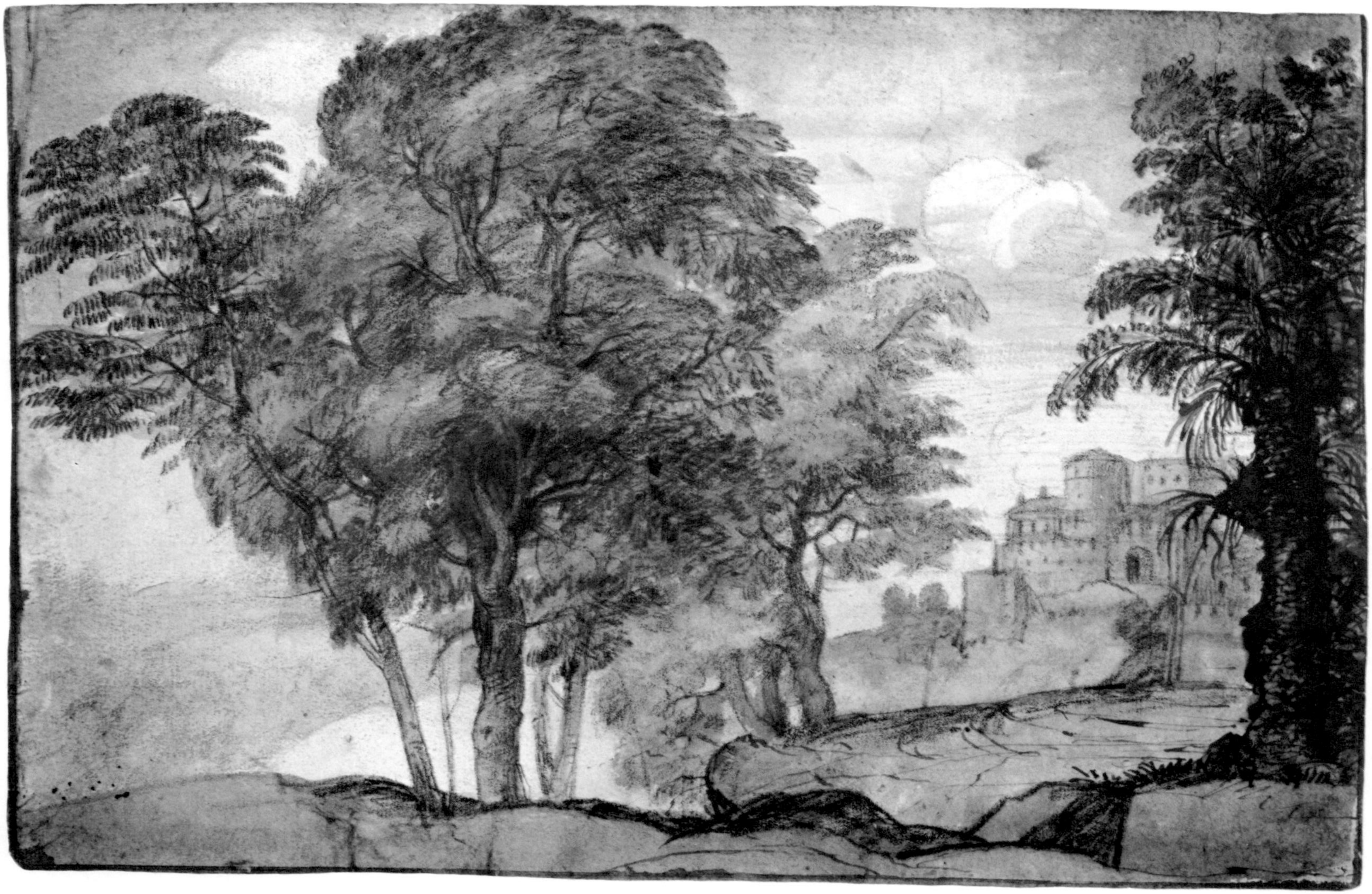

6 Claude Lorrain *Heroic Landscape*

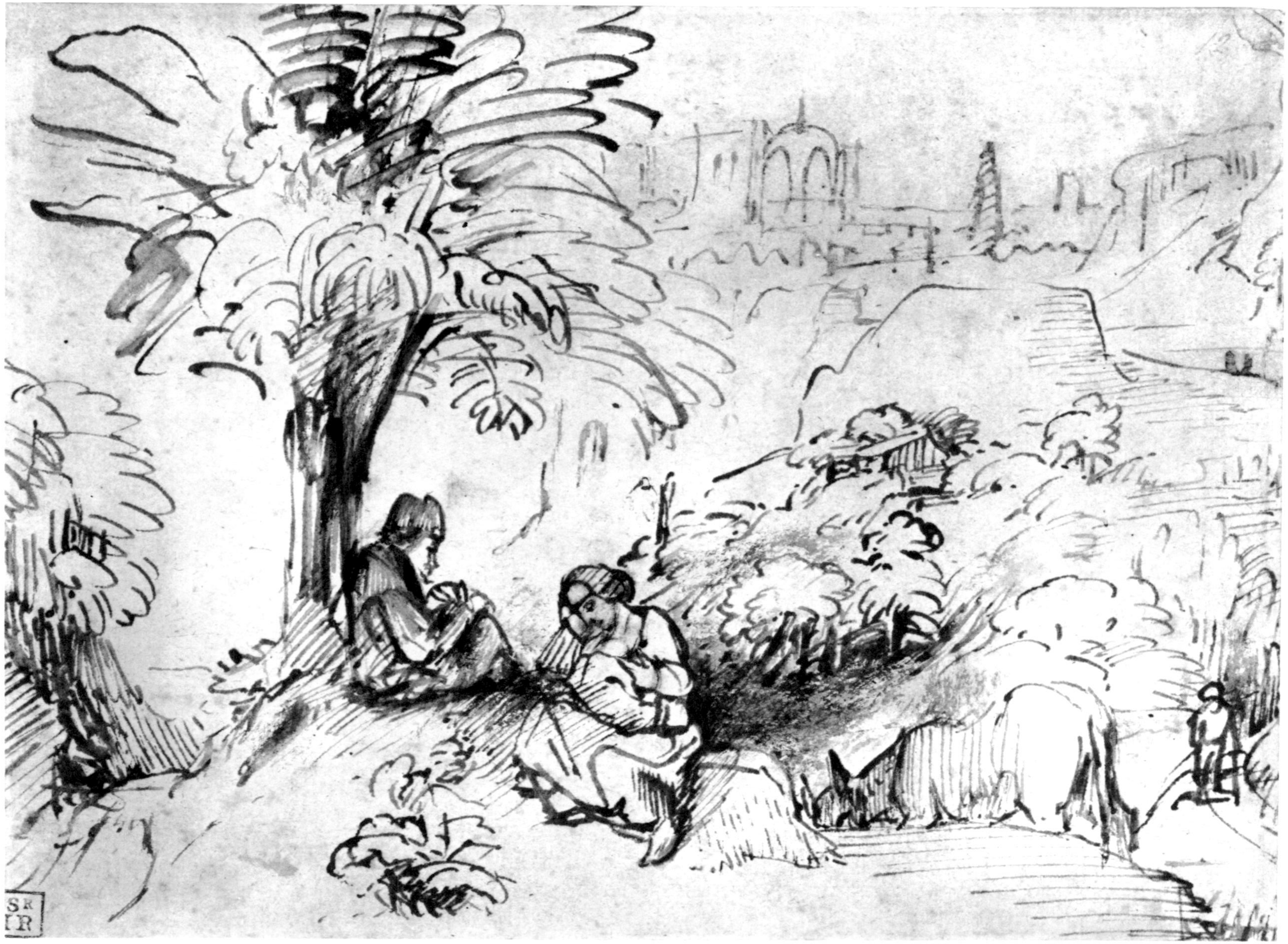

7 Rembrandt *The Rest on the Flight into Egypt*

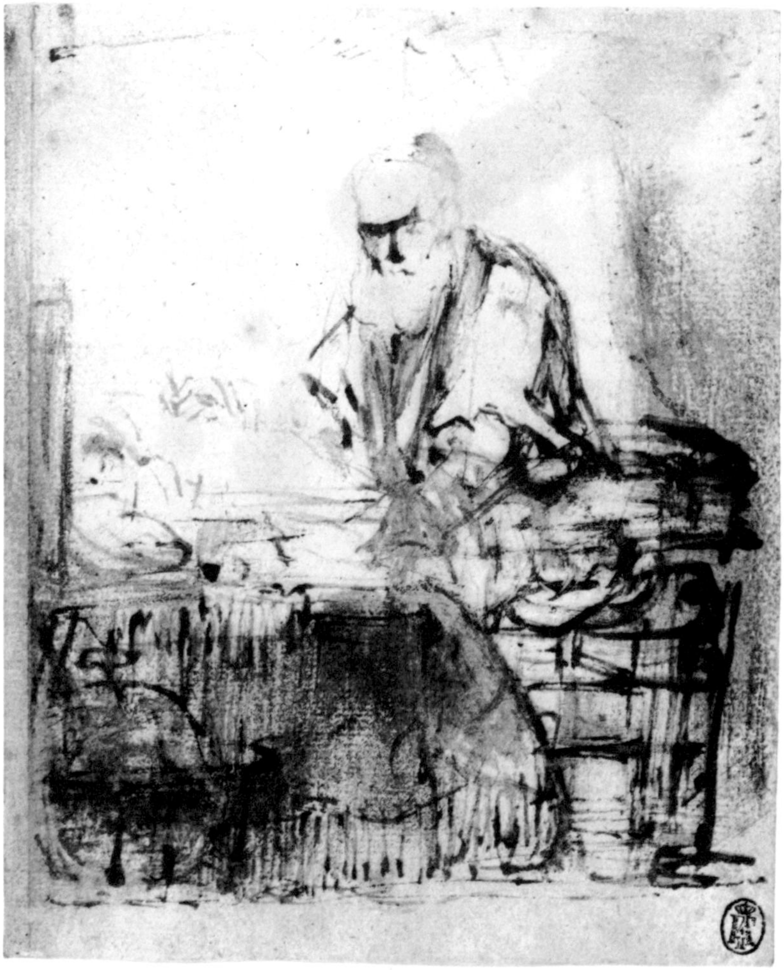

8 Rembrandt *Old Scholar at his Writing Table*

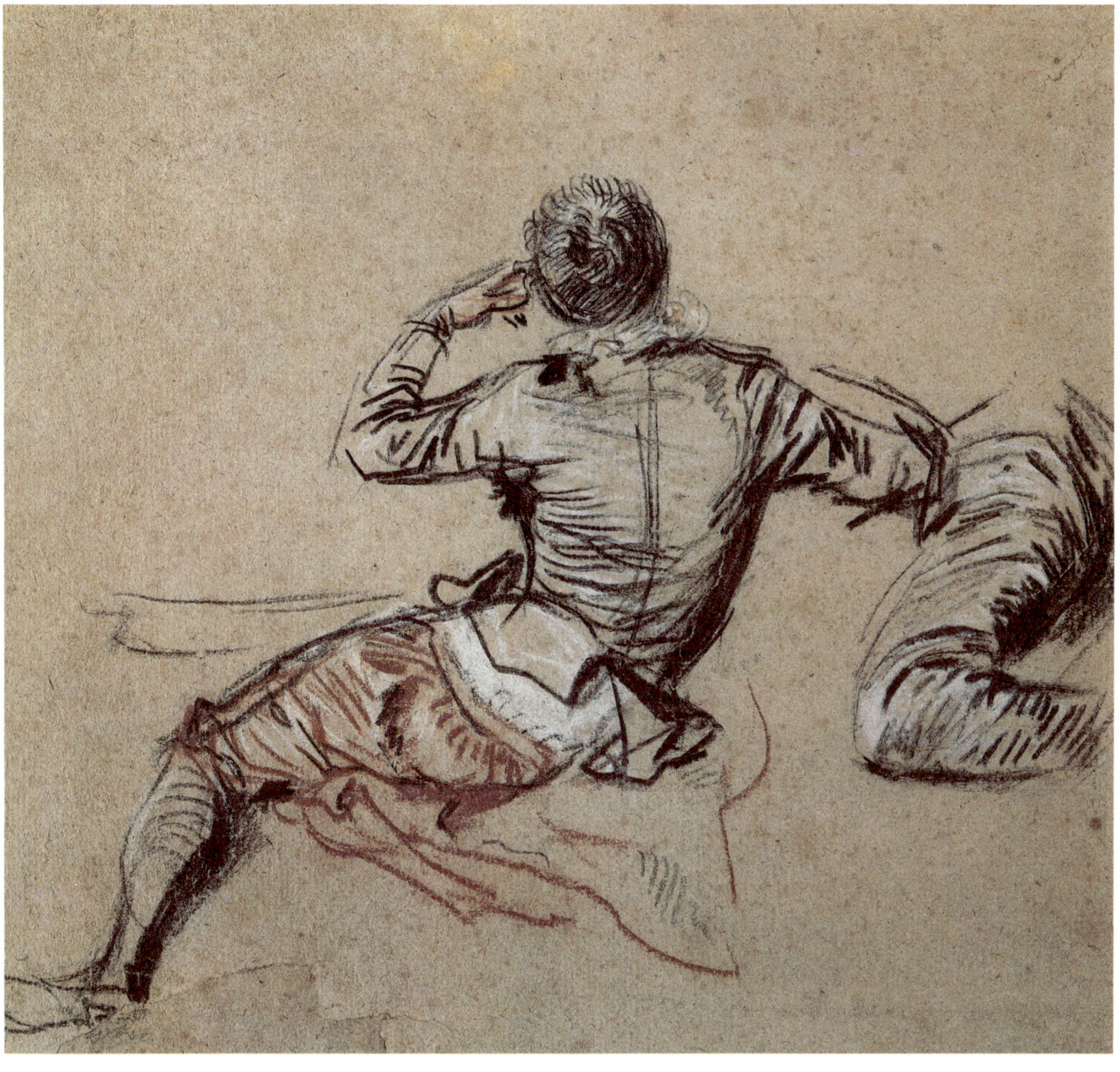

9 Jean-Antoine Watteau *Man Seen from Behind*

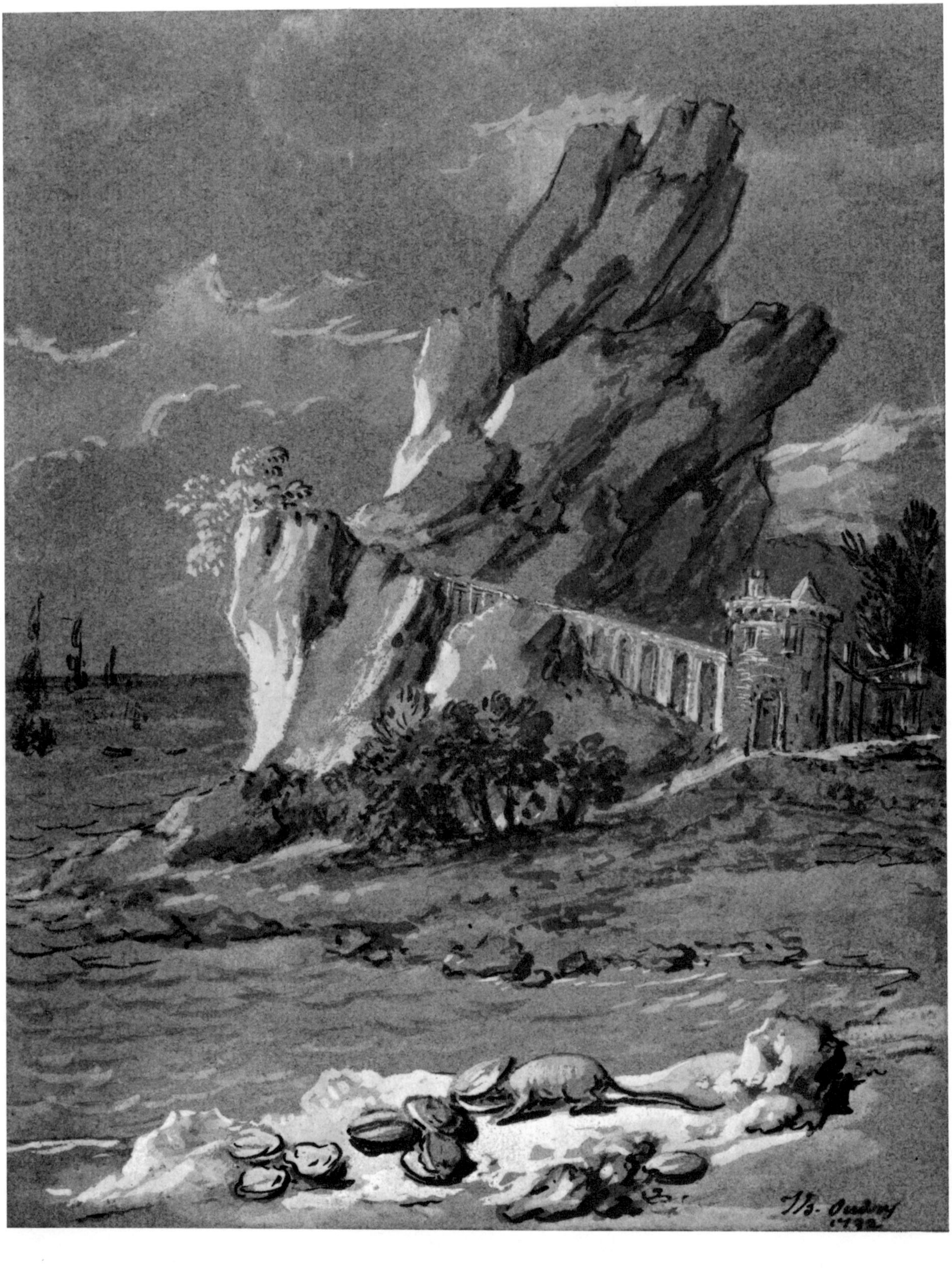

10 Jean-Baptiste Oudry *The Rat and the Oyster*

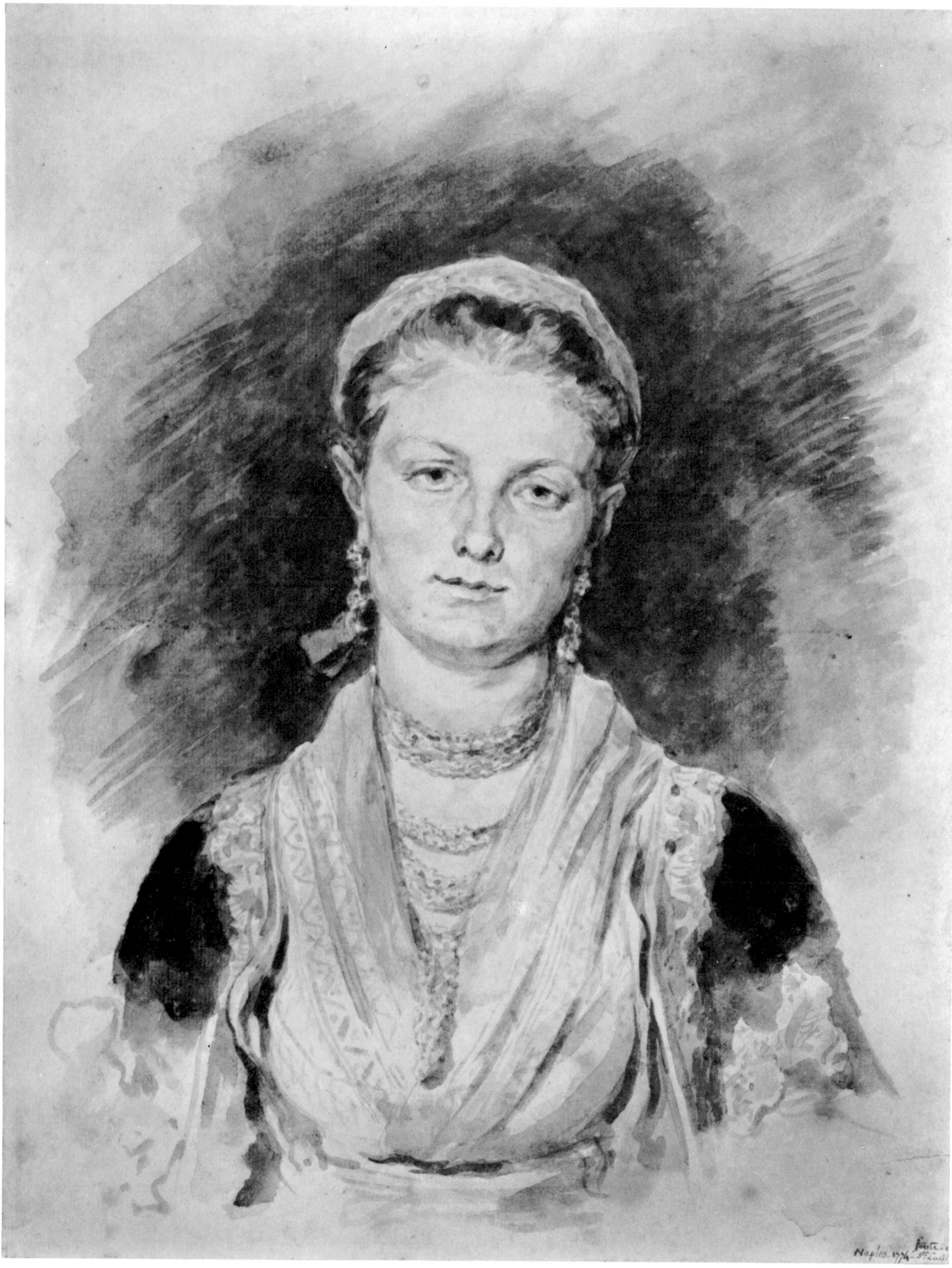

11 Jean-Honoré Fragonard *Portrait of a Neapolitan Girl*

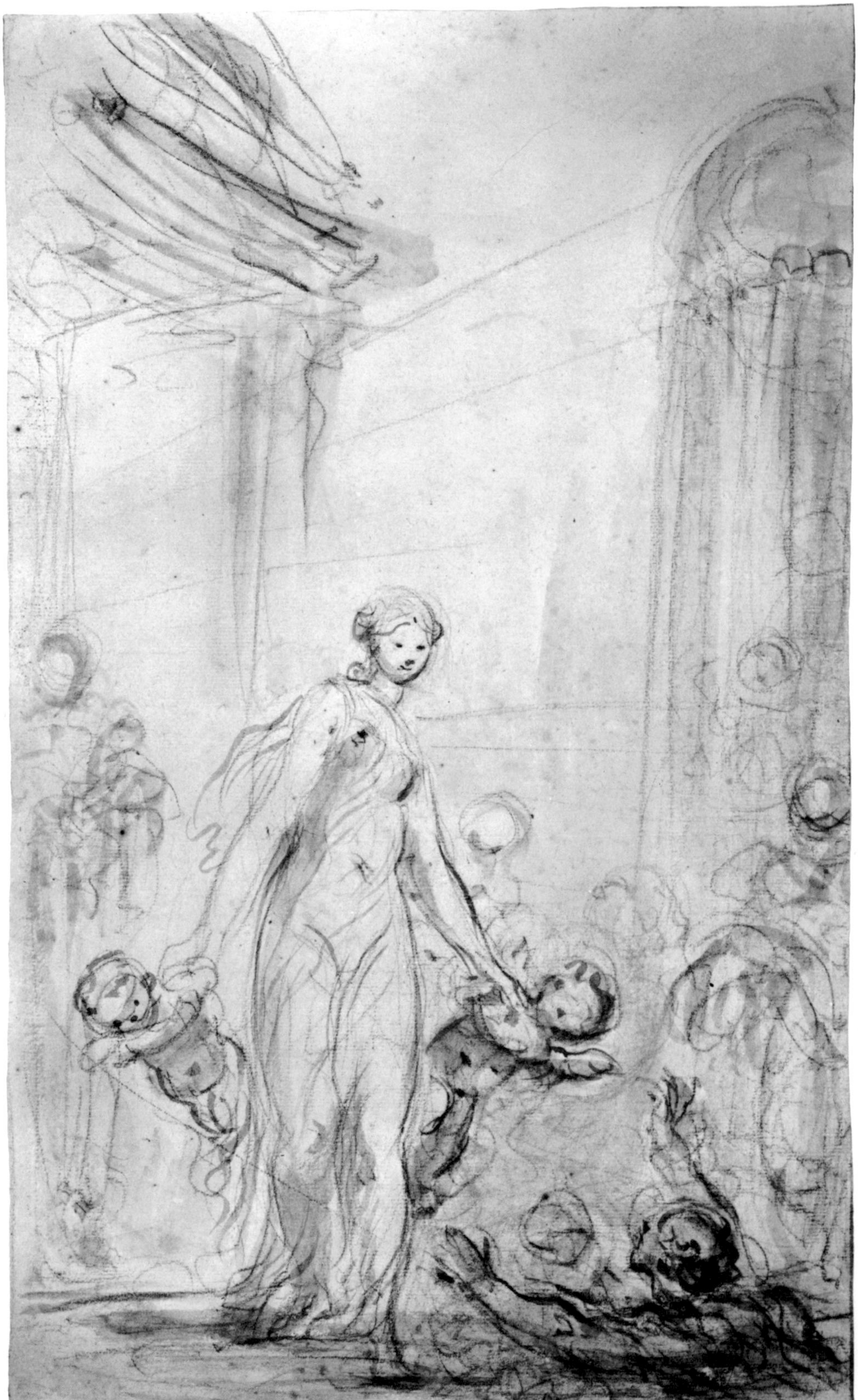

12 Jean-Honoré Fragonard *Ruggiero and Alcina at the Bath*

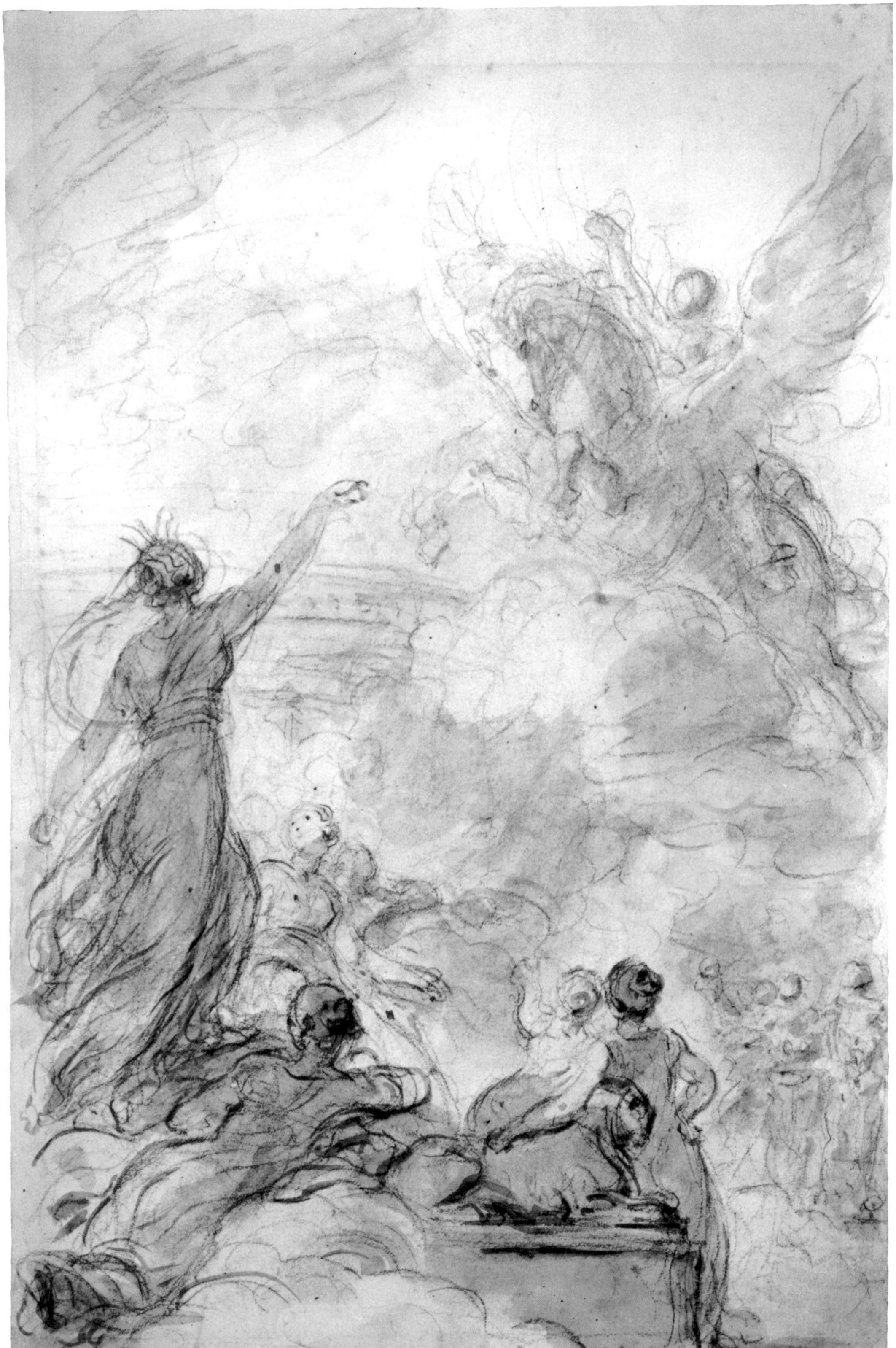

13 Jean-Honoré Fragonard *Ruggiero Masters the Hippogryph*

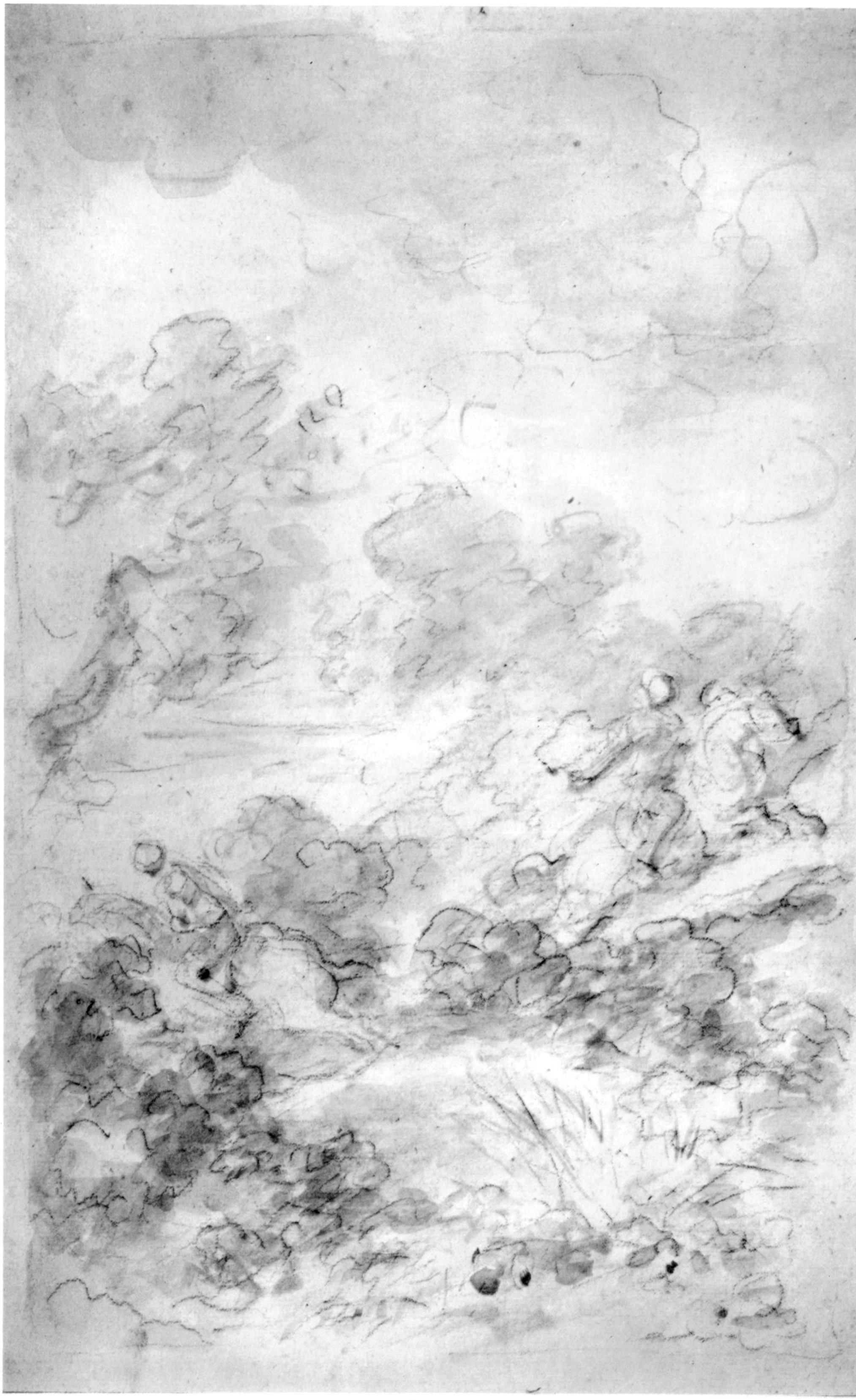

14 Jean-Honoré Fragonard *Ferrau and Orlando*

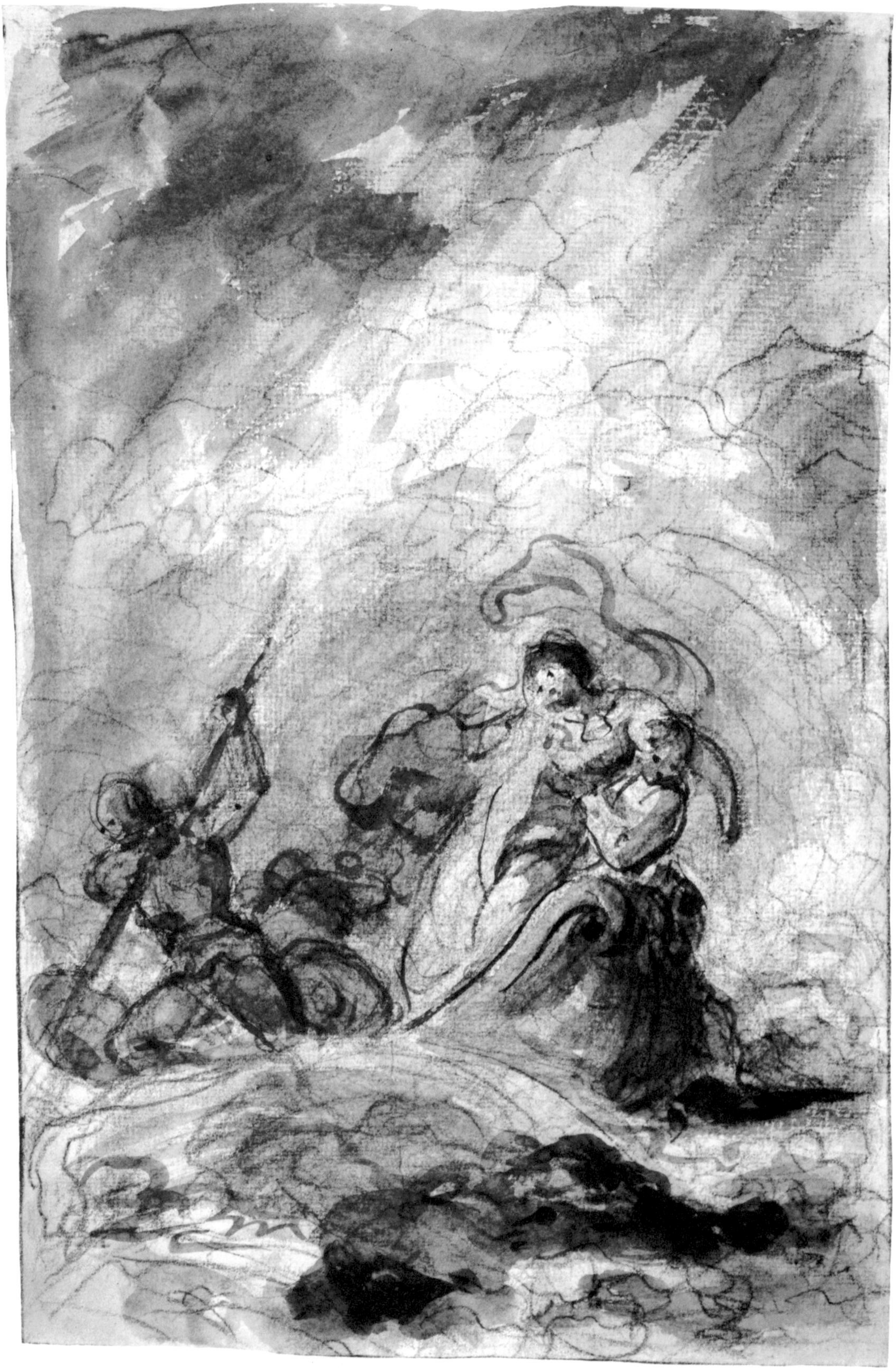

15 Jean-Honoré Fragonard *Isabella Rowed to Shore*

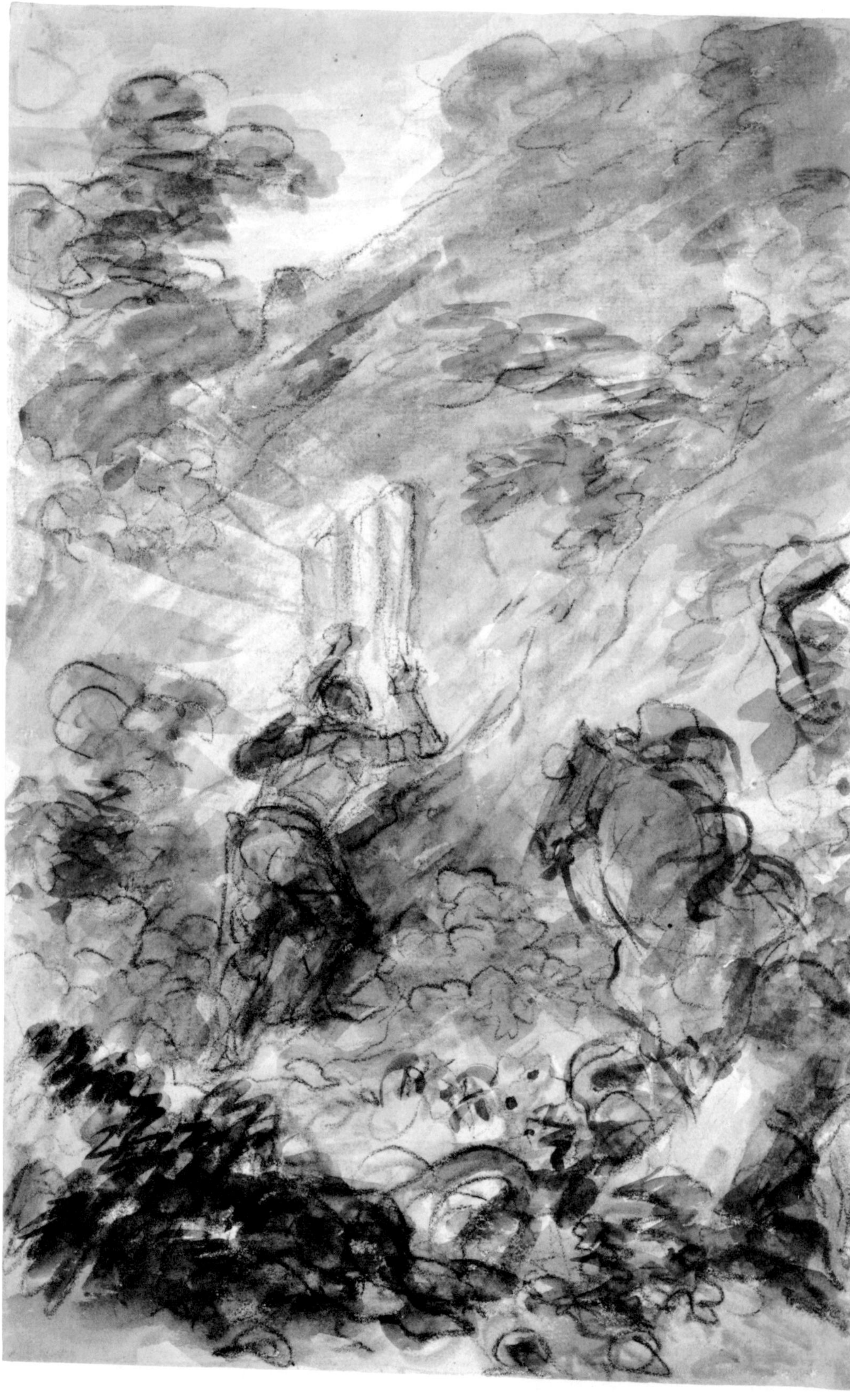

16 Jean-Honoré Fragonard *Orlando Discovers the Names of Angelica and Medoro*

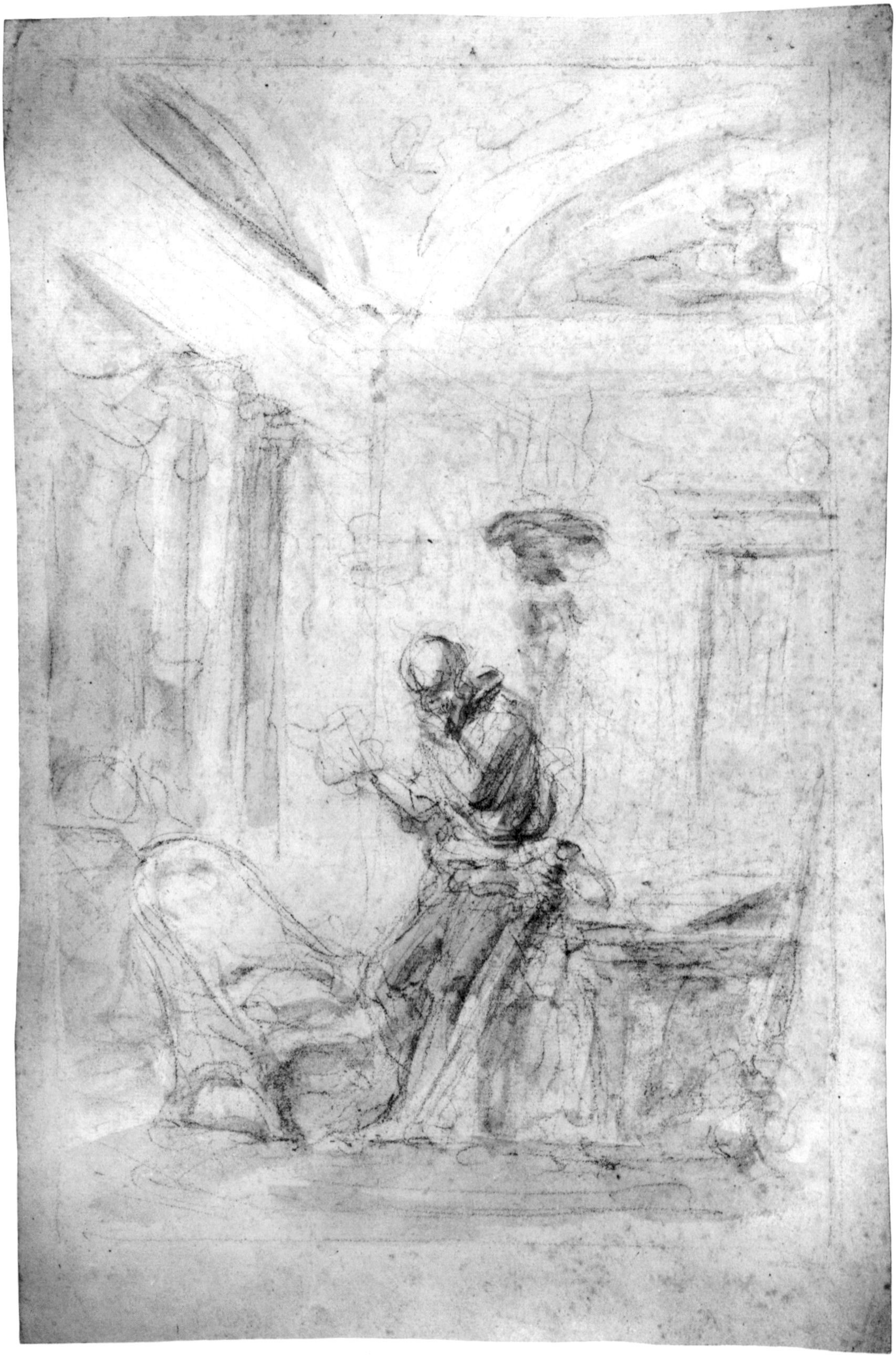

17 Jean-Honoré Fragonard *Bradamante Weeps . . .*

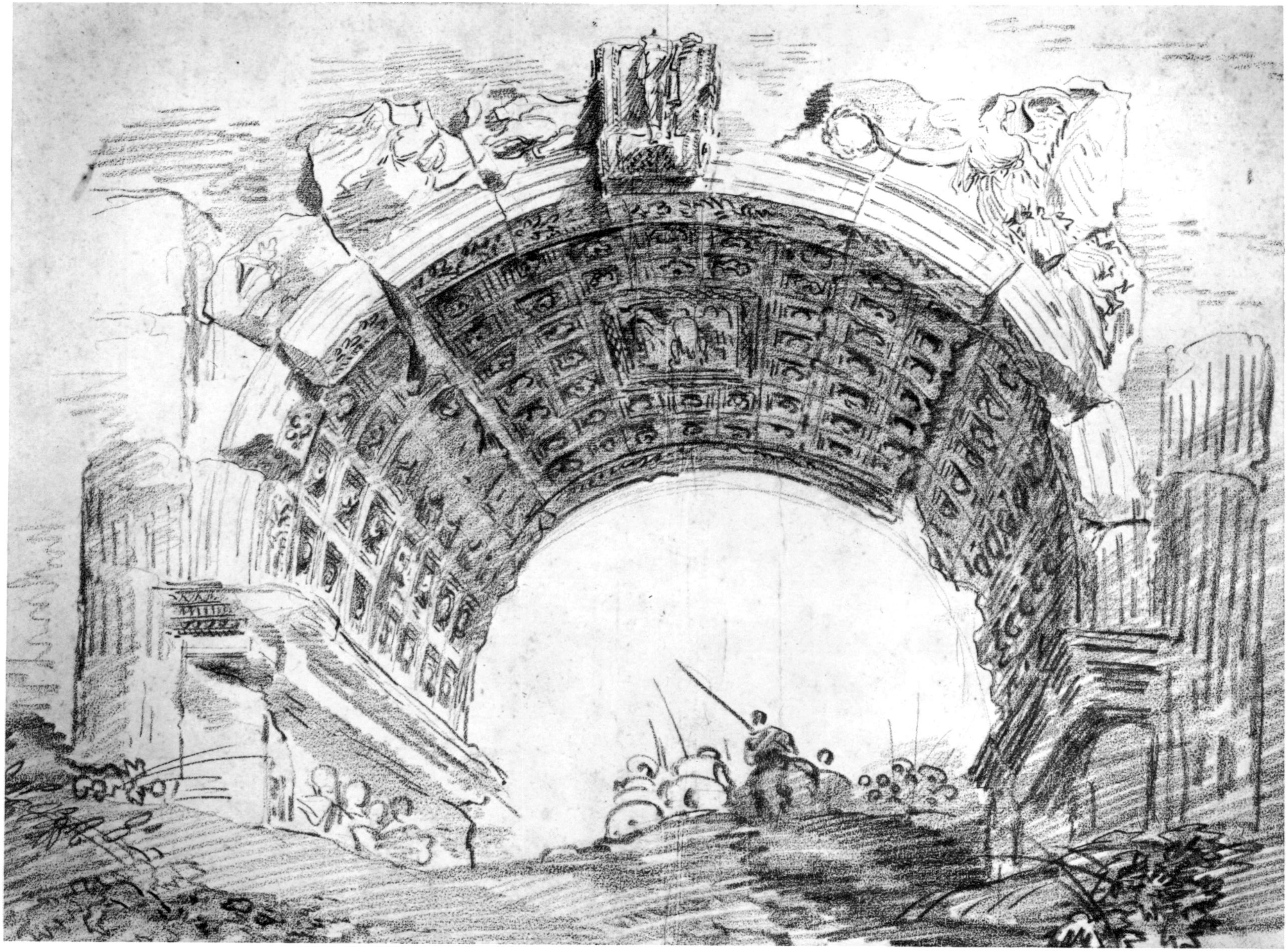

18 Hubert Robert *Arch of Titus*

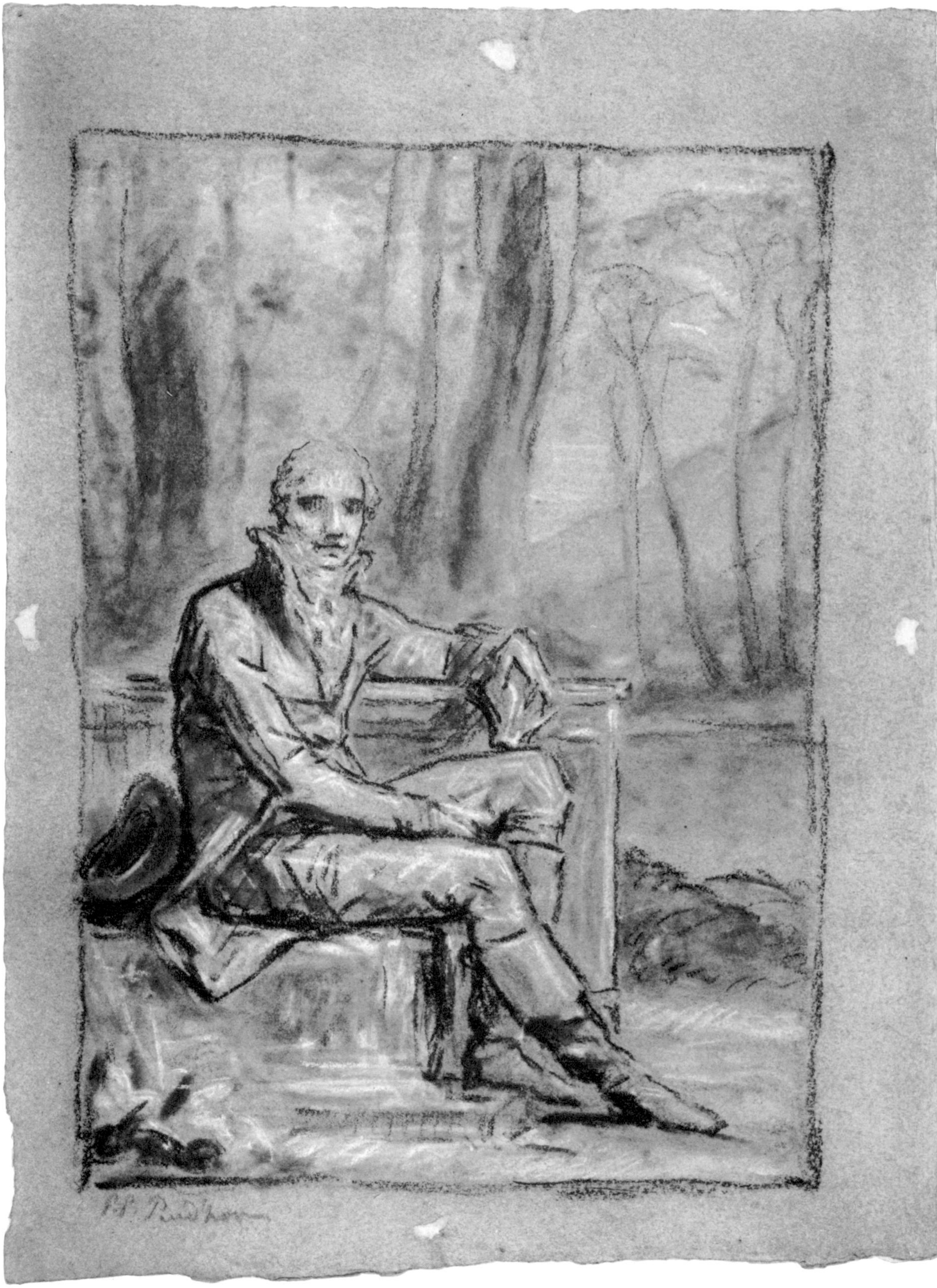

19 Pierre-Paul Prud'hon *Count Giovanni Battista Sommariva*

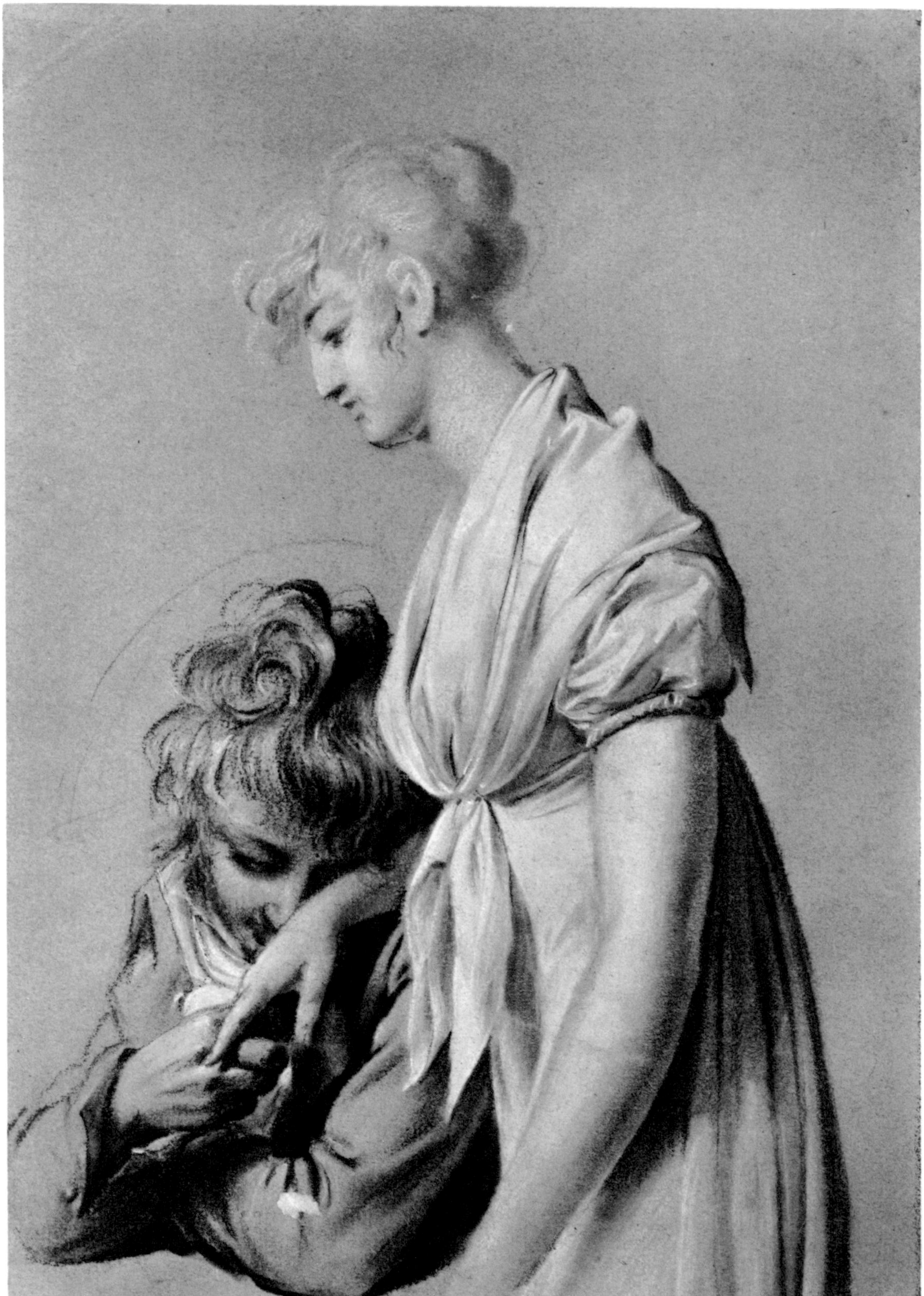

20 Louis Léopold Boilly *Les Fiancés*

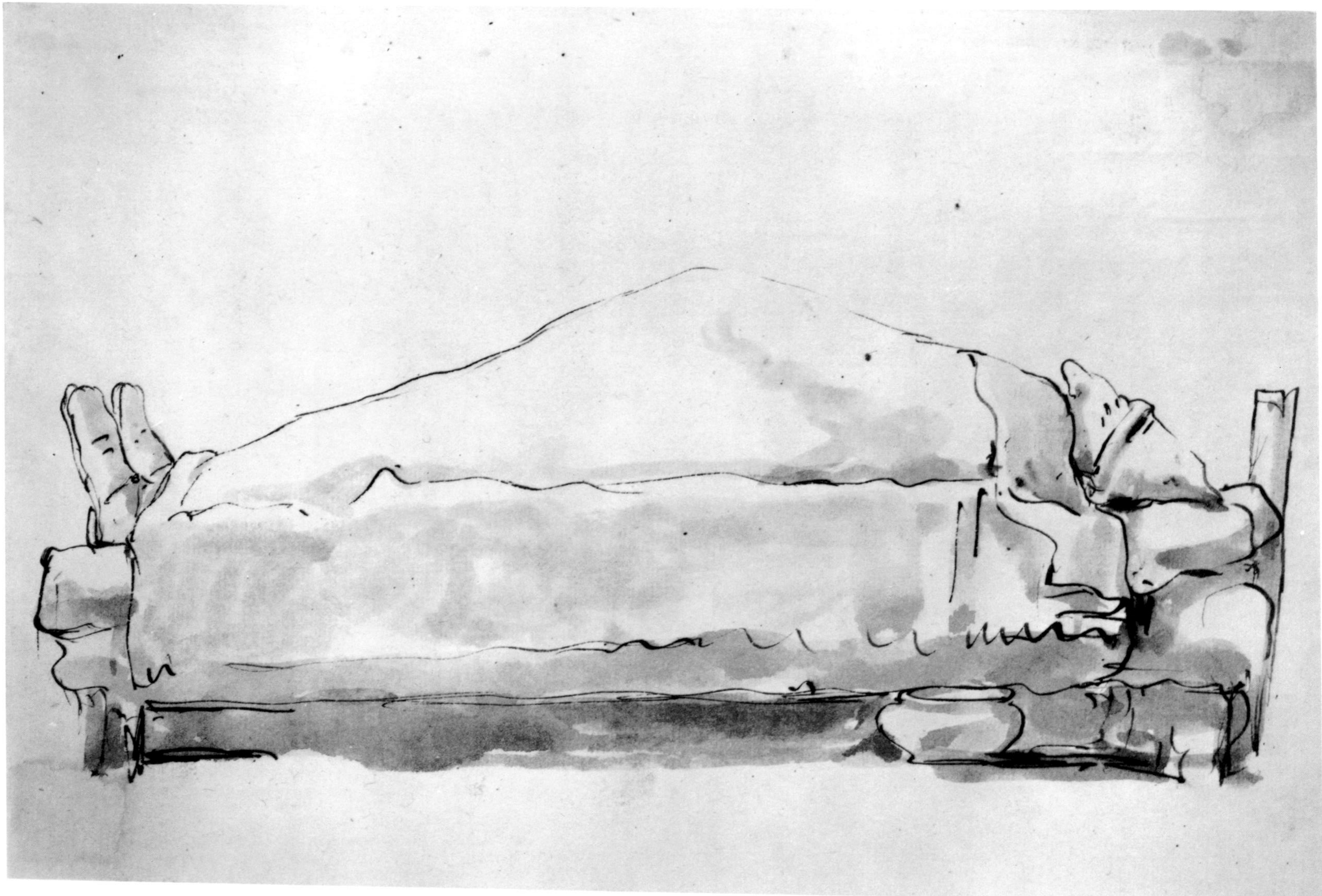

21 Giovanni Battista Tiepolo *Caricature of a Sleeping Man*

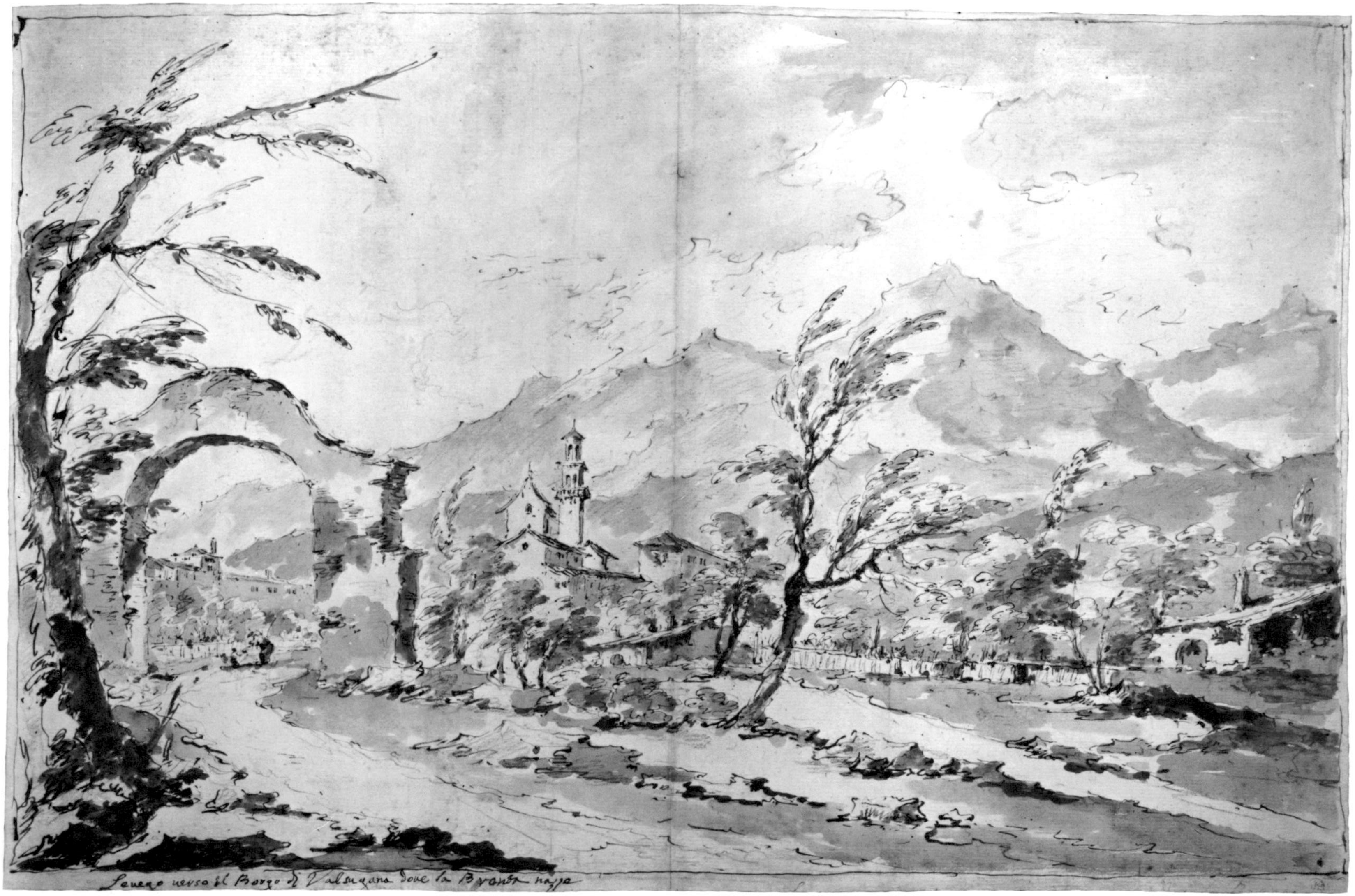

22 Francesco Guardi *View of Lévico*

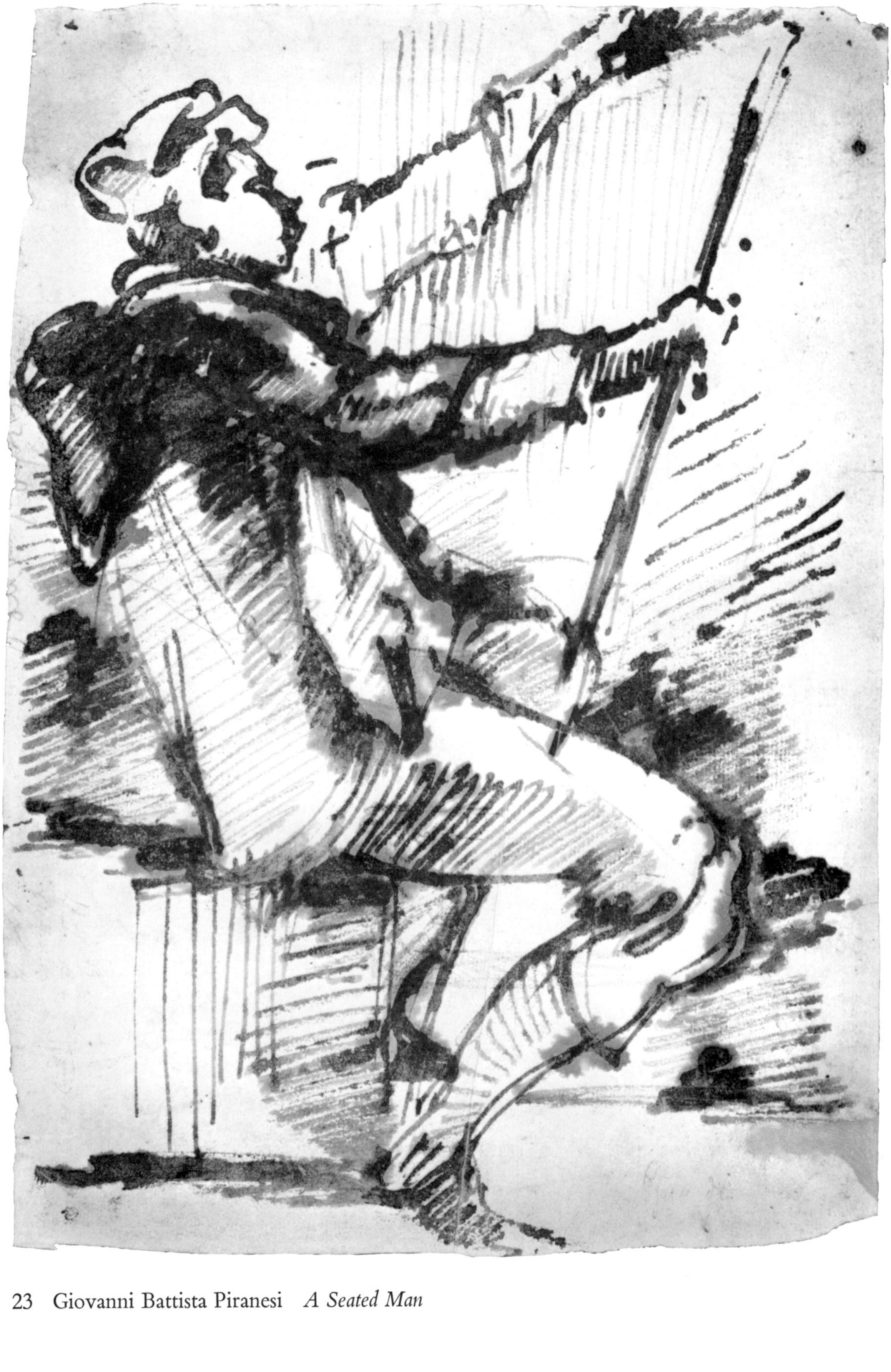

23 Giovanni Battista Piranesi *A Seated Man*

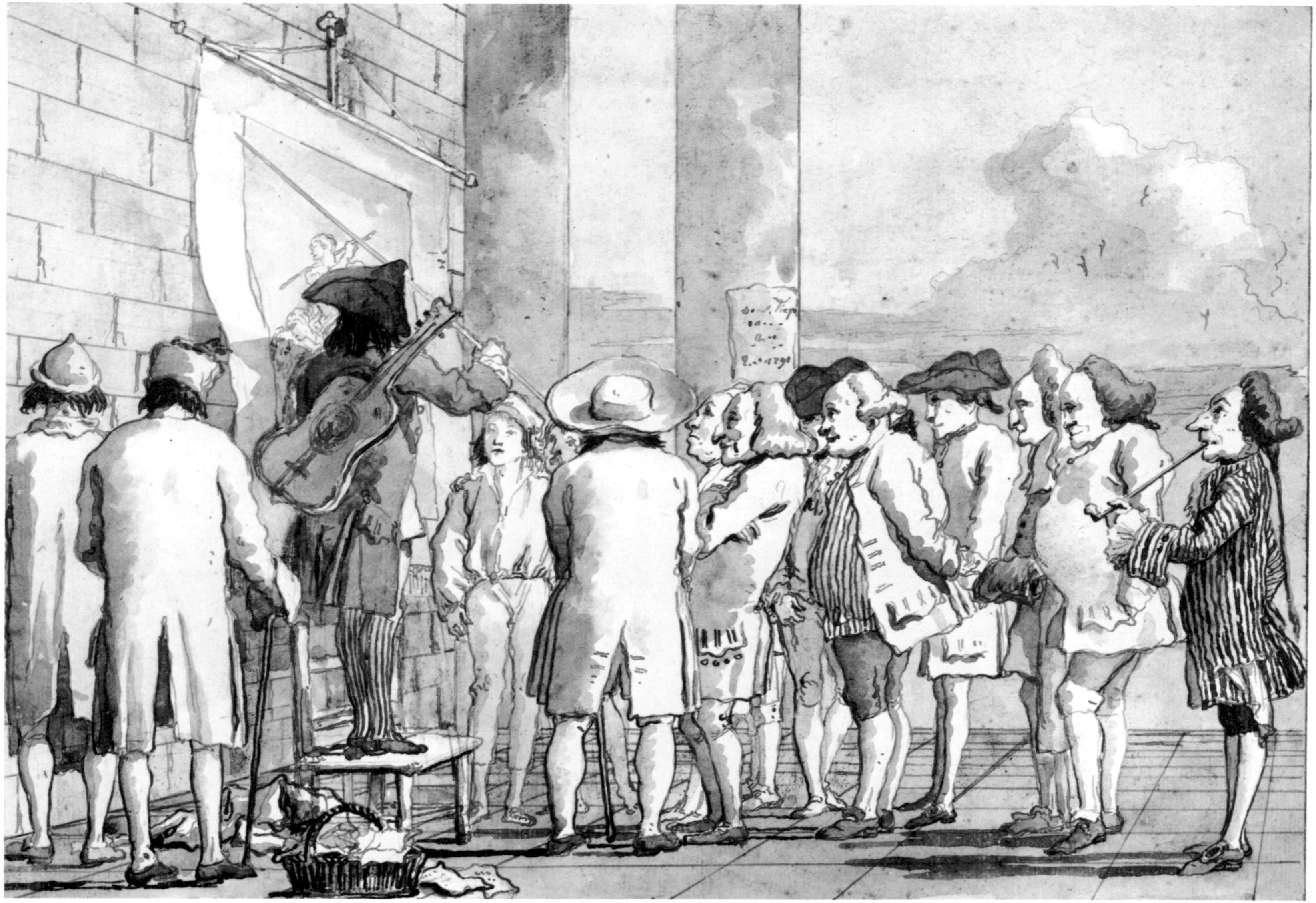

24 Giovanni Domenico Tiepolo *The Picture Show*

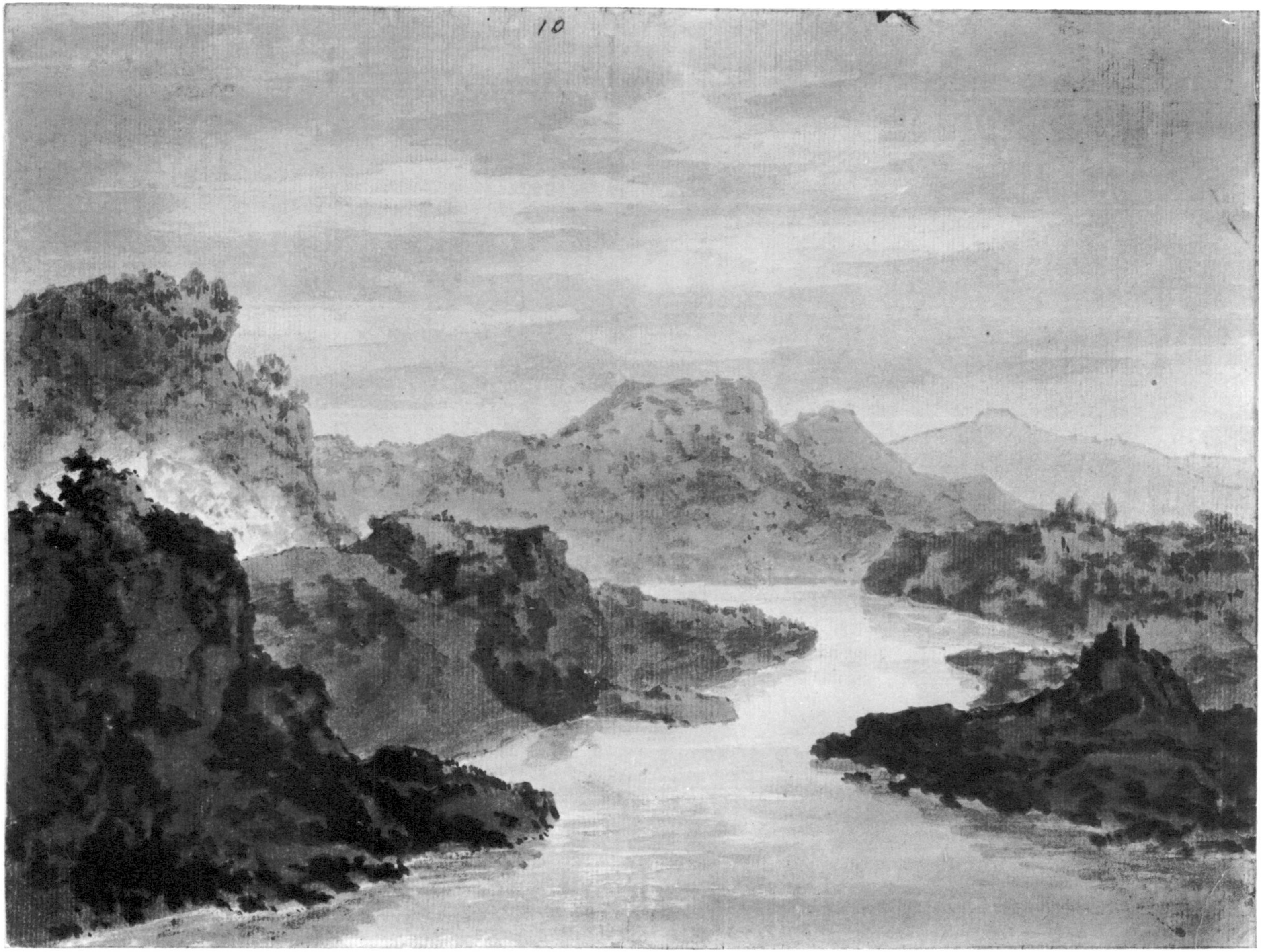

25 Alexander Cozens *A River between Hills*

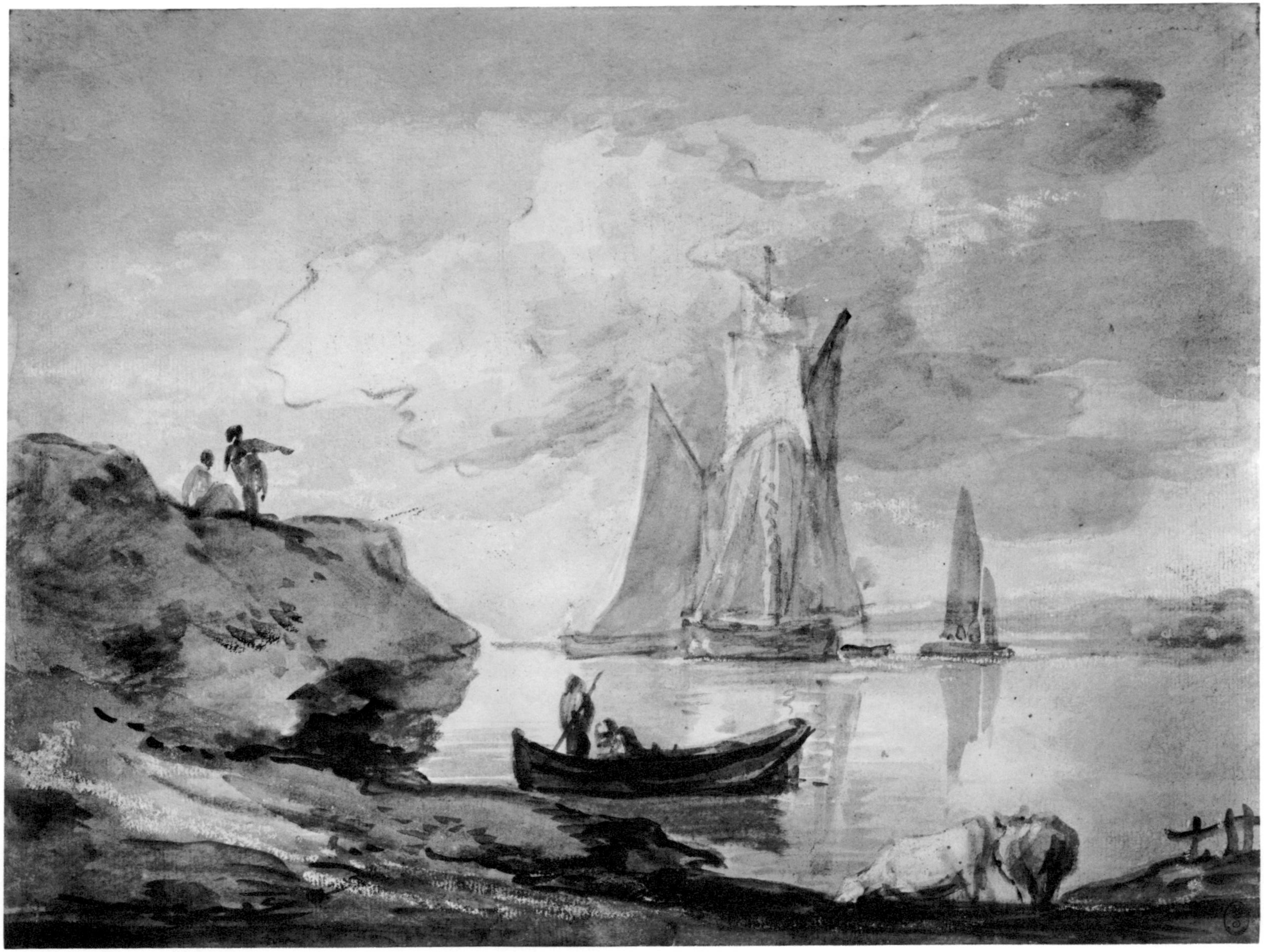

26 Thomas Gainsborough *Coastal Scene*

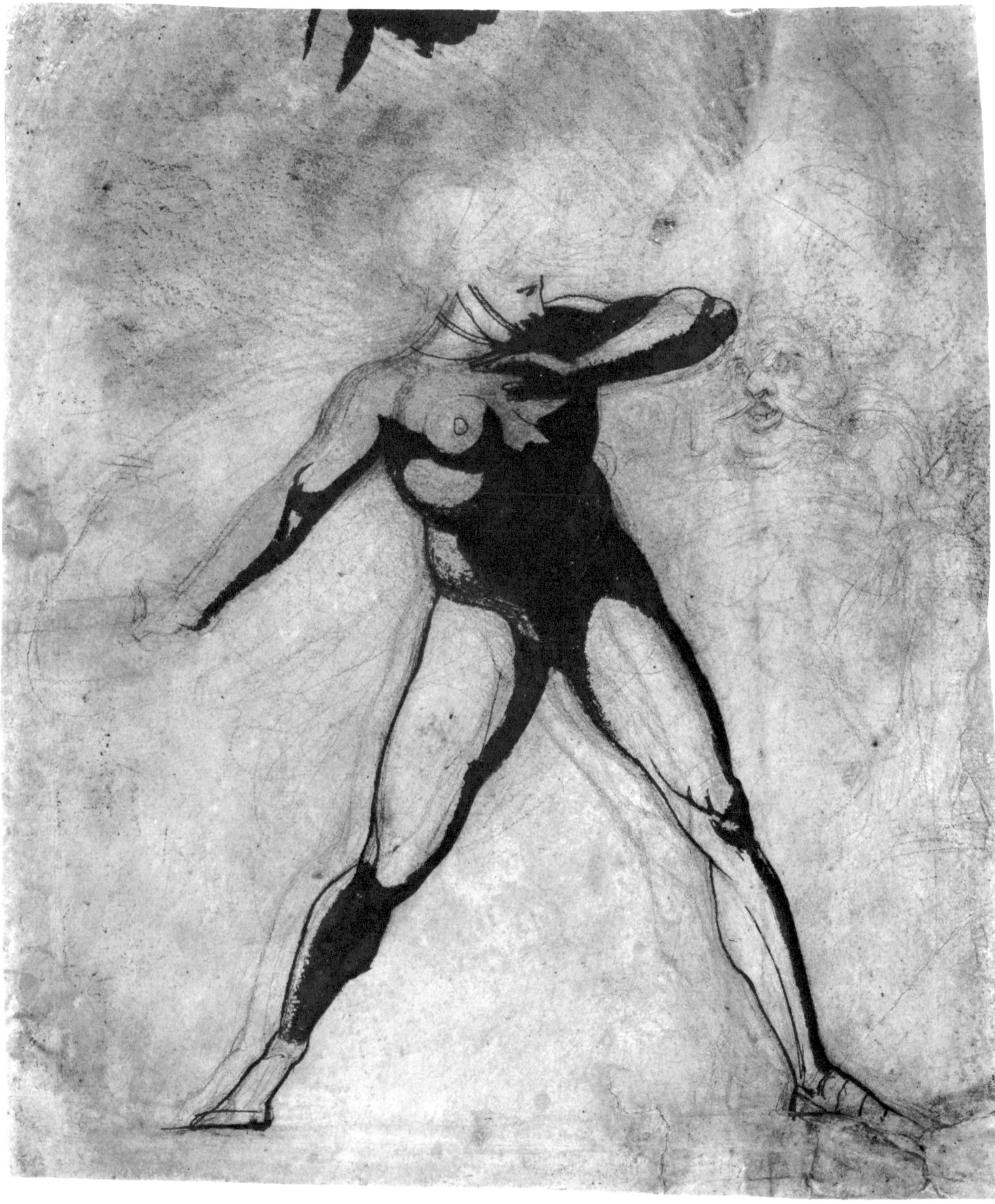

27 Henry Fuseli *Britomart Frees Amoret*

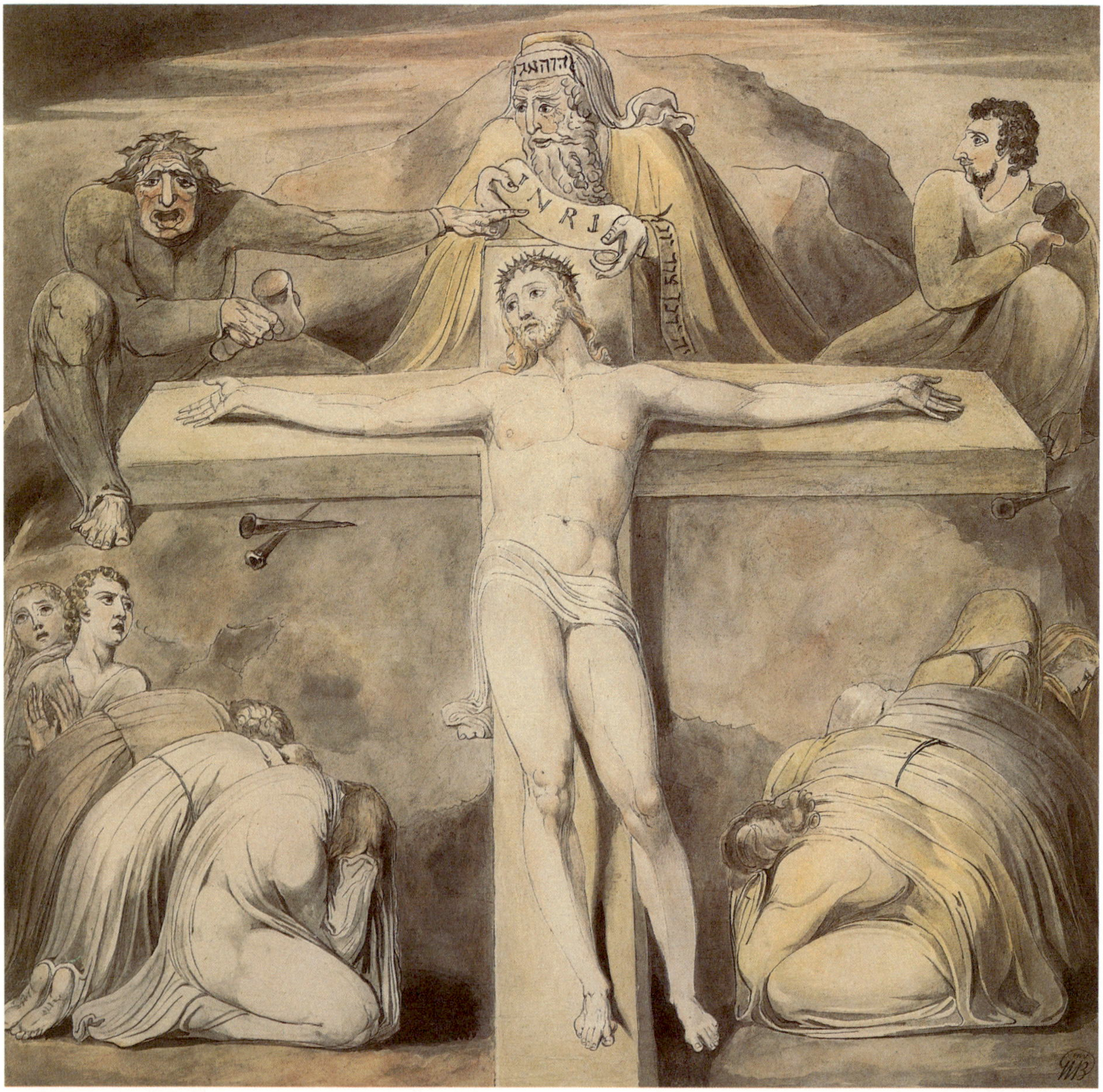

28 William Blake *The Crucifixion*

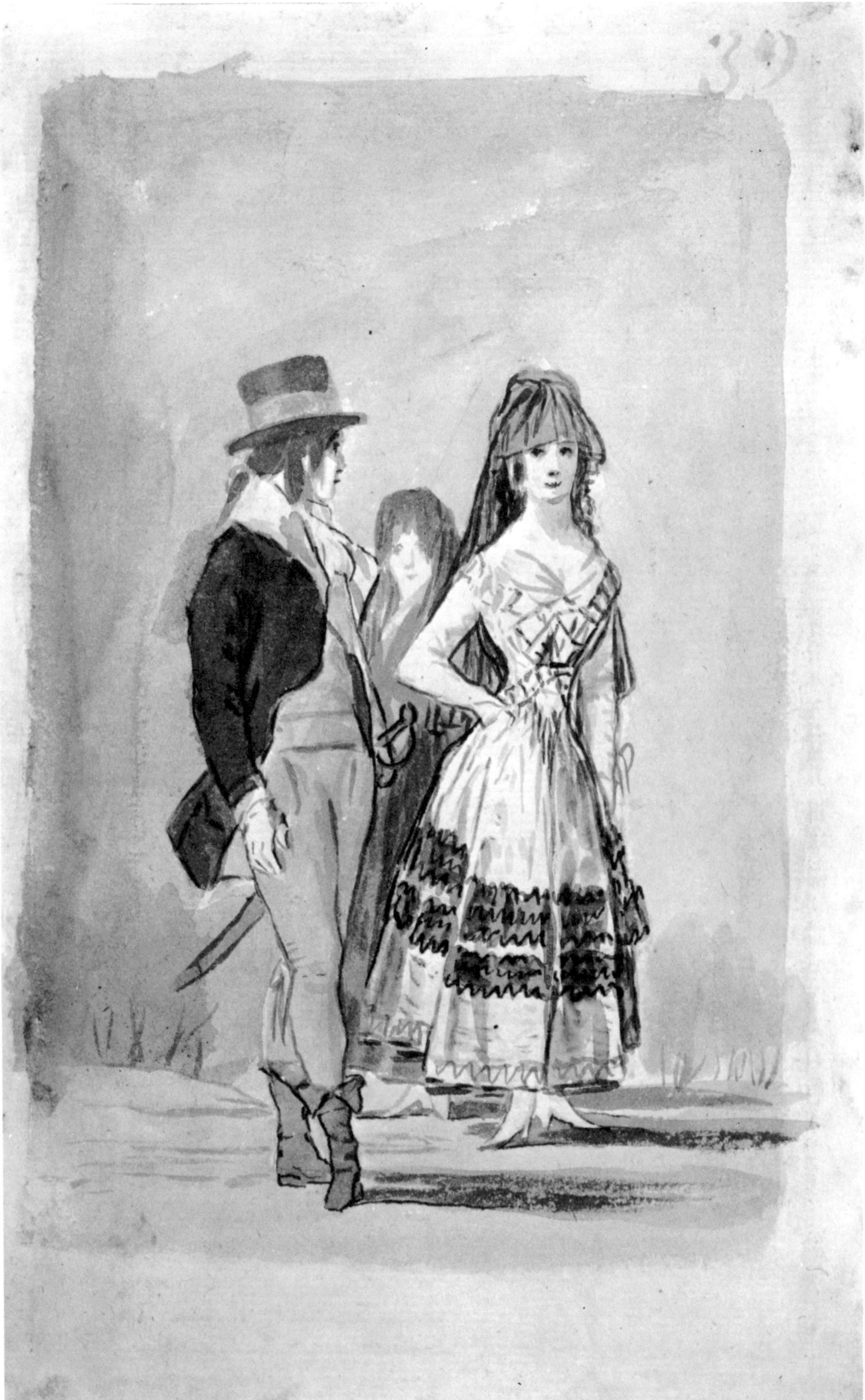

29 Francisco de Goya y Lucientes *A Young Man with Two Majas*

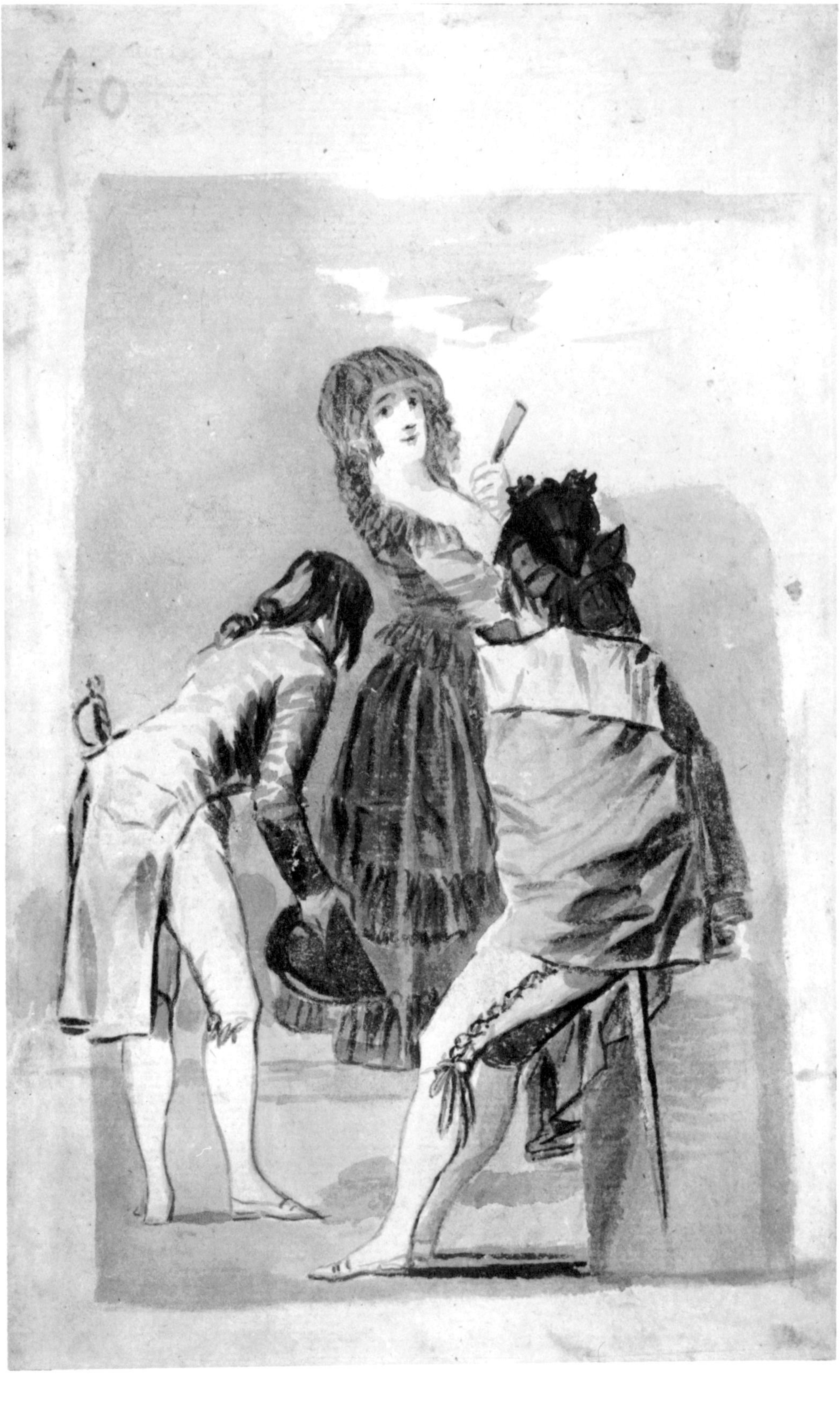

29 (verso) Francisco de Goya y Lucientes *Majo Watching a Gallant Bowing to a Maja*

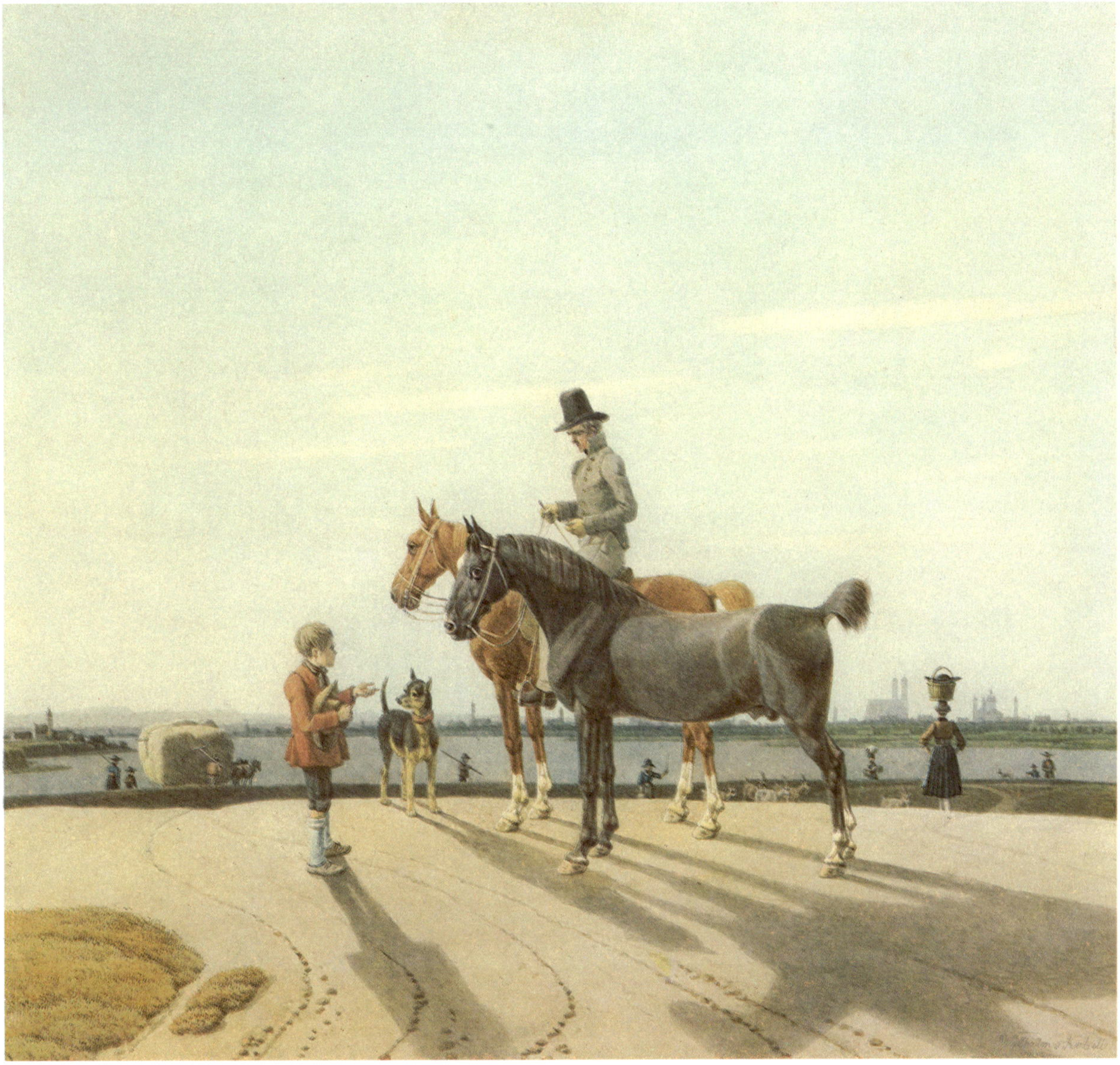

30 Wilhelm von Kobell *Man on Horseback*

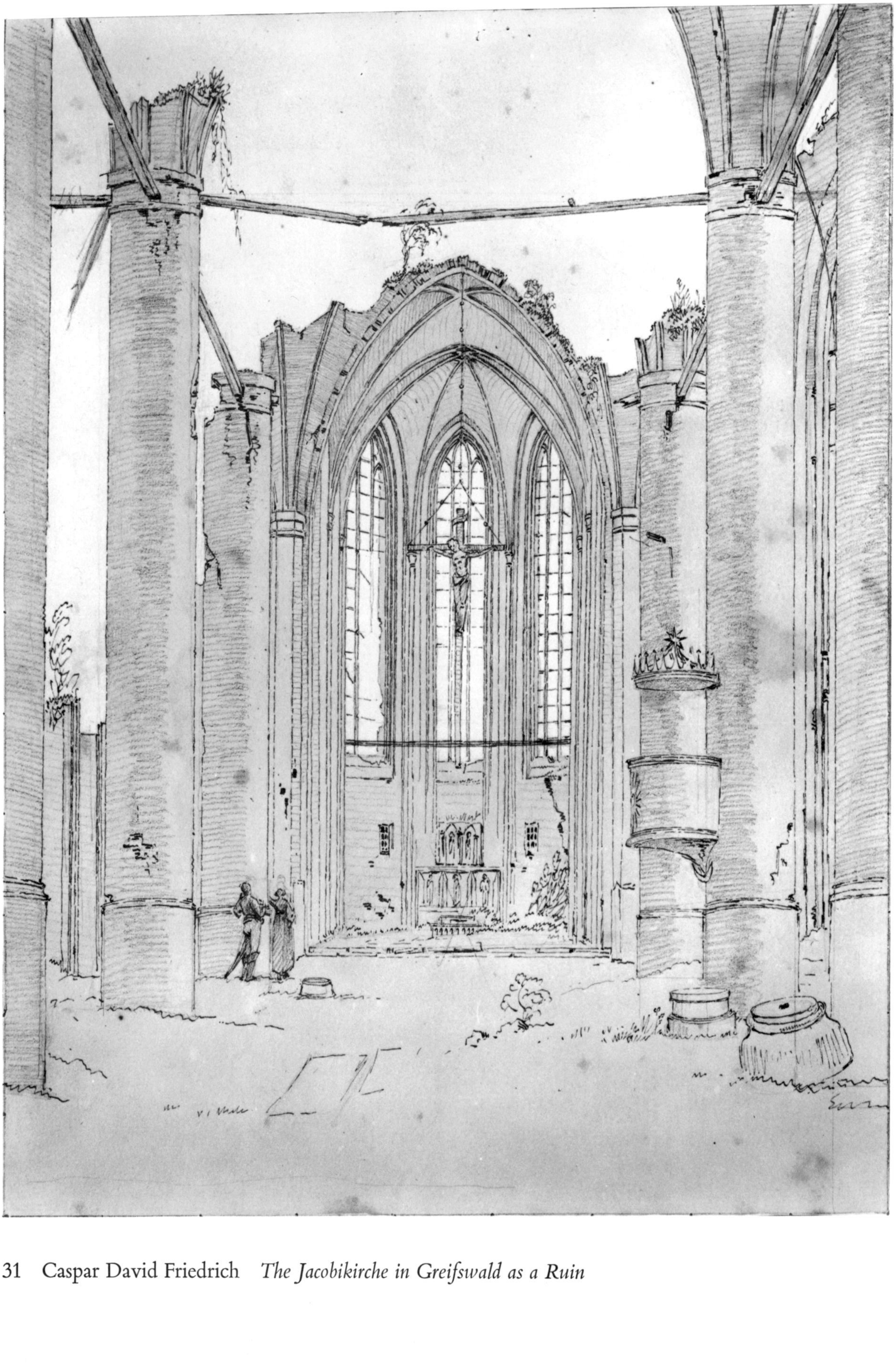

31 Caspar David Friedrich *The Jacobikirche in Greifswald as a Ruin*

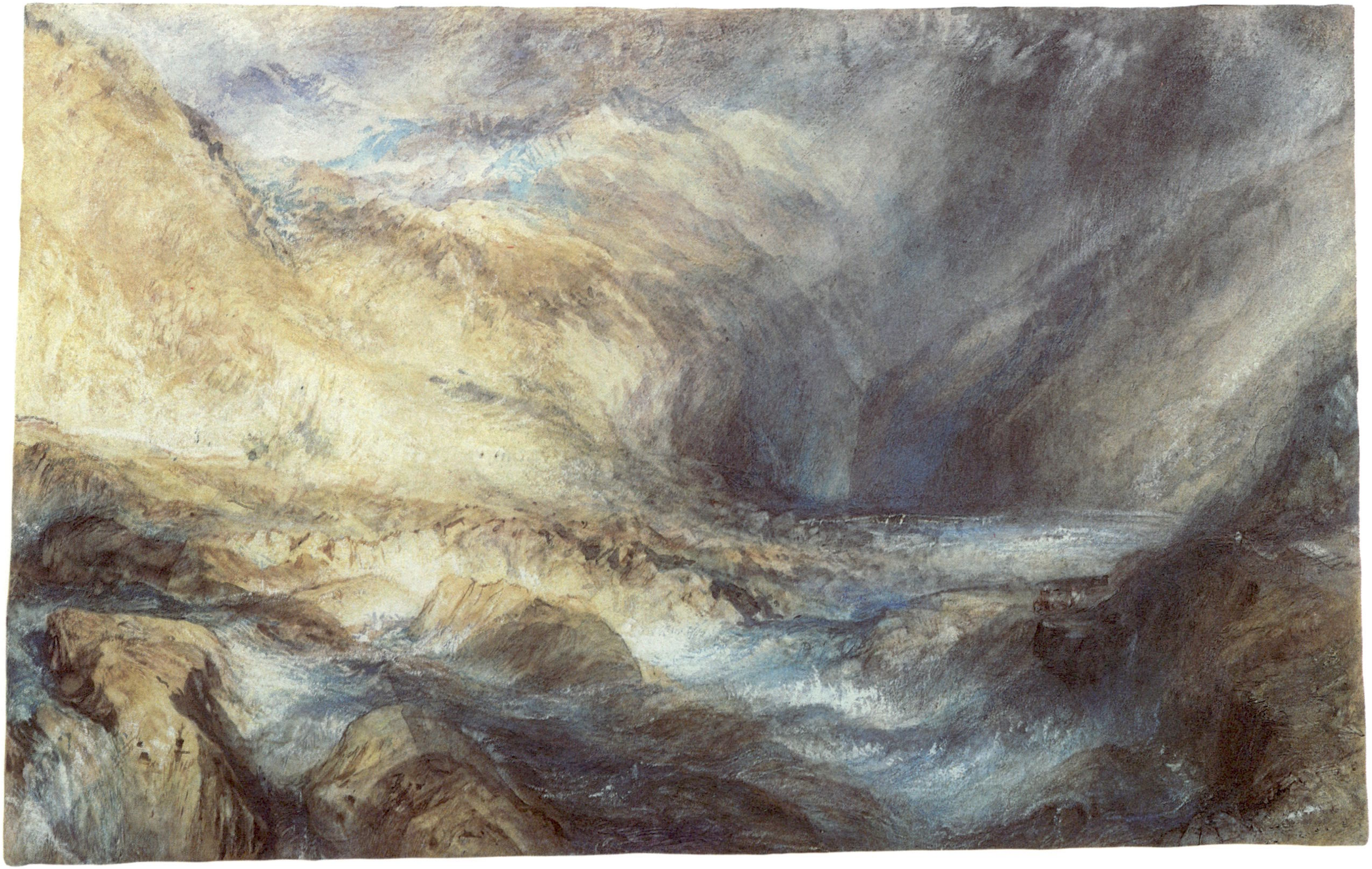

32 Joseph Mallord William Turner *The Pass at Faido, St. Gotthard*

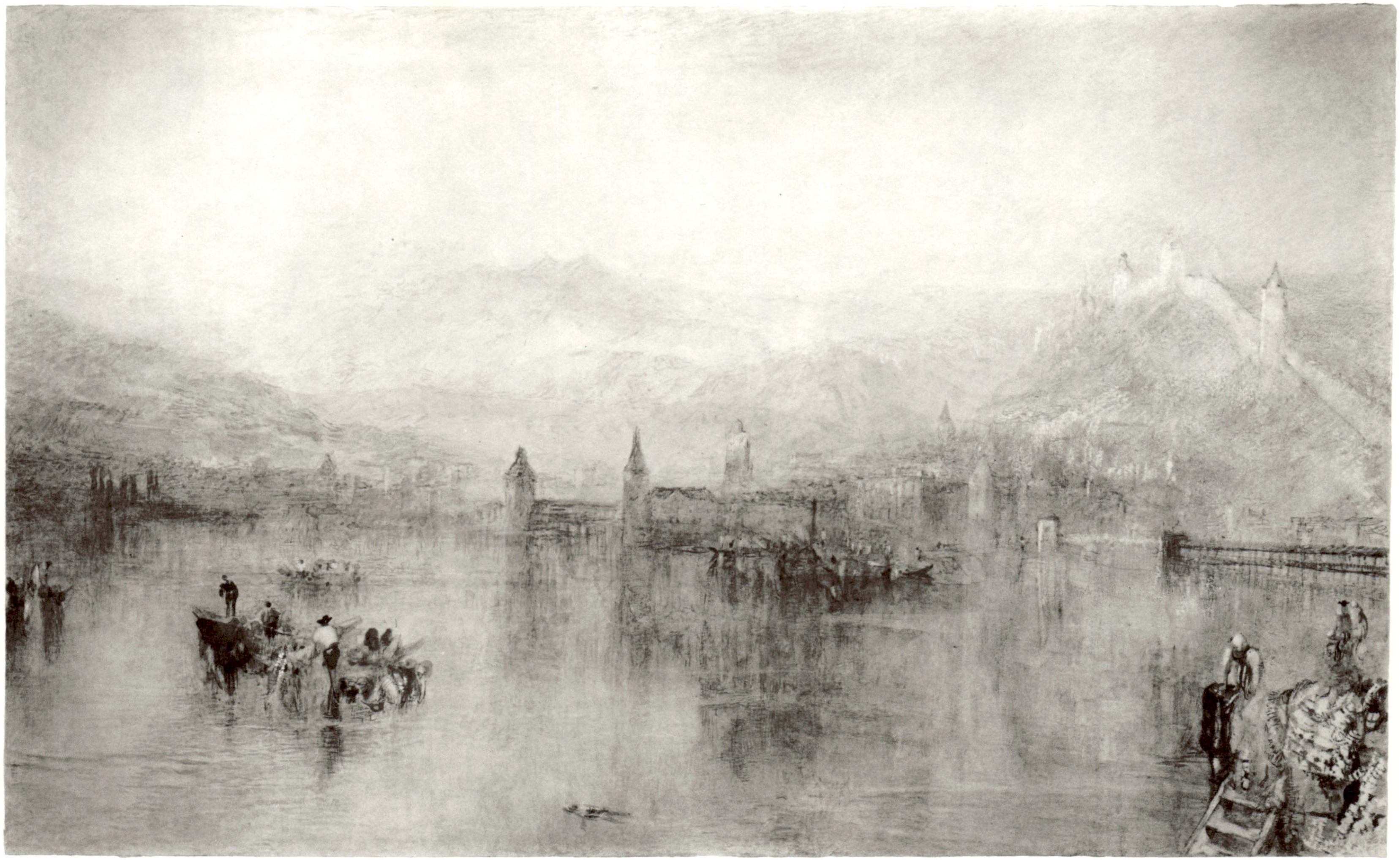

33 Joseph Mallord William Turner *Lucerne from the Lake*

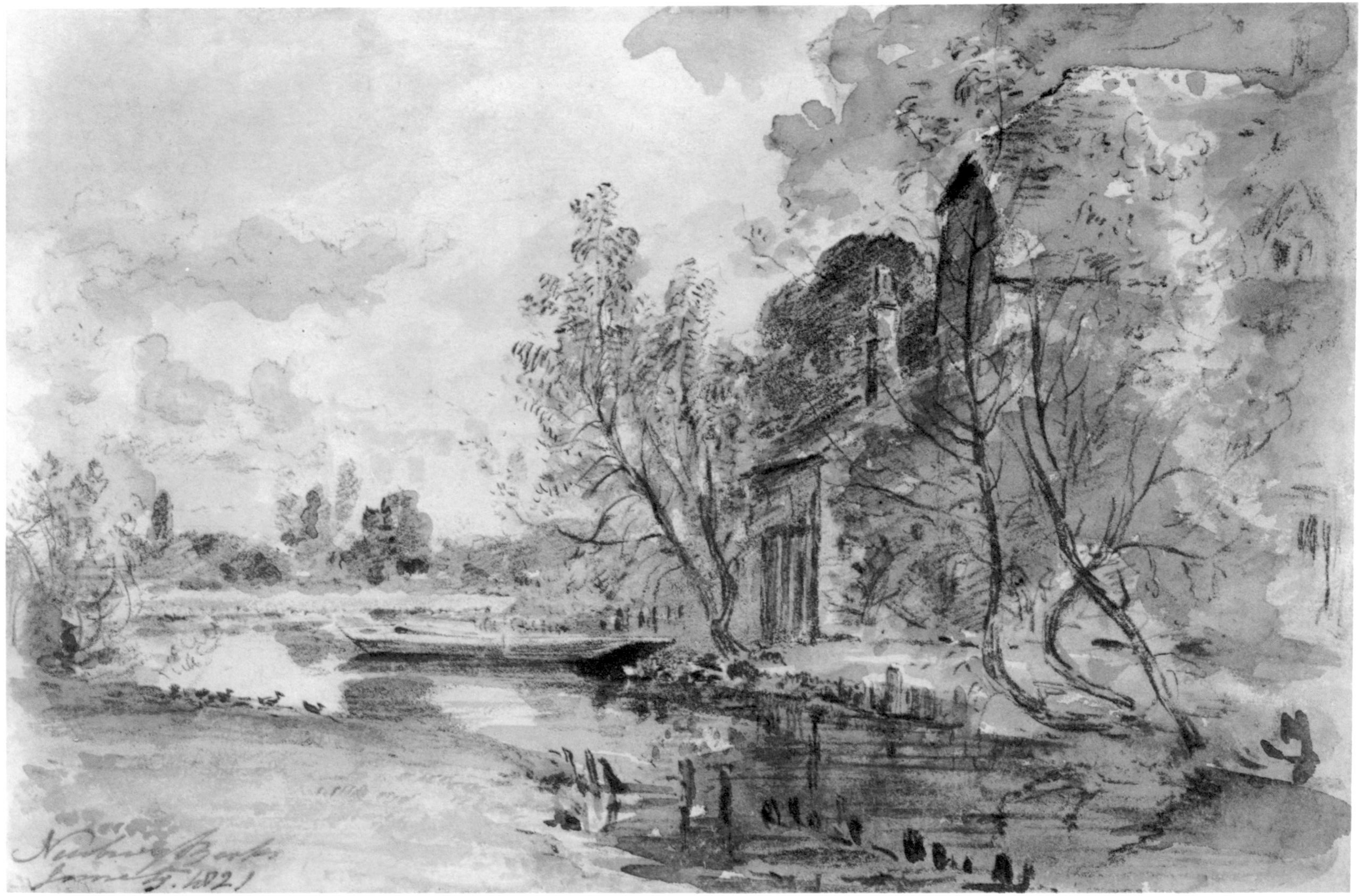

34 John Constable *A View of the Canal, Newbury*

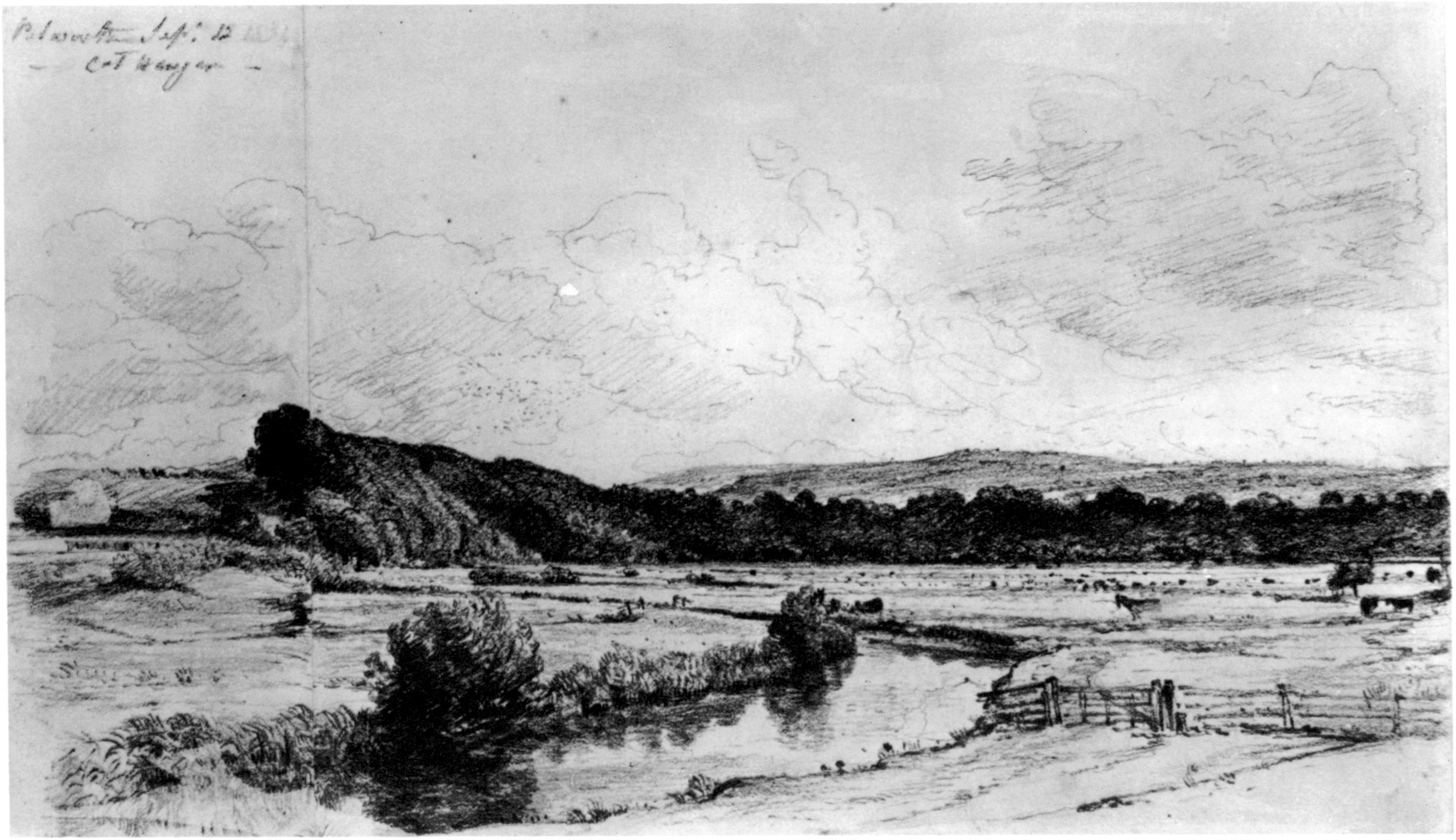

35 John Constable *View of Cathanger near Petworth*

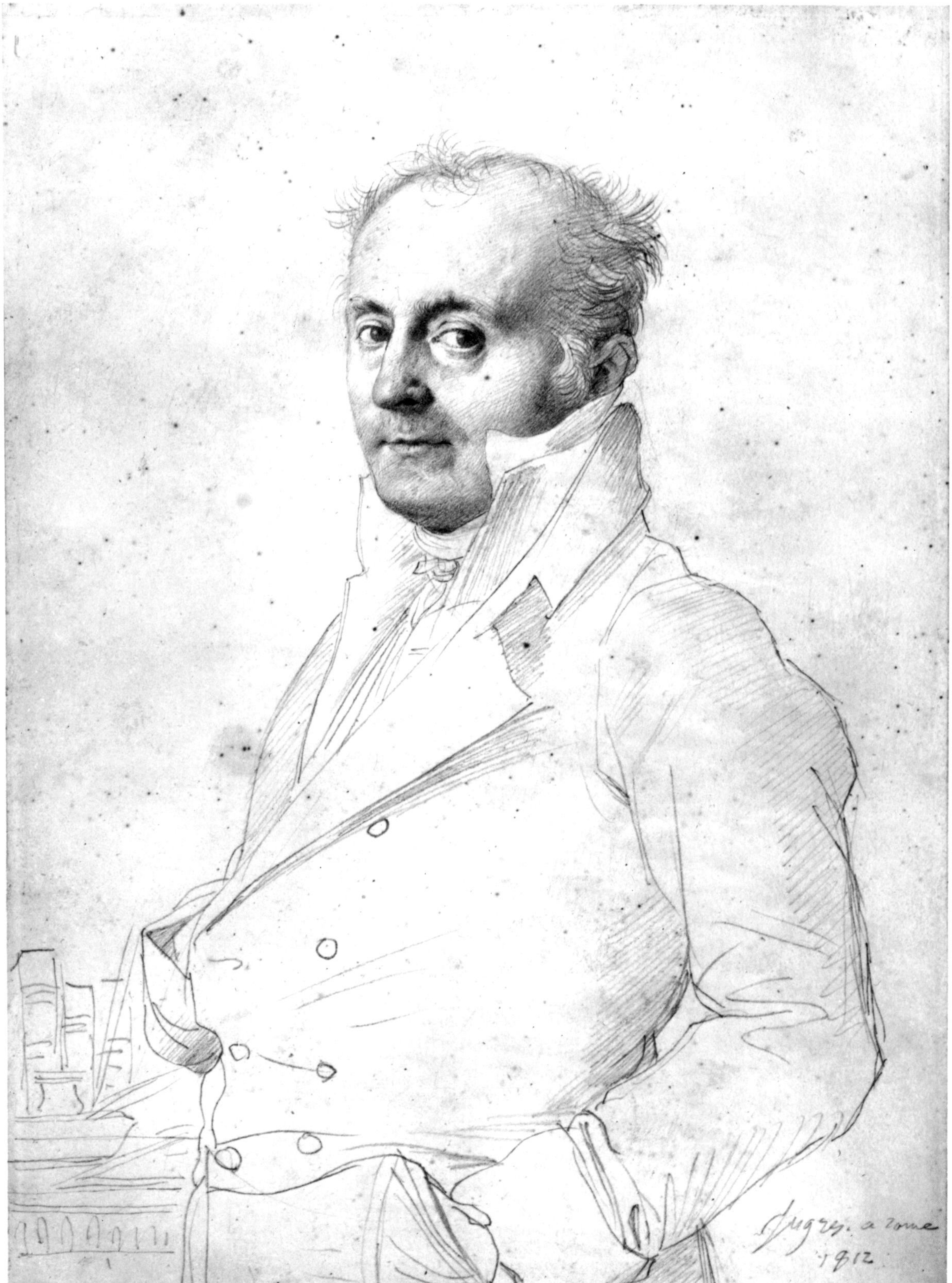

36 Jean-Auguste-Dominique Ingres *Portrait of Hippolyte-François Devillers*

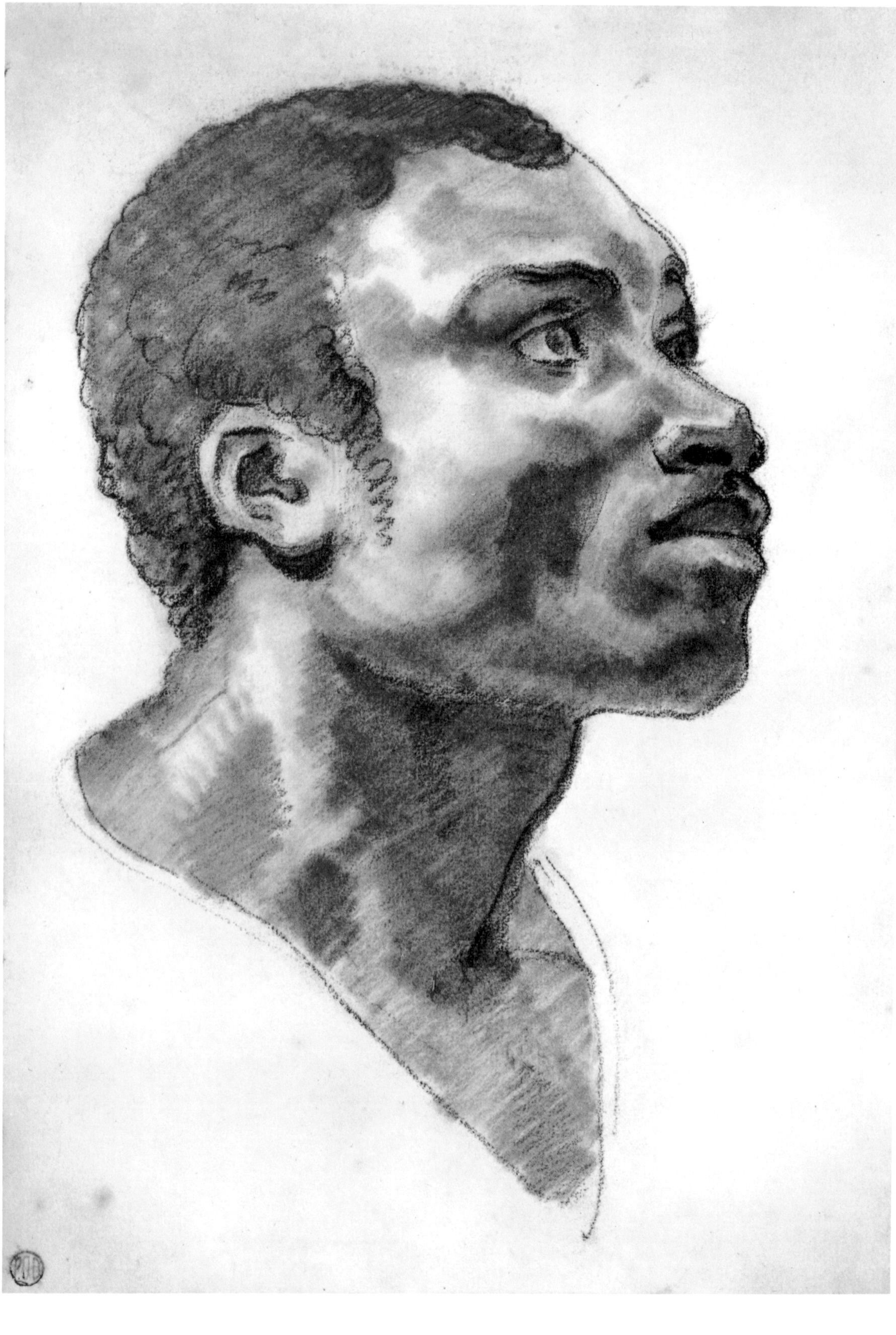

37 Théodore Gericault *Head of a Negro*

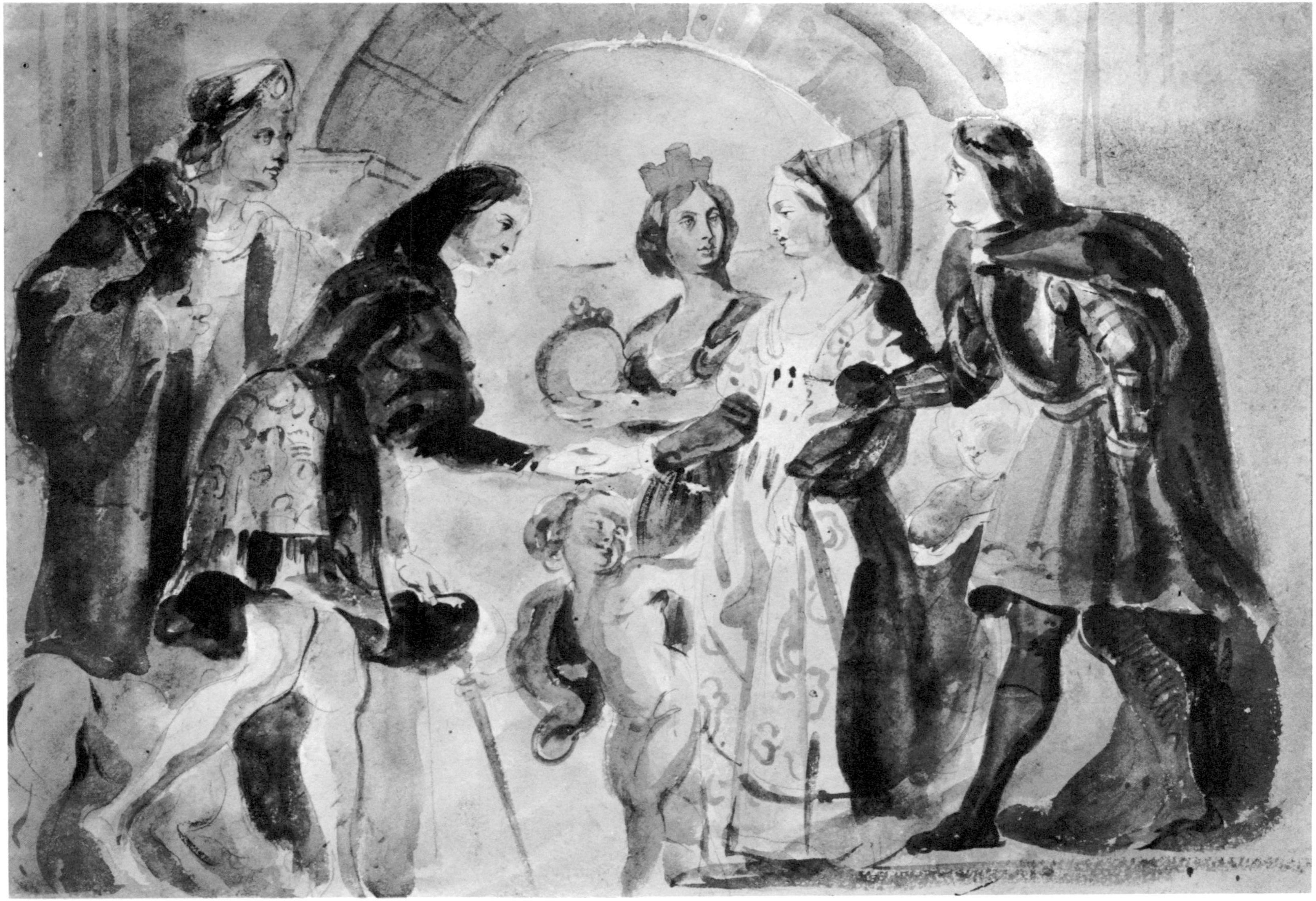

38 Eugène Delacroix *Compositional Study*

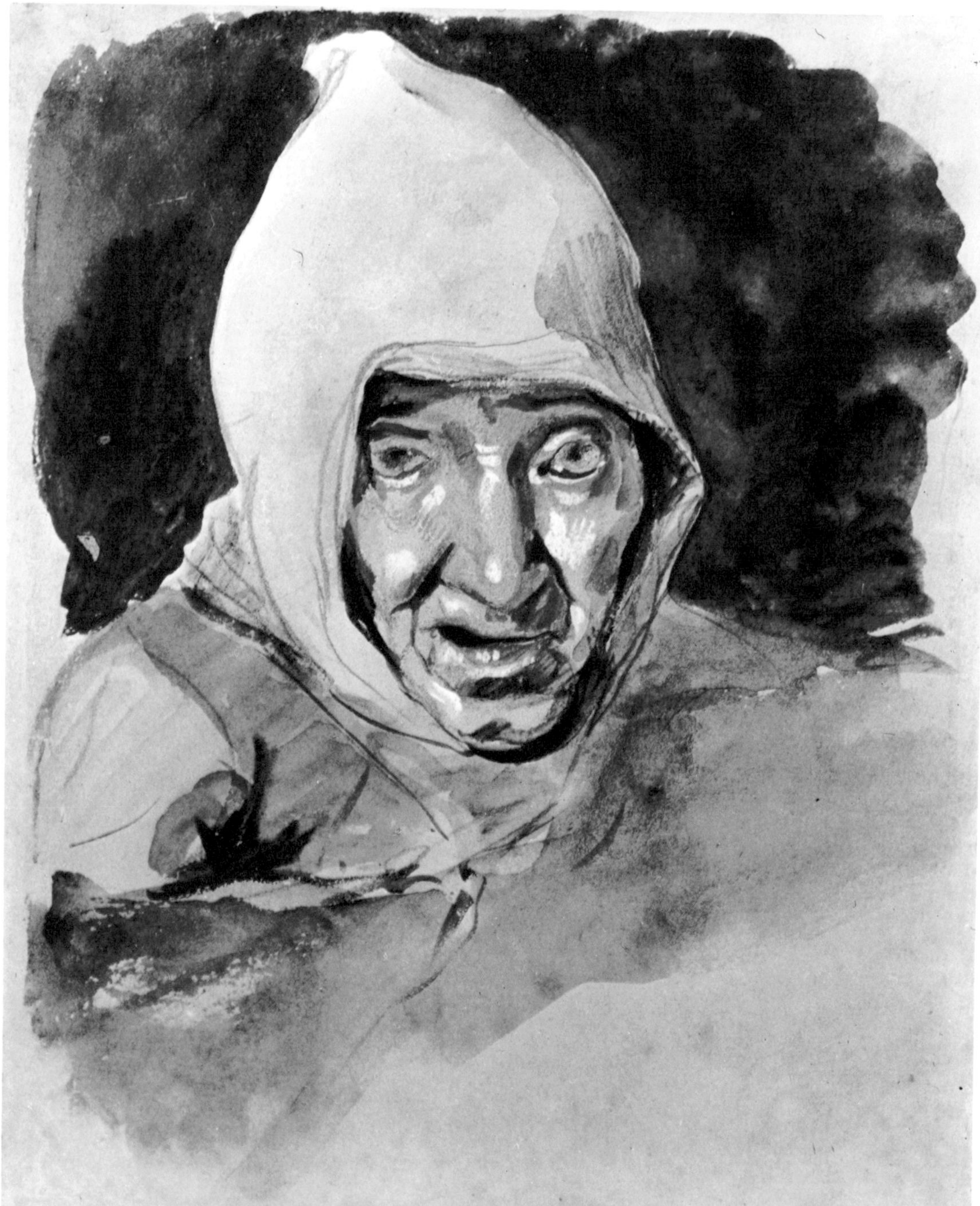

39 Eugène Delacroix *Head of a Woman*

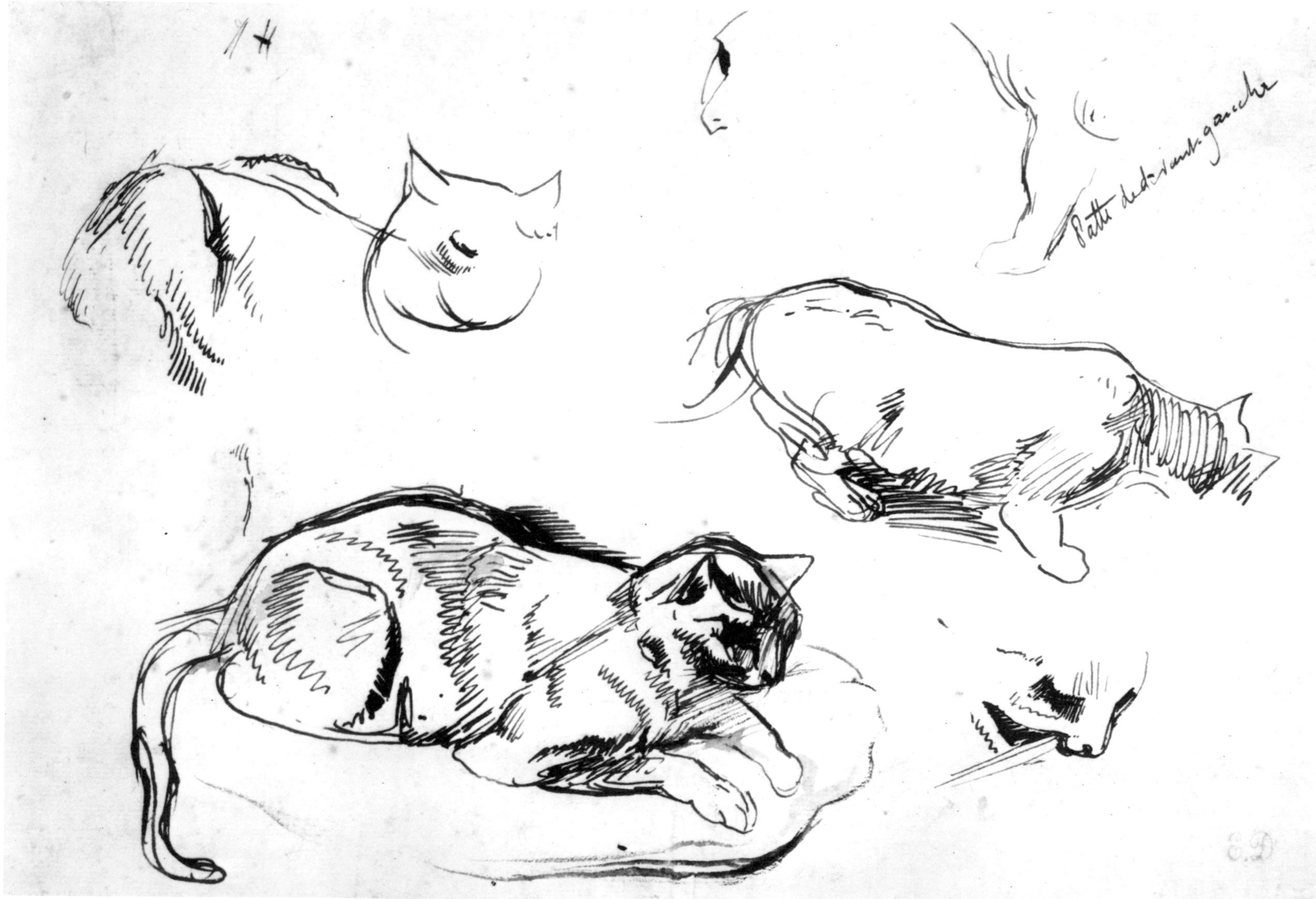

40 Eugène Delacroix *Studies of a Cat*

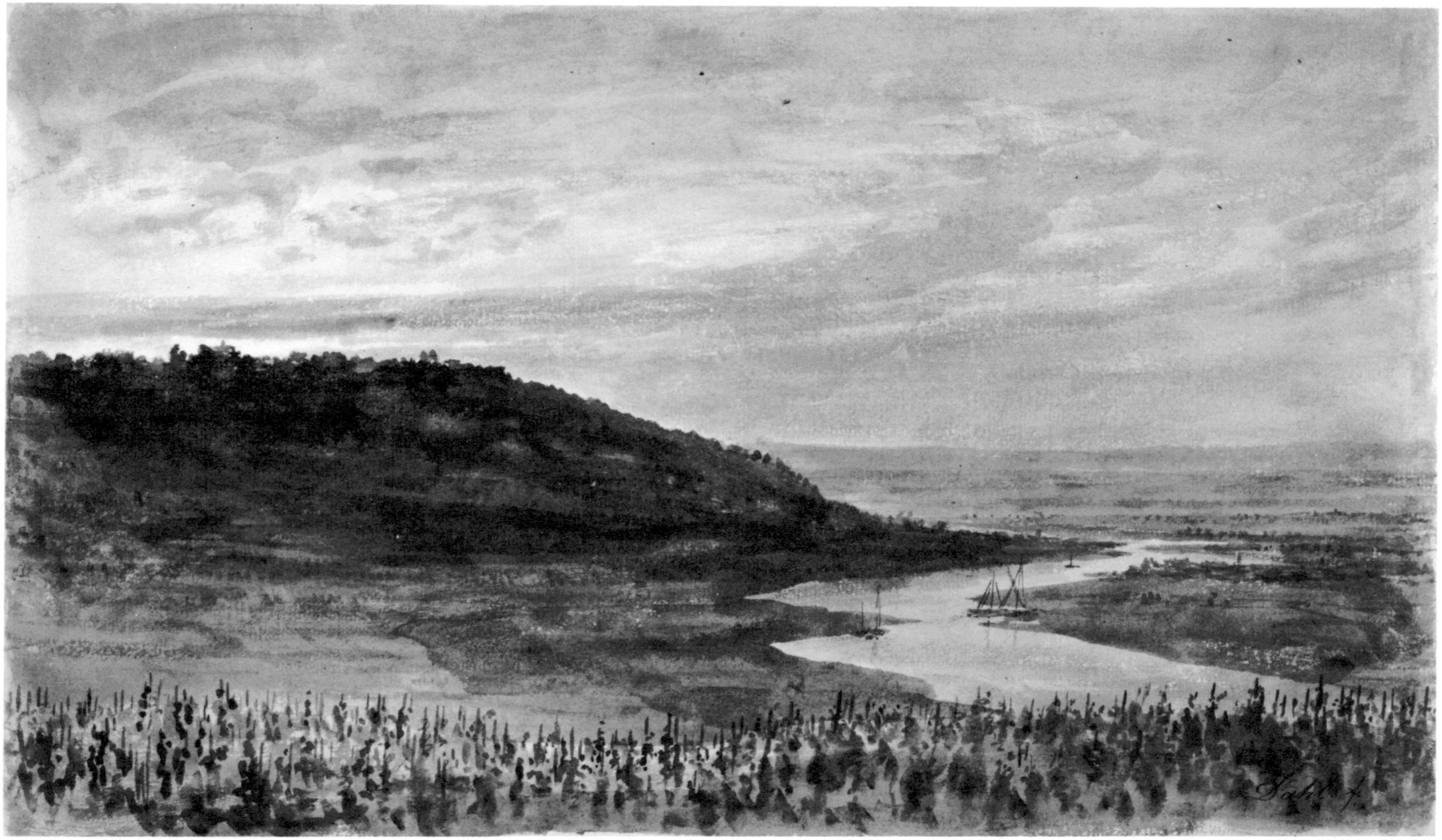

41 Johan Christian Claussen Dahl *A View of the Elbe Valley*

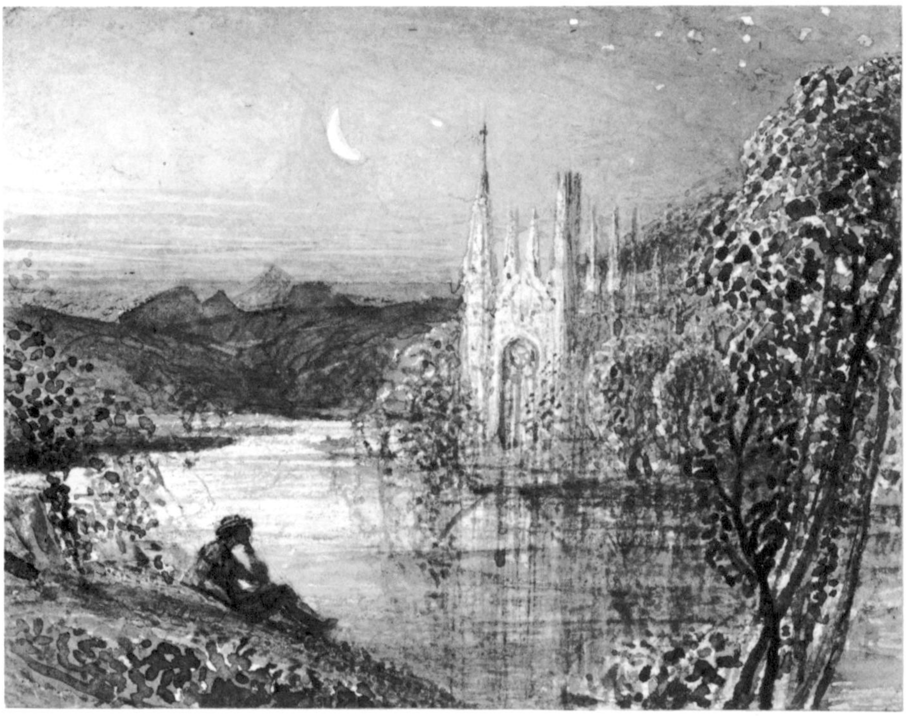

42 Samuel Palmer *The Haunted Stream*

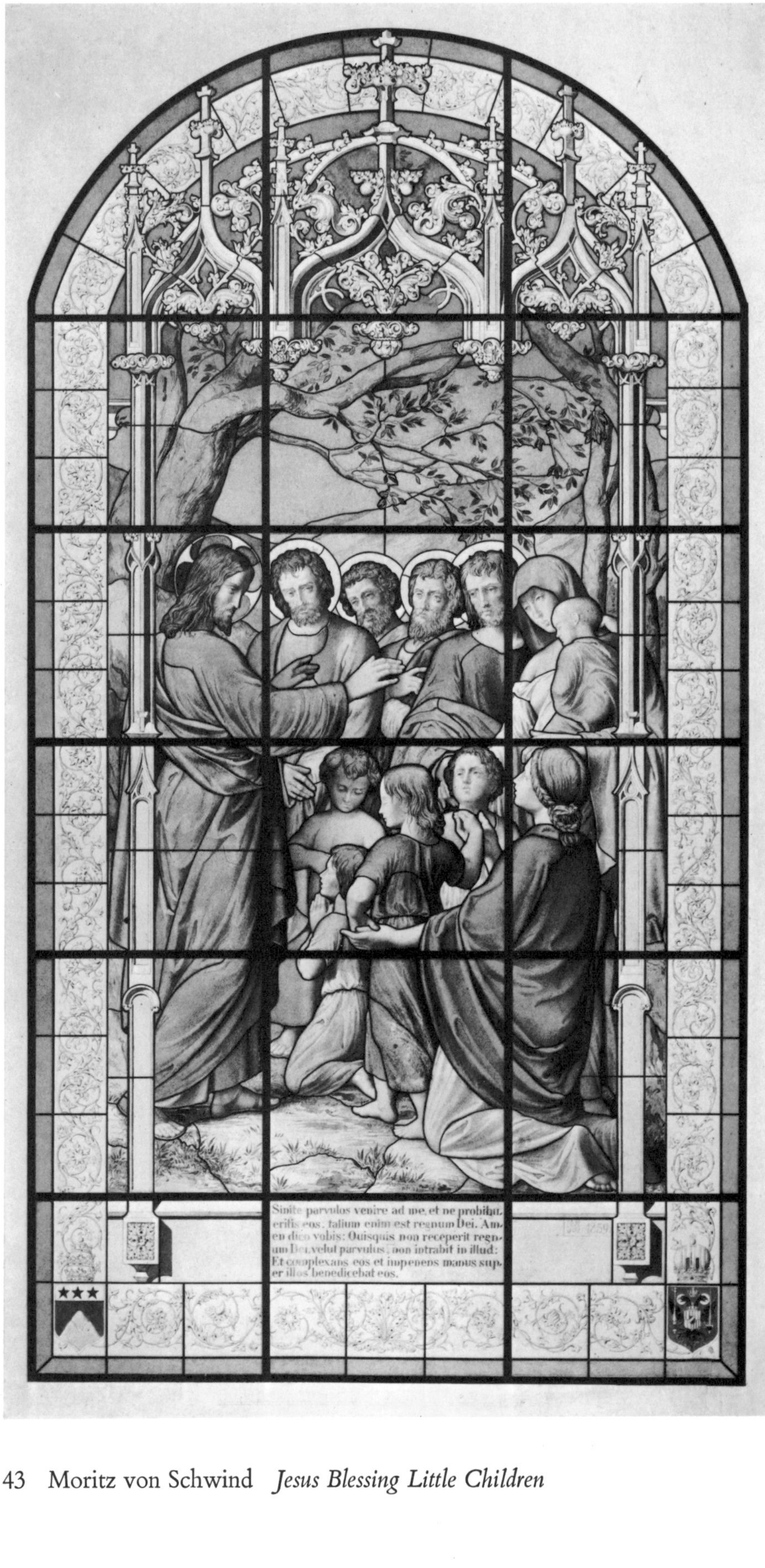

43 Moritz von Schwind *Jesus Blessing Little Children*

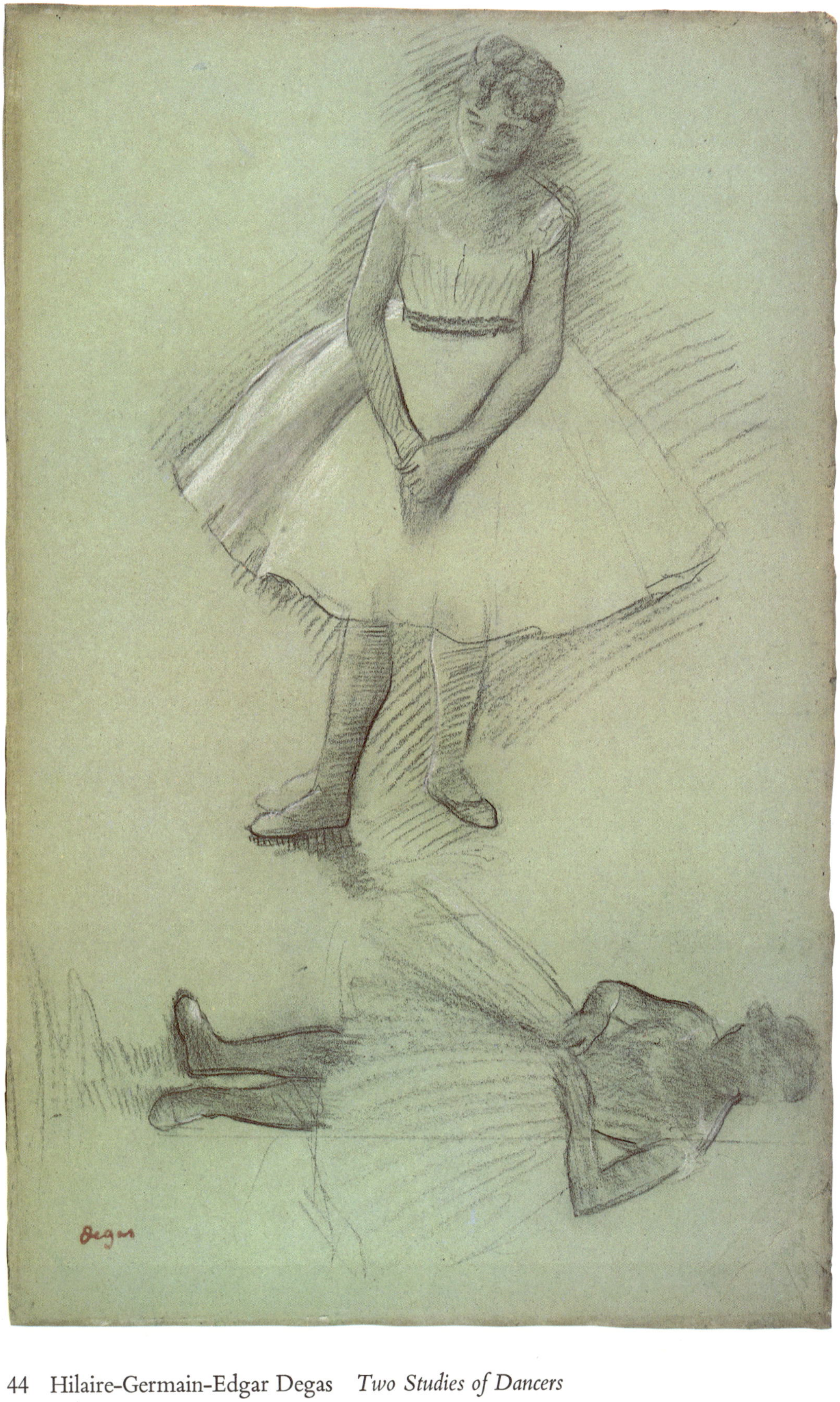

44 Hilaire-Germain-Edgar Degas *Two Studies of Dancers*

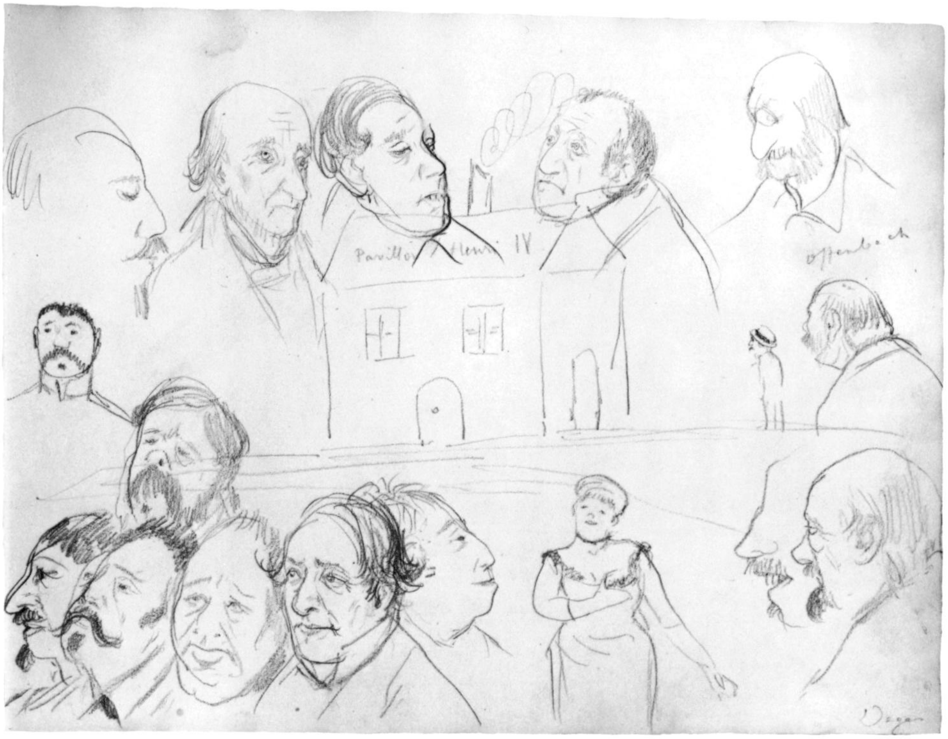

45 Degas Sketchbook, fol. 2 *The Pavillon Henri IV*

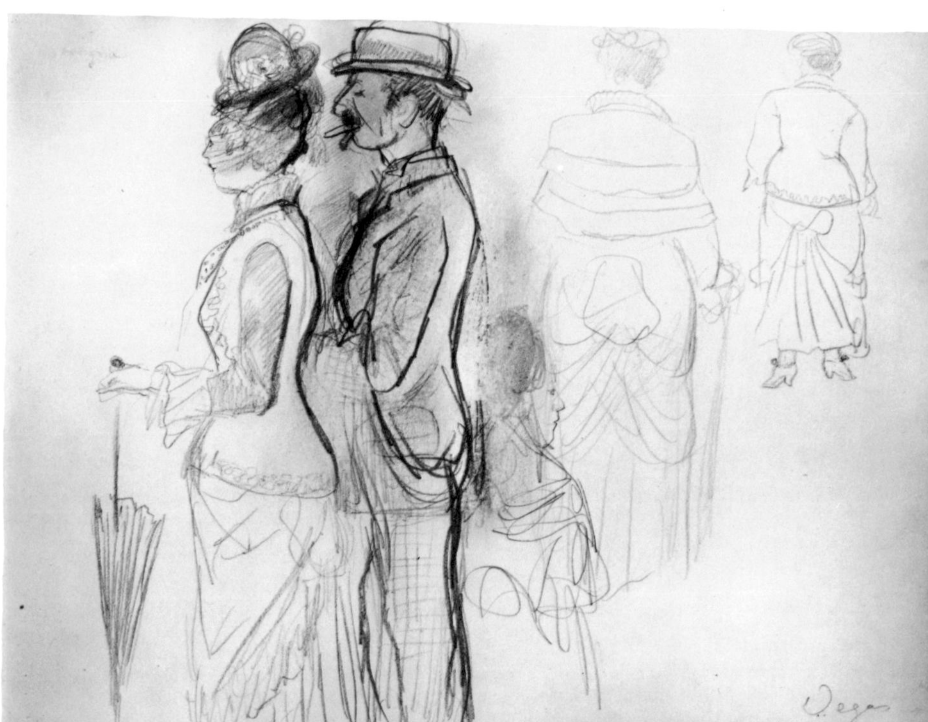

45 Degas Sketchbook, fol. 4 *A Prostitute*

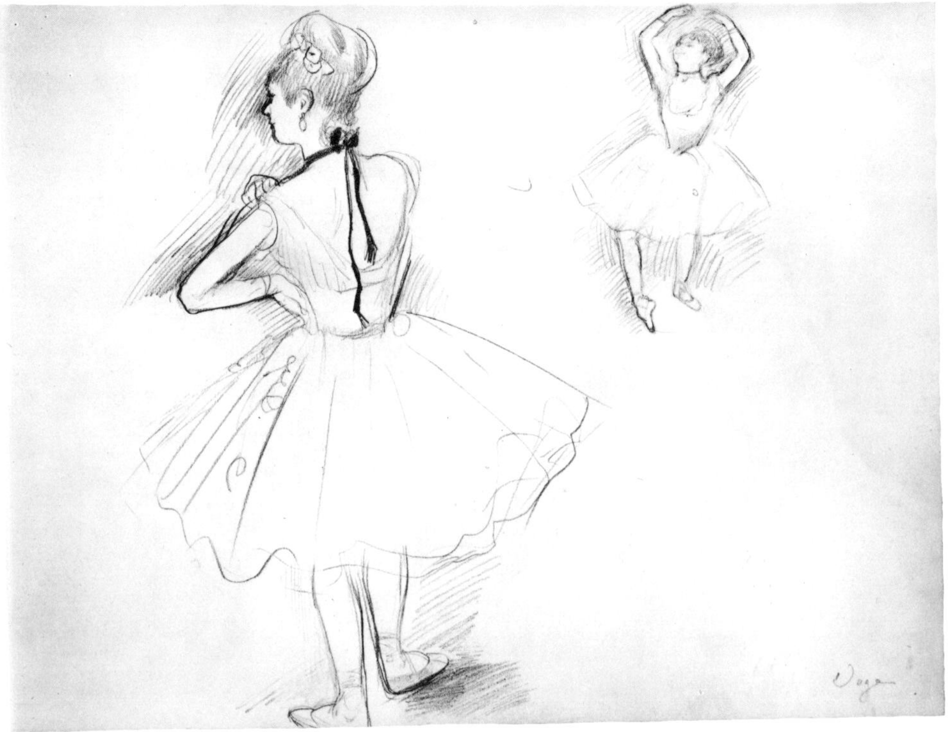

45 Degas Sketchbook, fol. 13 *Two Studies of Dancers*

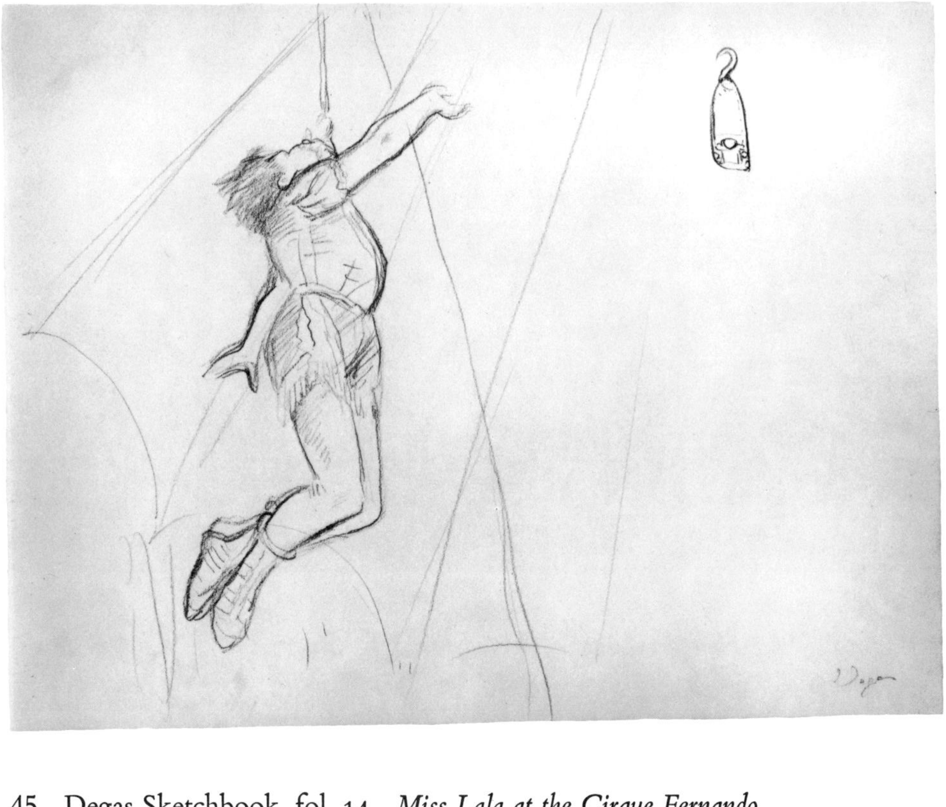

45 Degas Sketchbook, fol. 14 *Miss Lala at the Cirque Fernando*

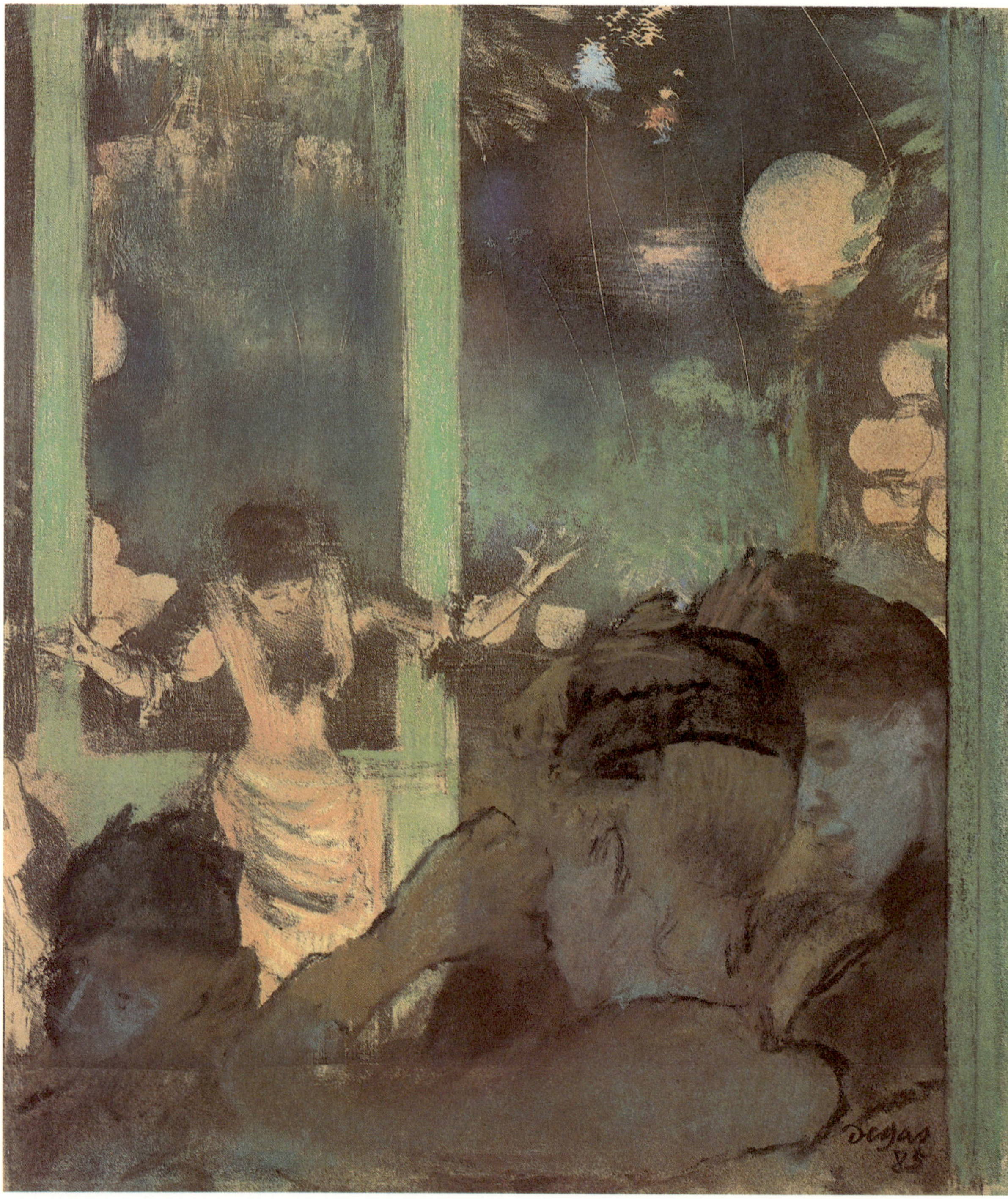

46 Hilaire-Germain-Edgar Degas *Aux Ambassadeurs: Mlle Bécat*

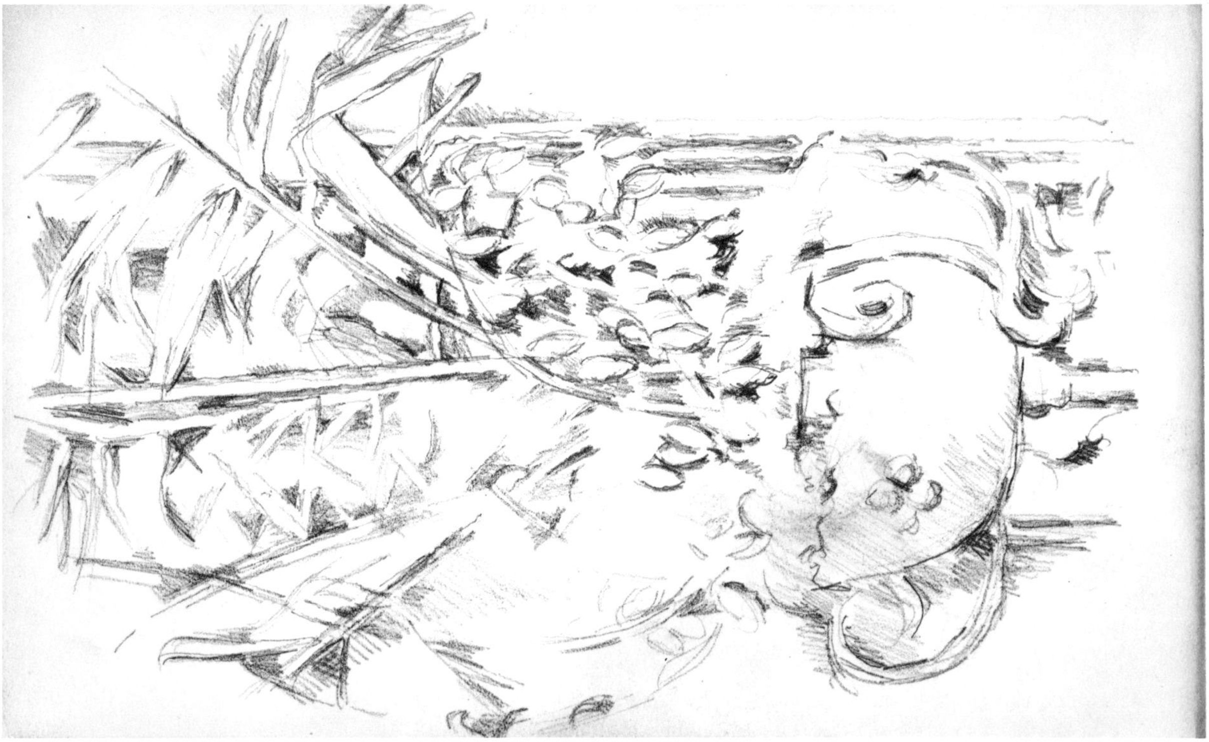

47 Cézanne Sketchbook, fol. 11, (verso) *Flower Stand with Plants*

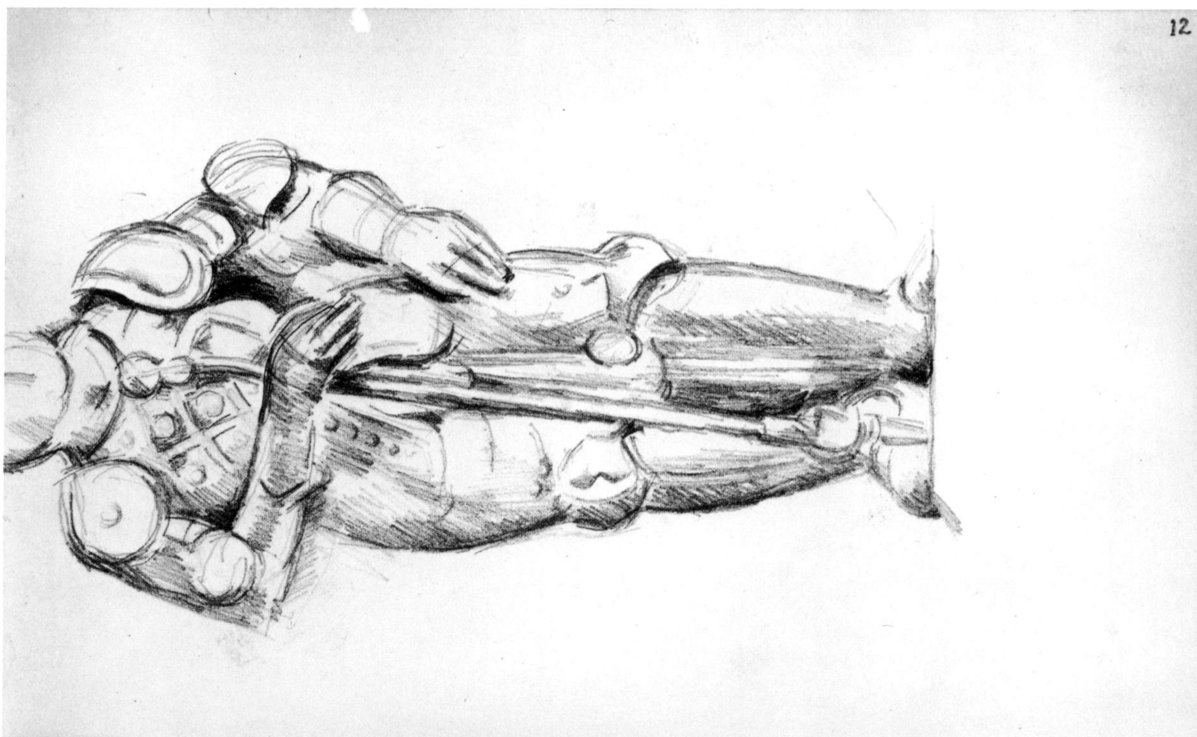

47 Cézanne Sketchbook, fol. 12 *Suit of Armor*

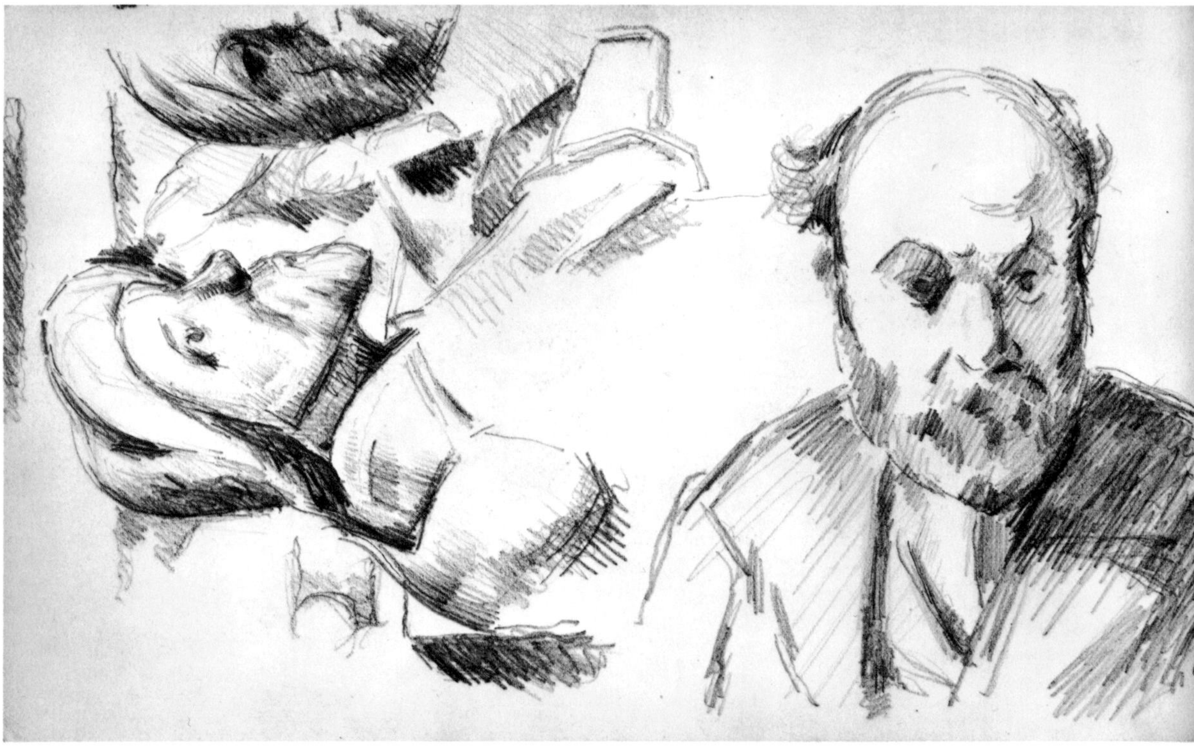

47 Cézanne Sketchbook, fol. 13, (verso) *Self-Portrait (right); Two Busts*

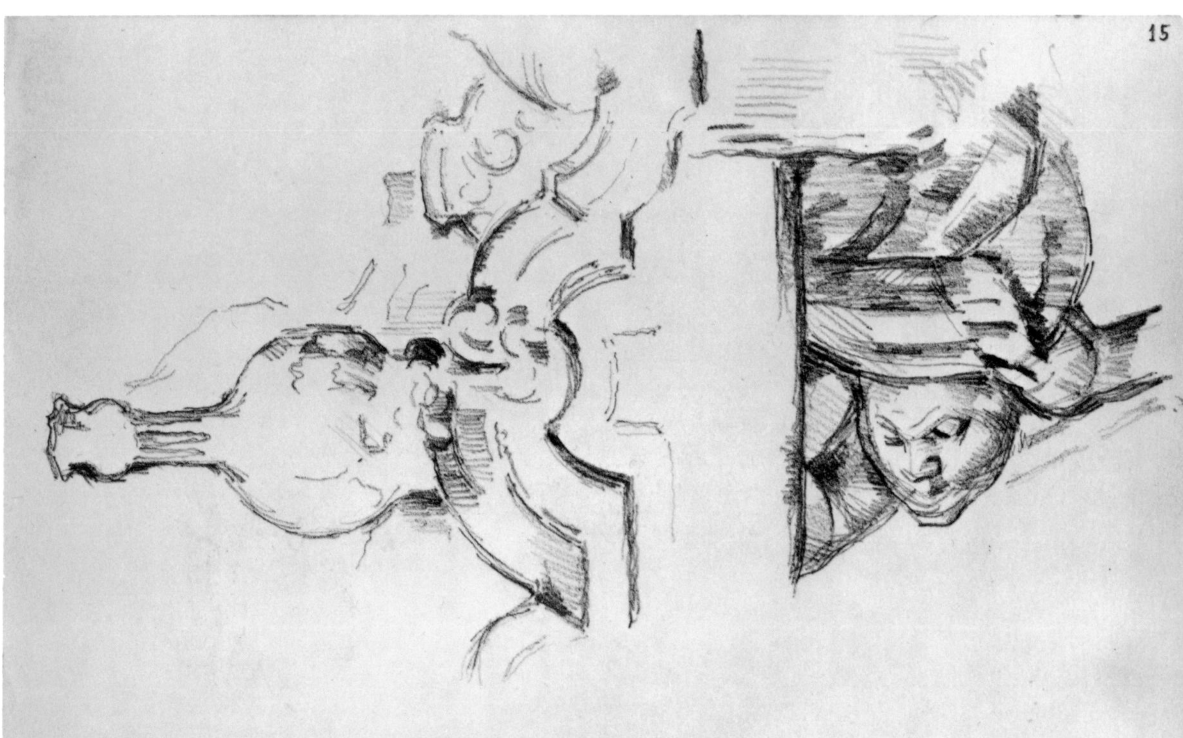

47 Cézanne Sketchbook, fol. 15 *Sculpted Furniture with Vase and a Head*

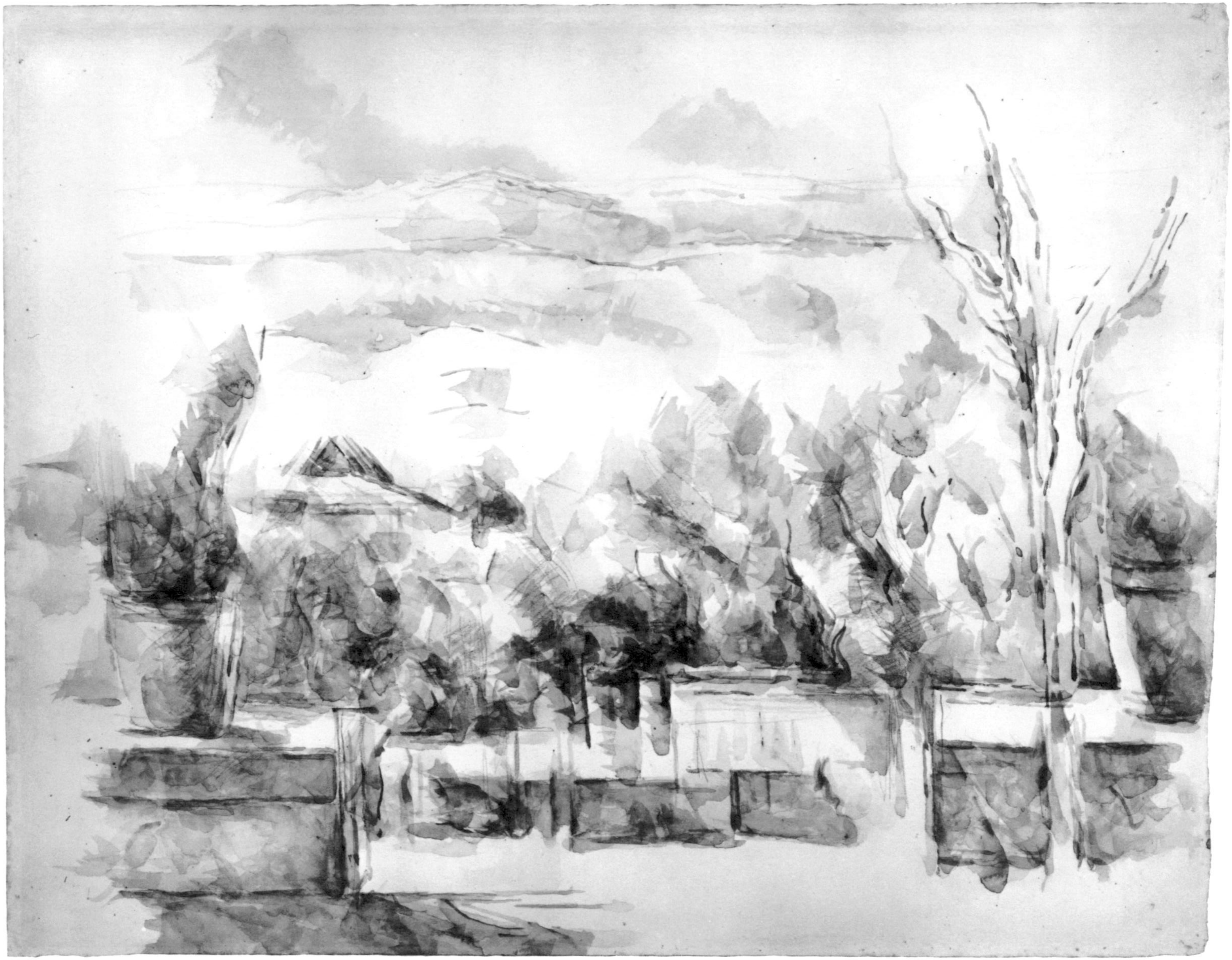

48 Paul Cézanne *The Terrace of the Garden at Les Lauves*

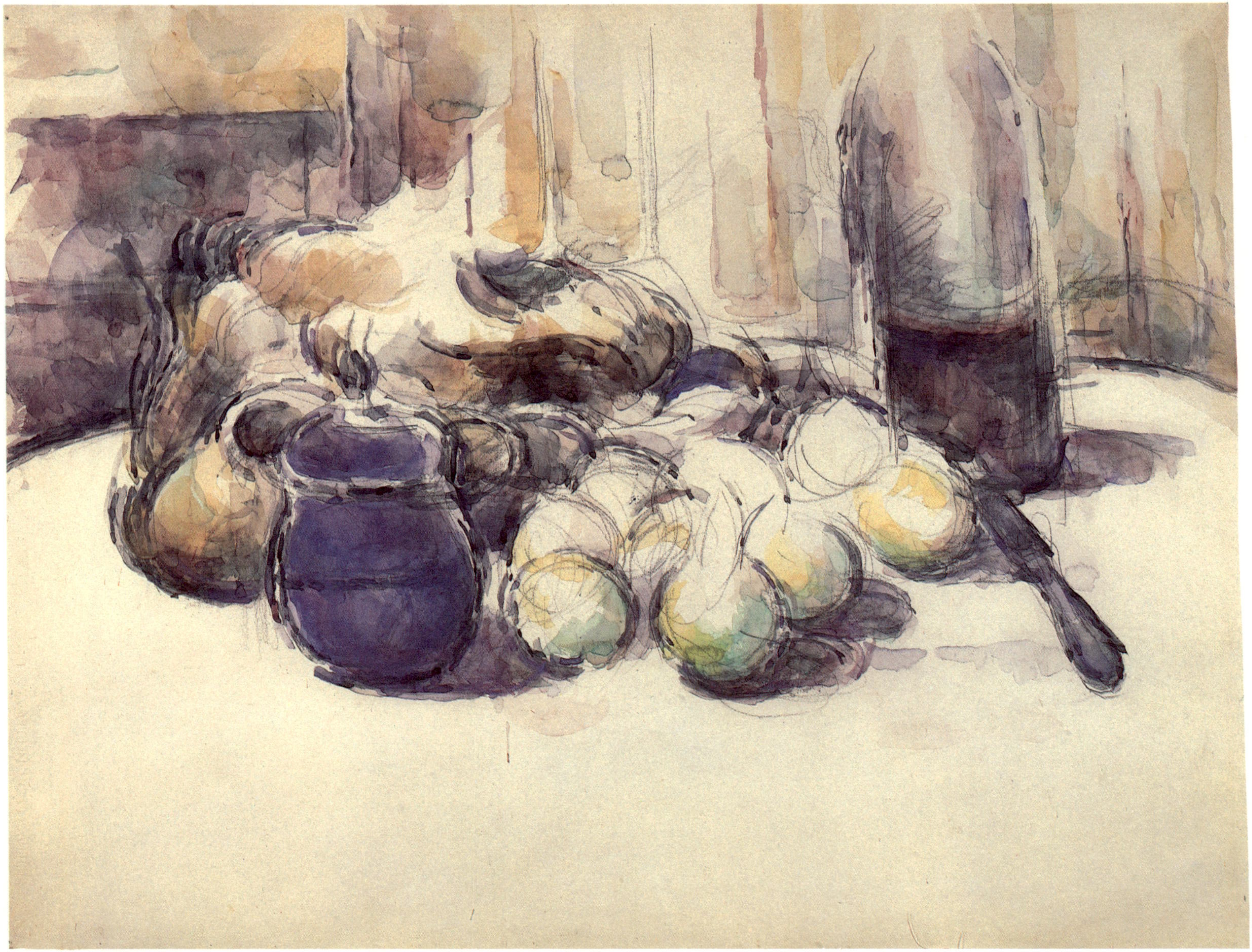

49 Paul Cézanne *Still Life*

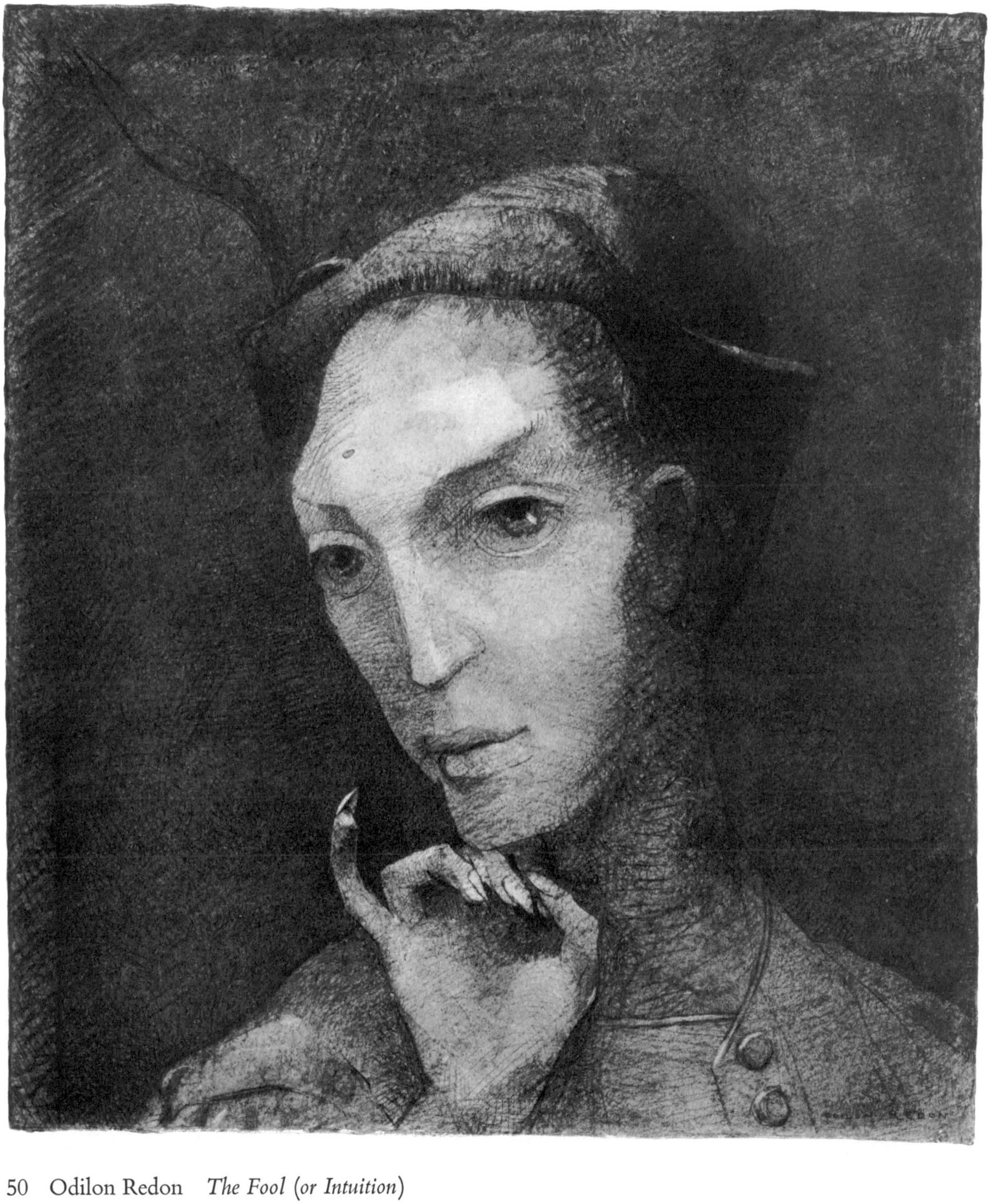

50 Odilon Redon *The Fool (or Intuition)*

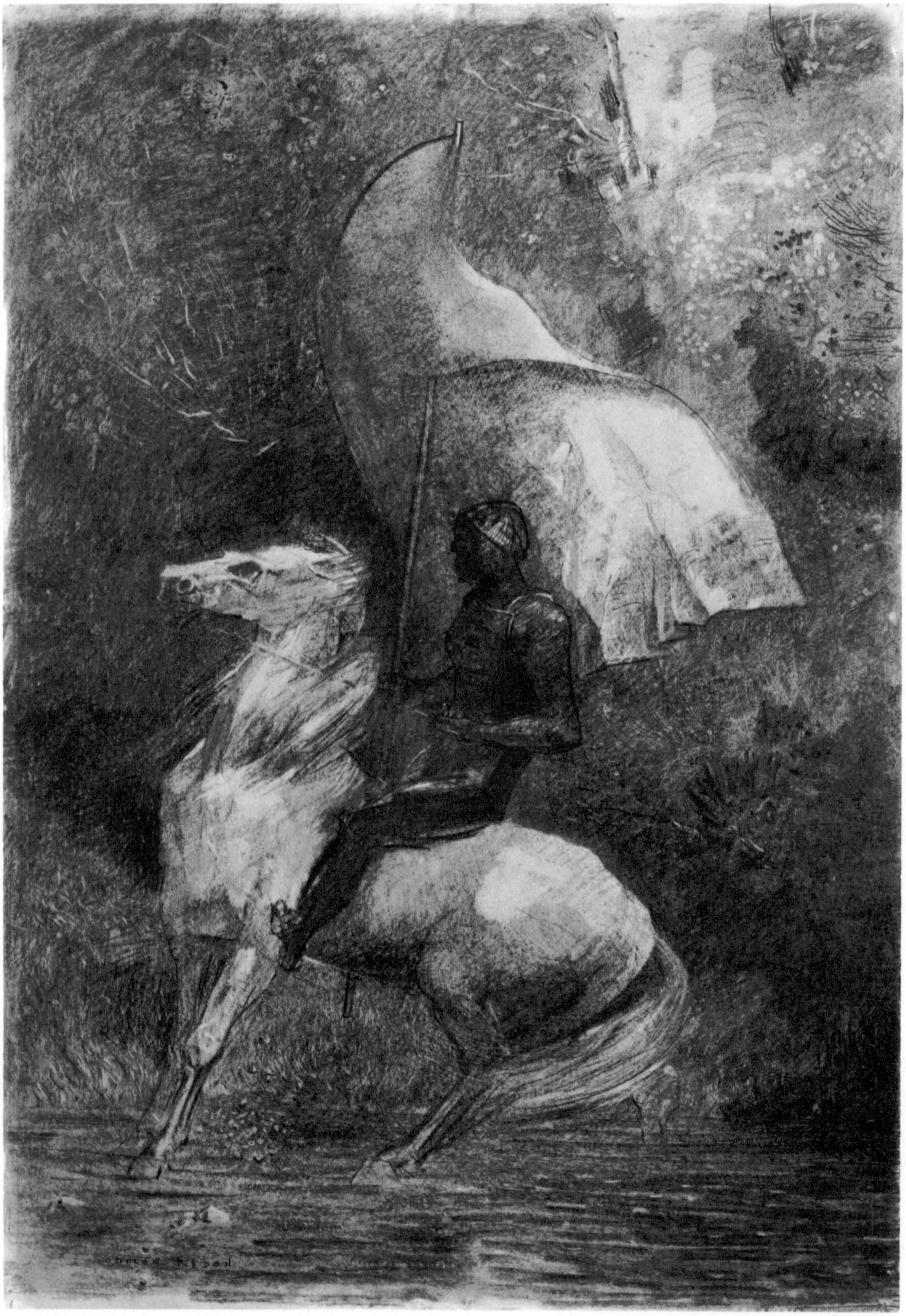

51 Odilon Redon *Cavalier*

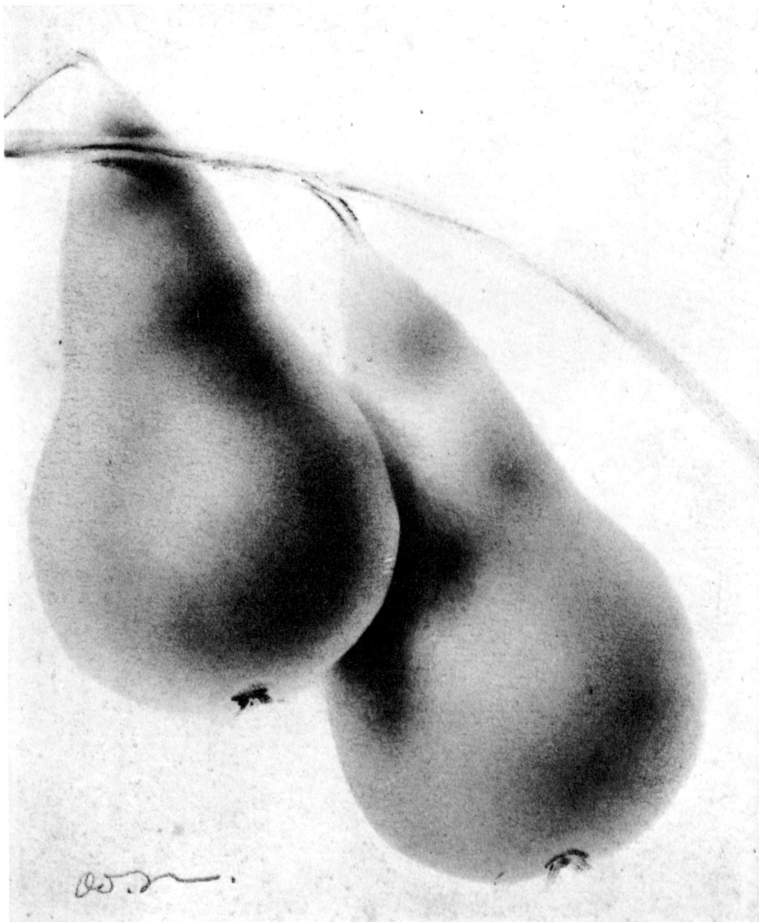

52 Odilon Redon *Two Pears*

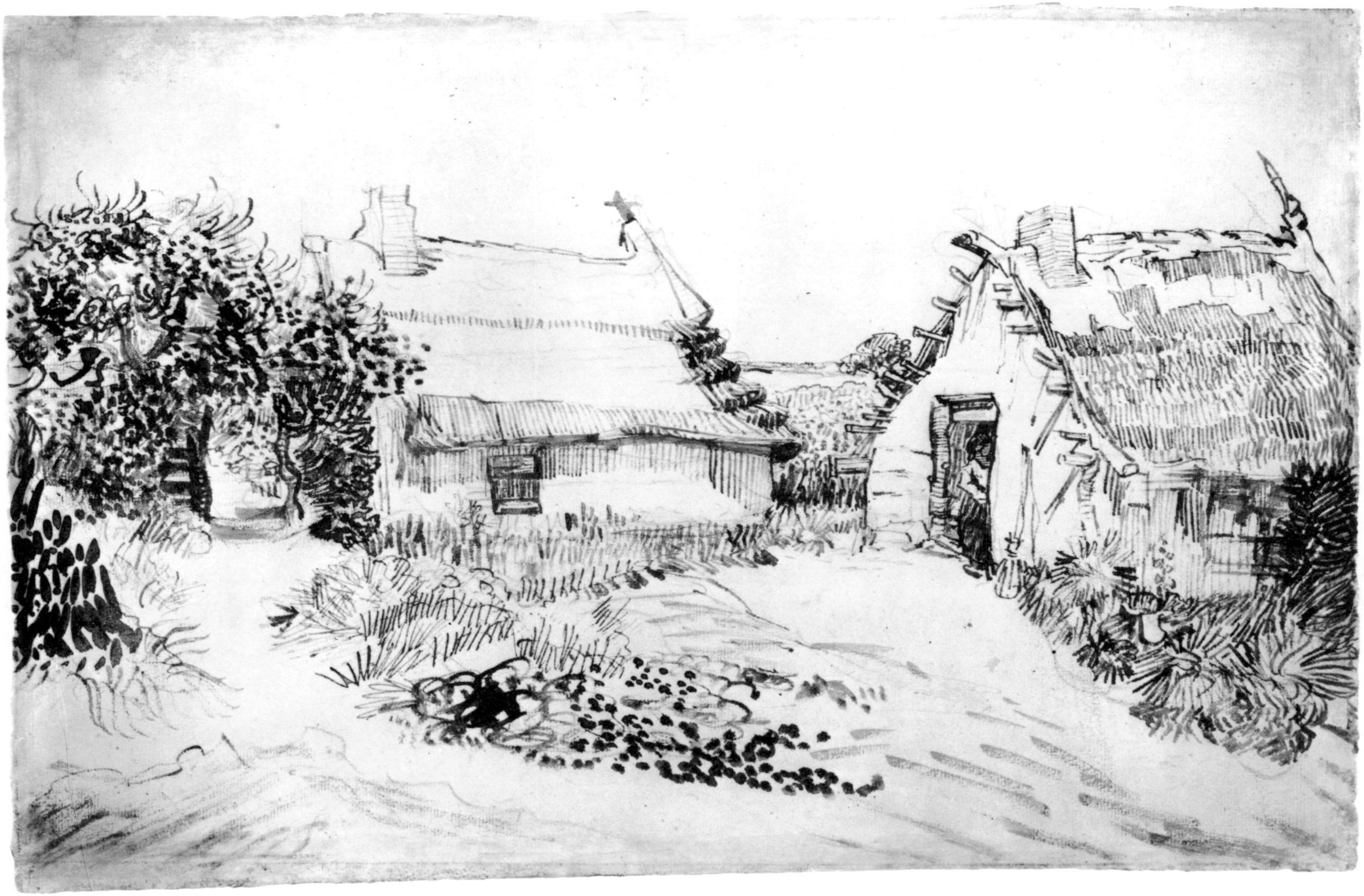

53 Vincent van Gogh *Two Cottages*

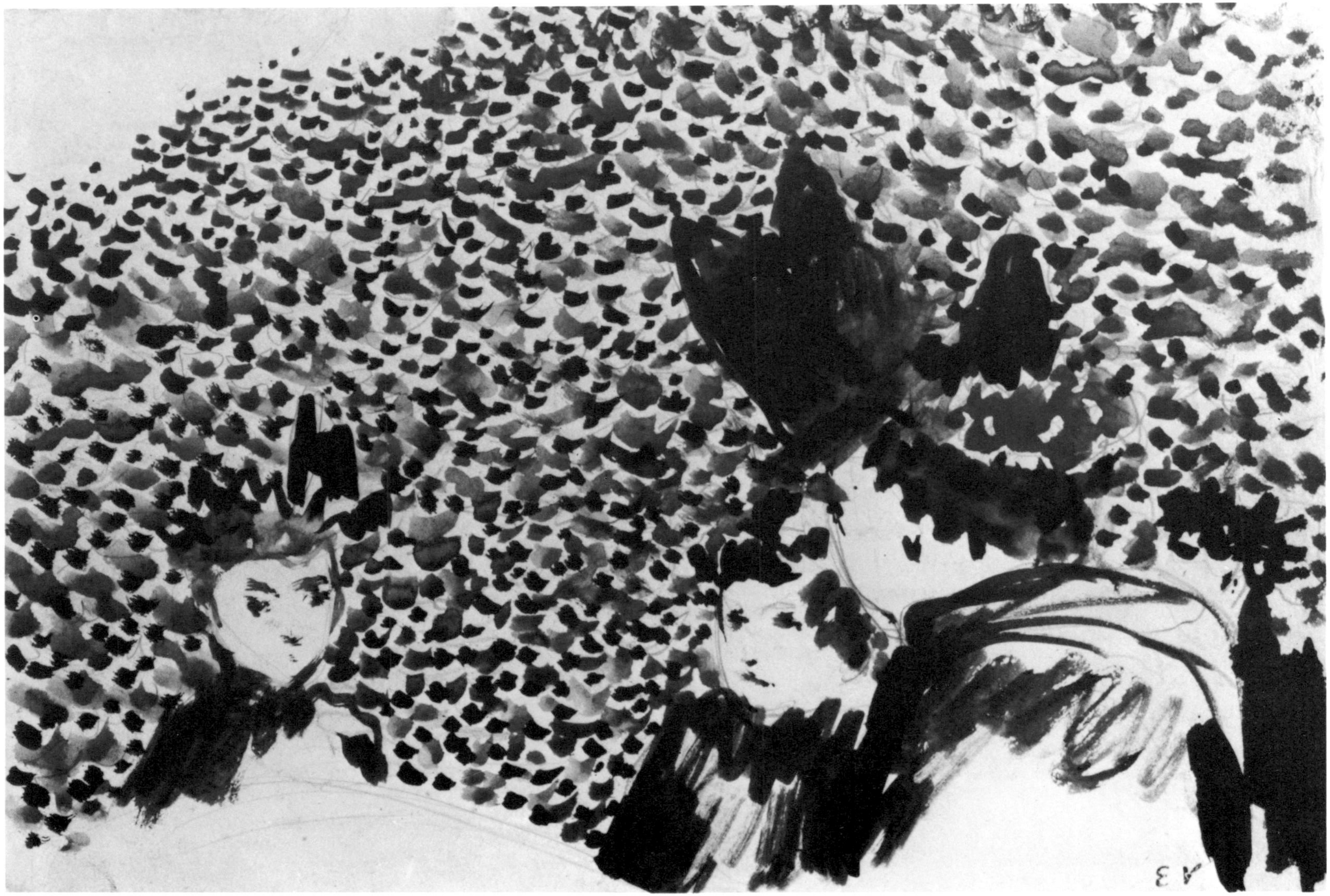

54 Edouard Vuillard *Les Chapeaux*

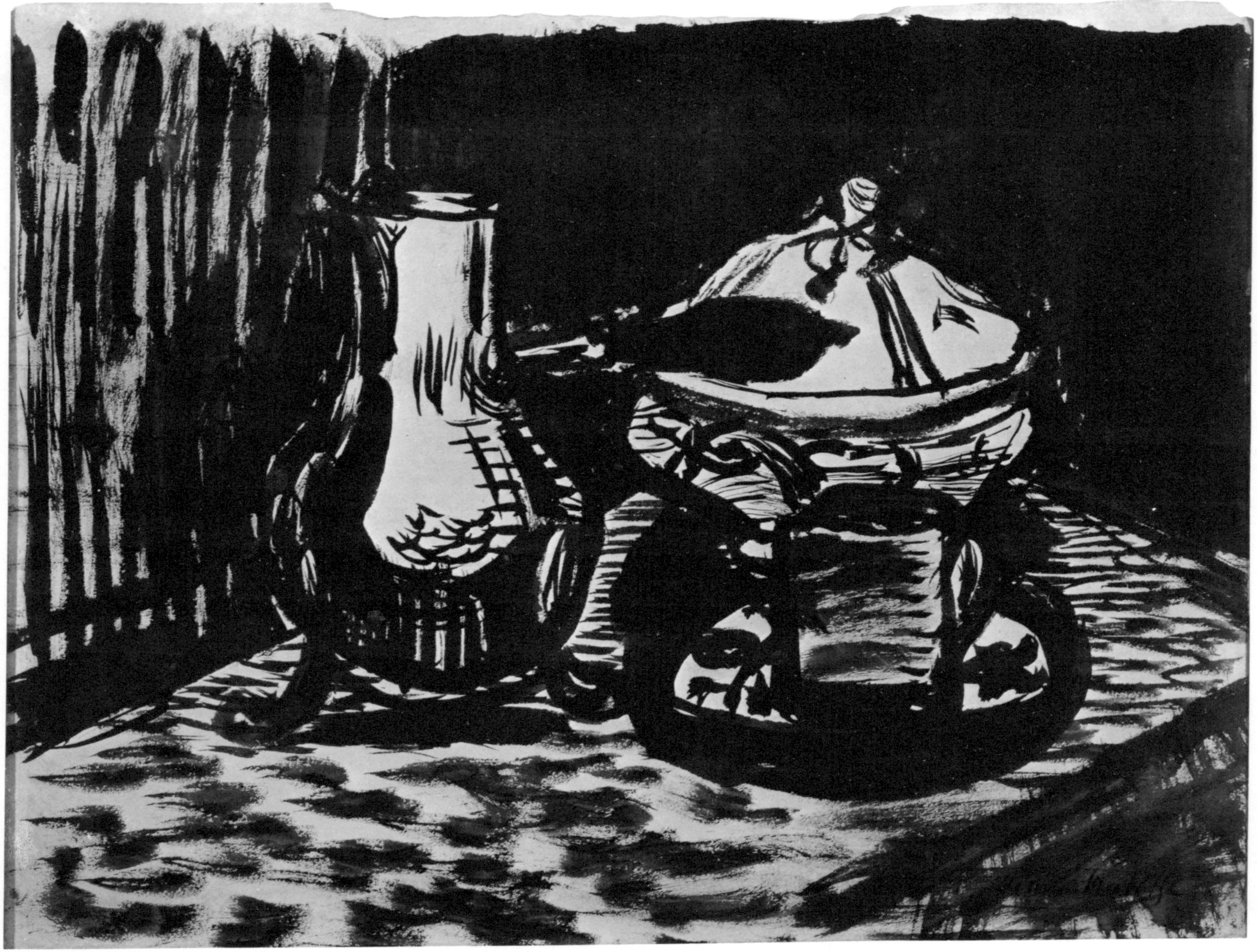

55 Henri Matisse *Still-Life with a Chocolatière*

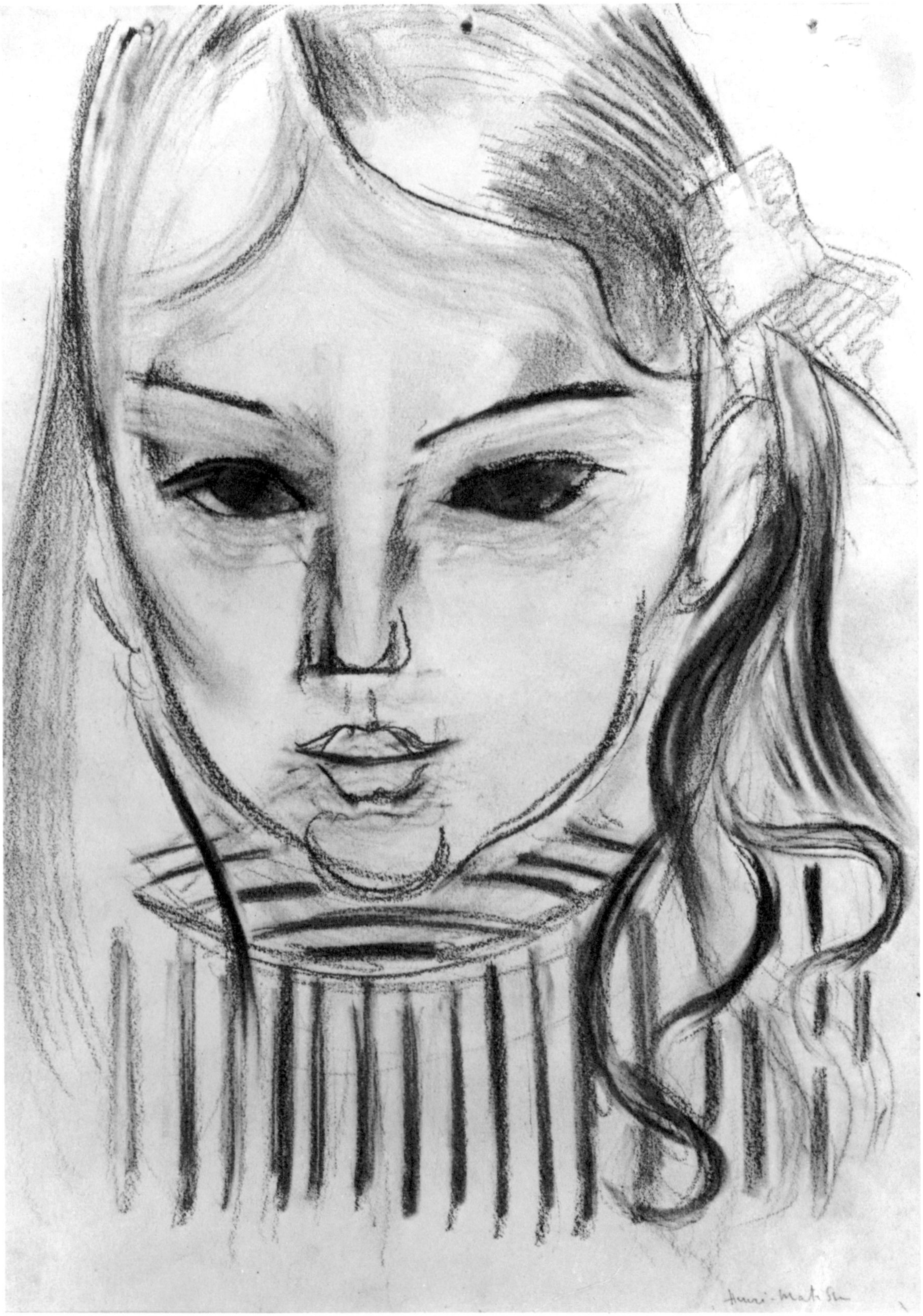

56 Henri Matisse *Portrait of a Girl*

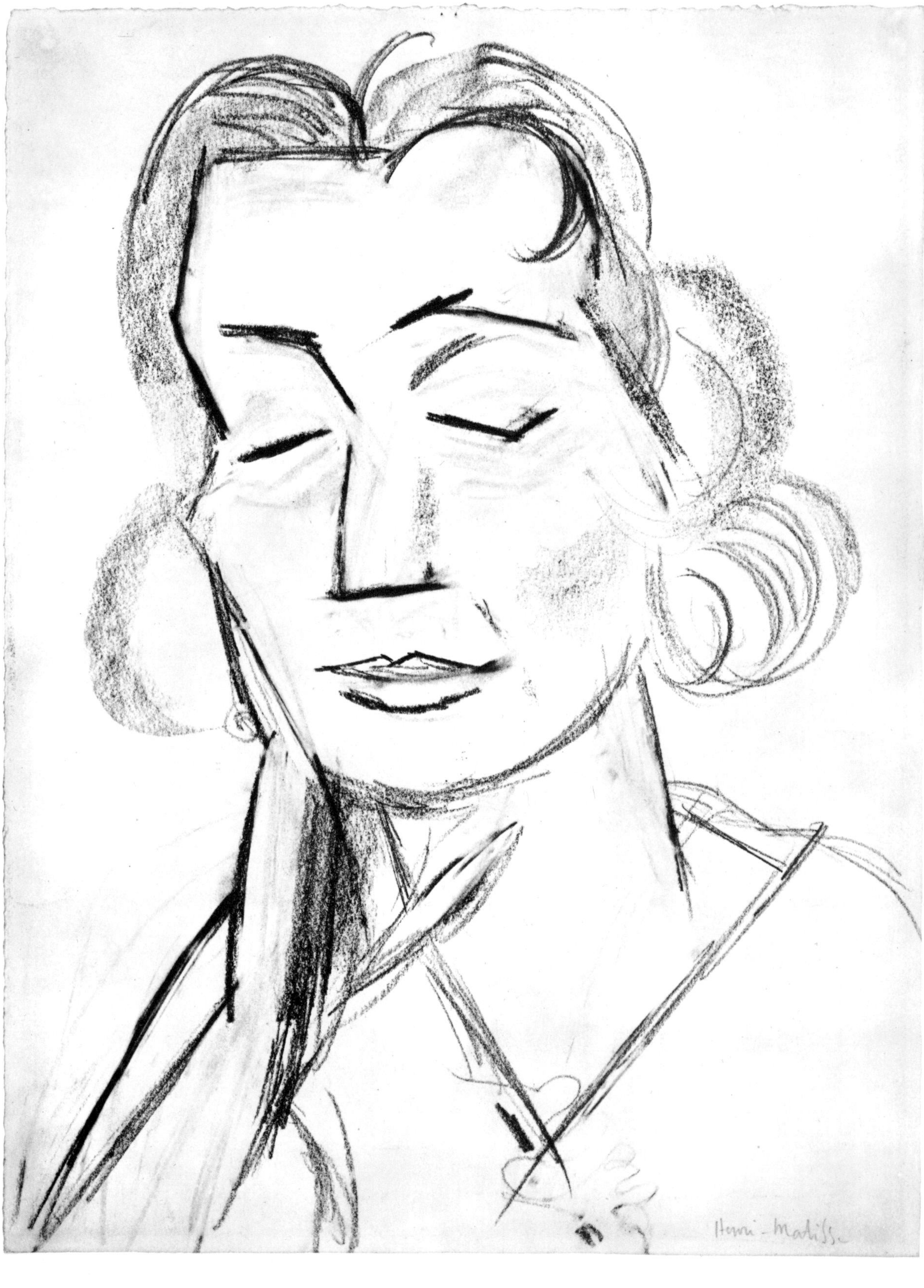

57 Henri Matisse *Portrait of Eva Mudocci*

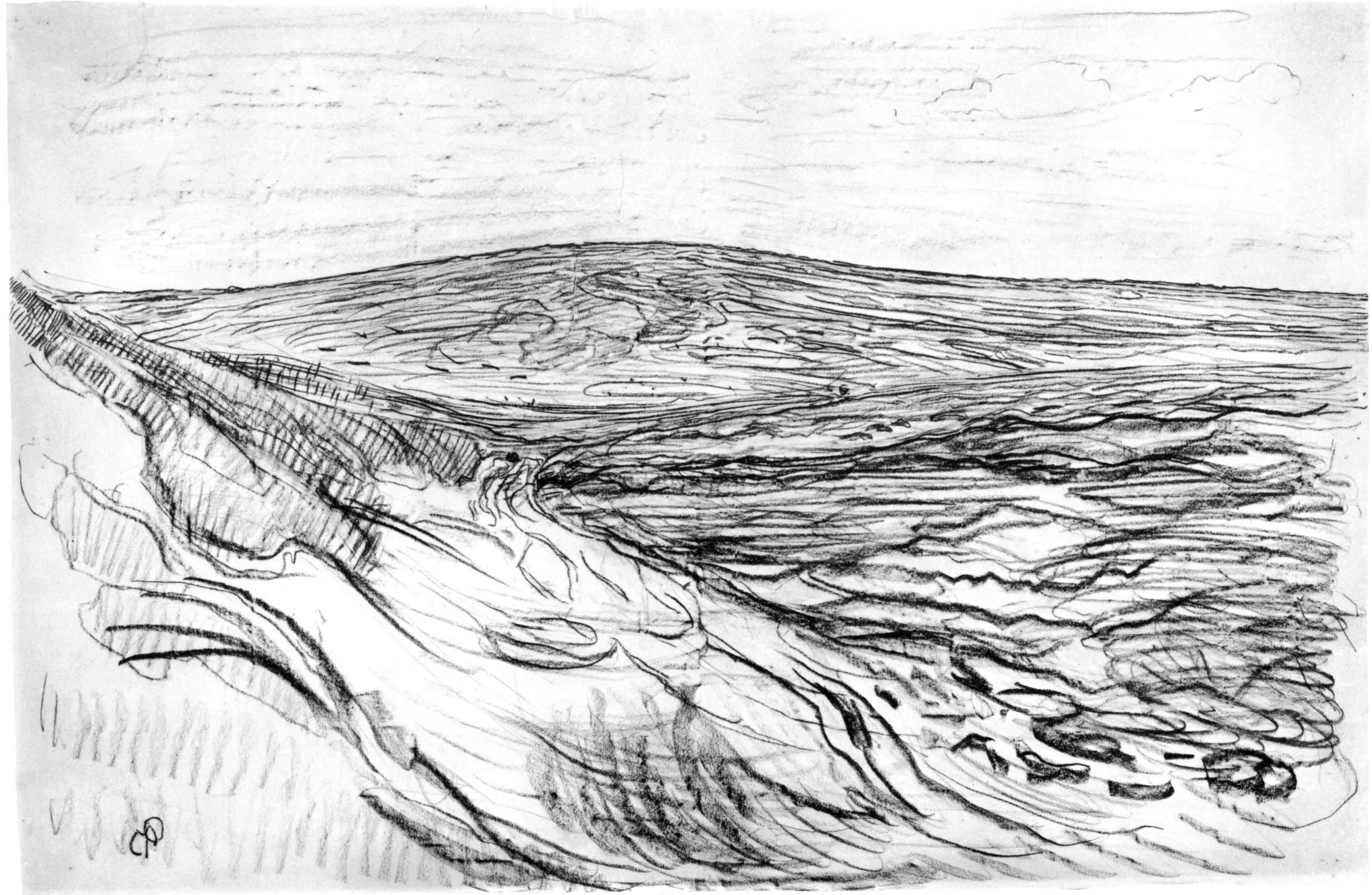

58 Piet Mondrian *The Dunes at Domburg*

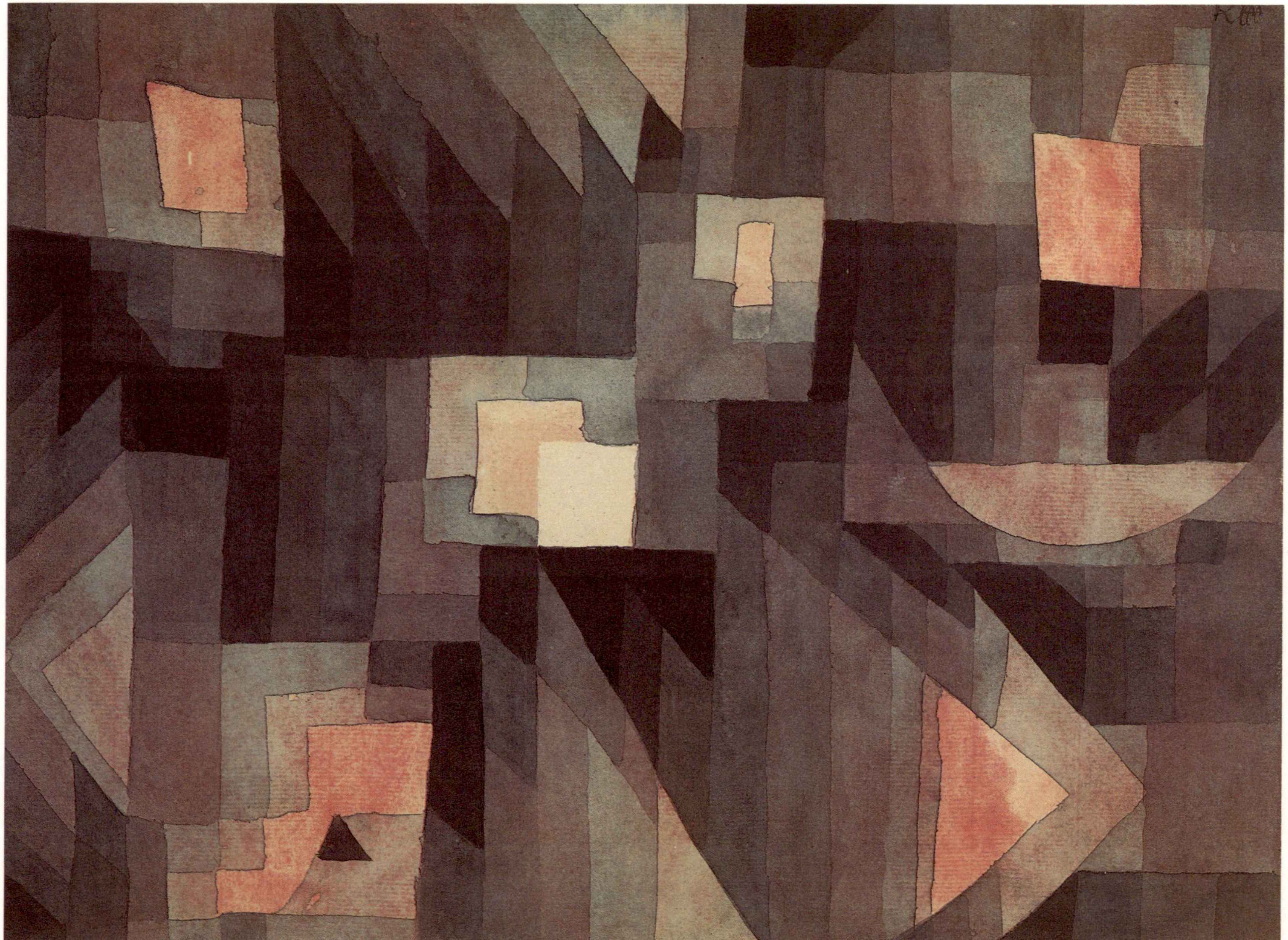

59 Paul Klee *Red, Green Gradation*

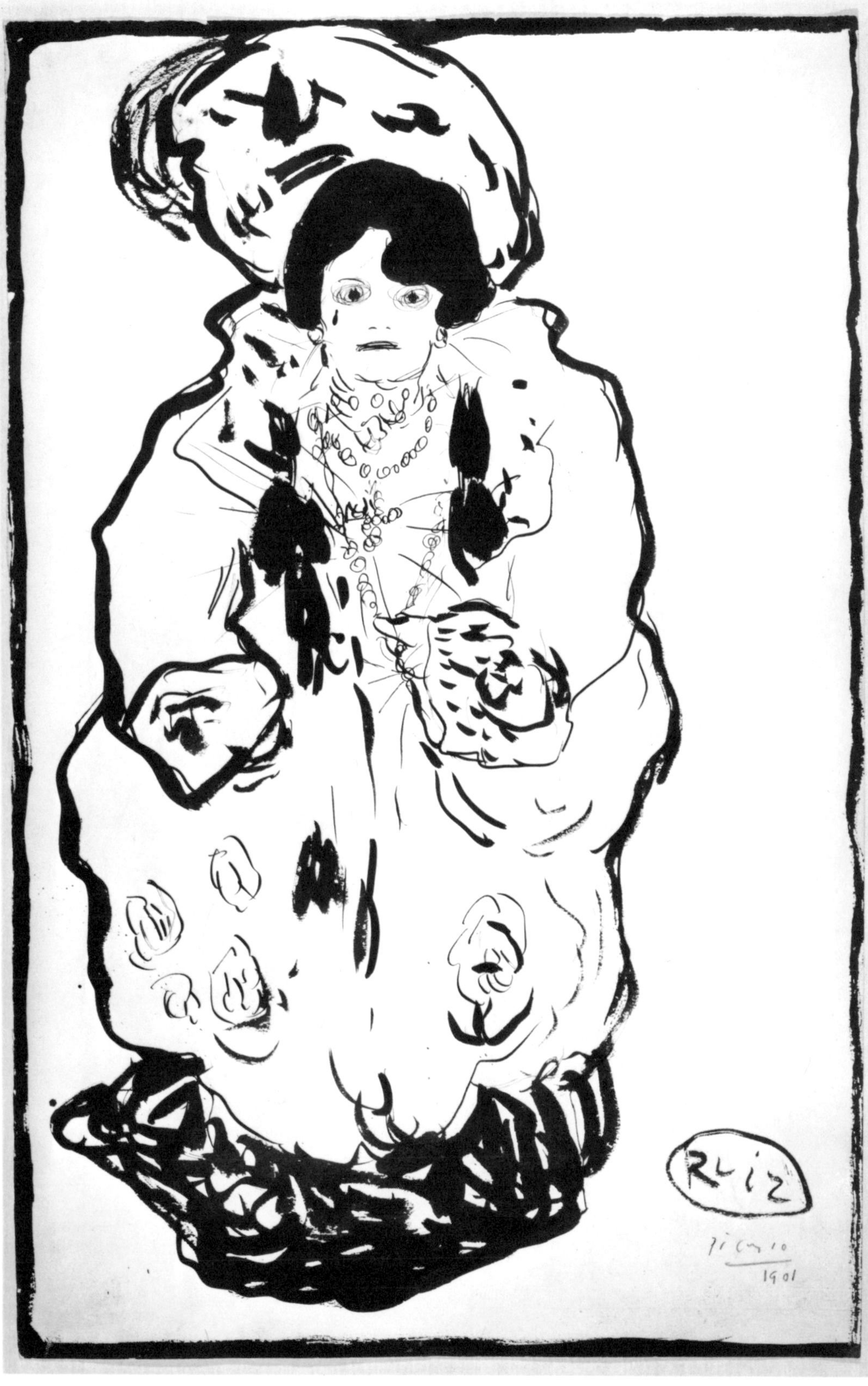

60 Pablo Picasso *Portrait of Marie Derval*

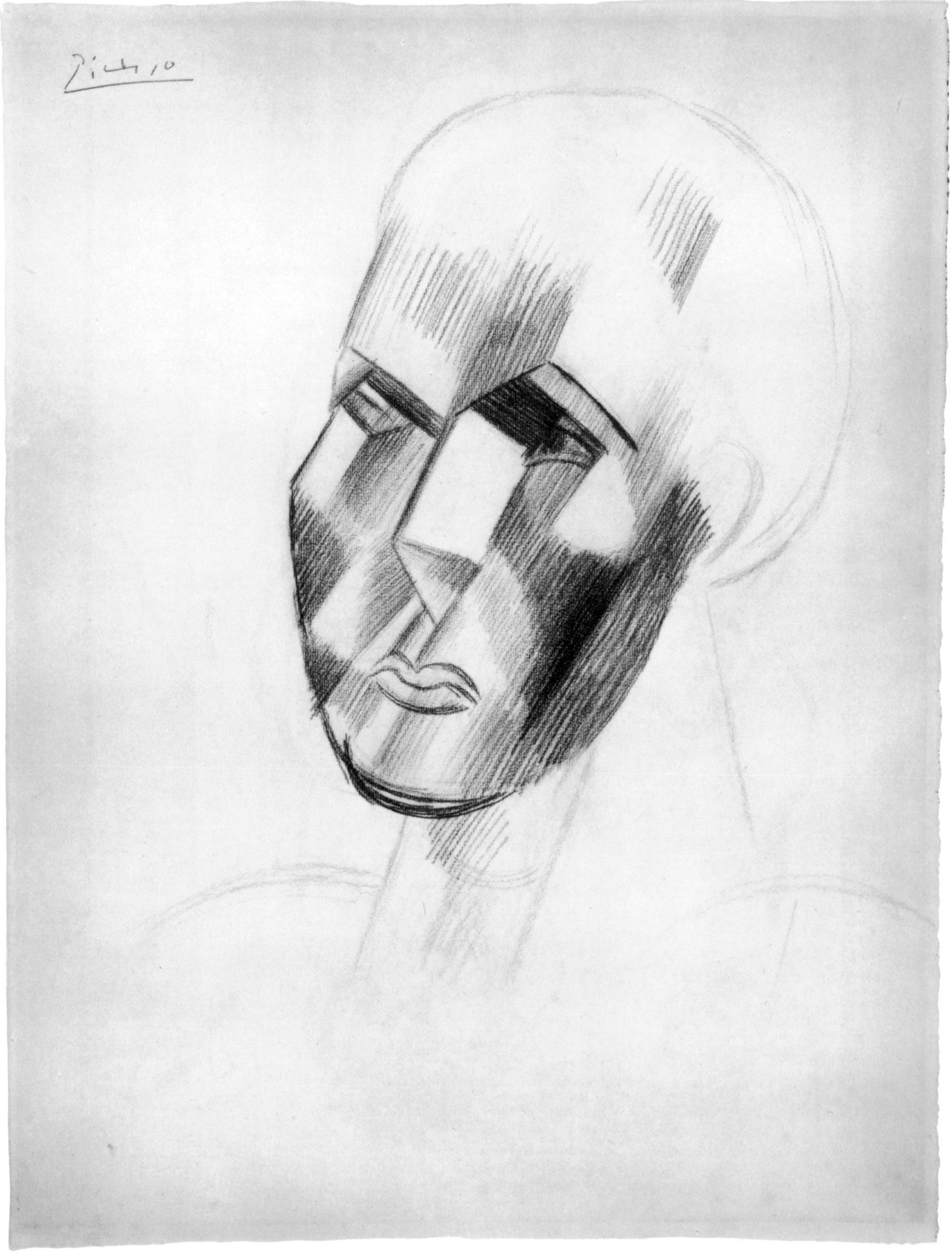

61 Pablo Picasso *Head of a Man*

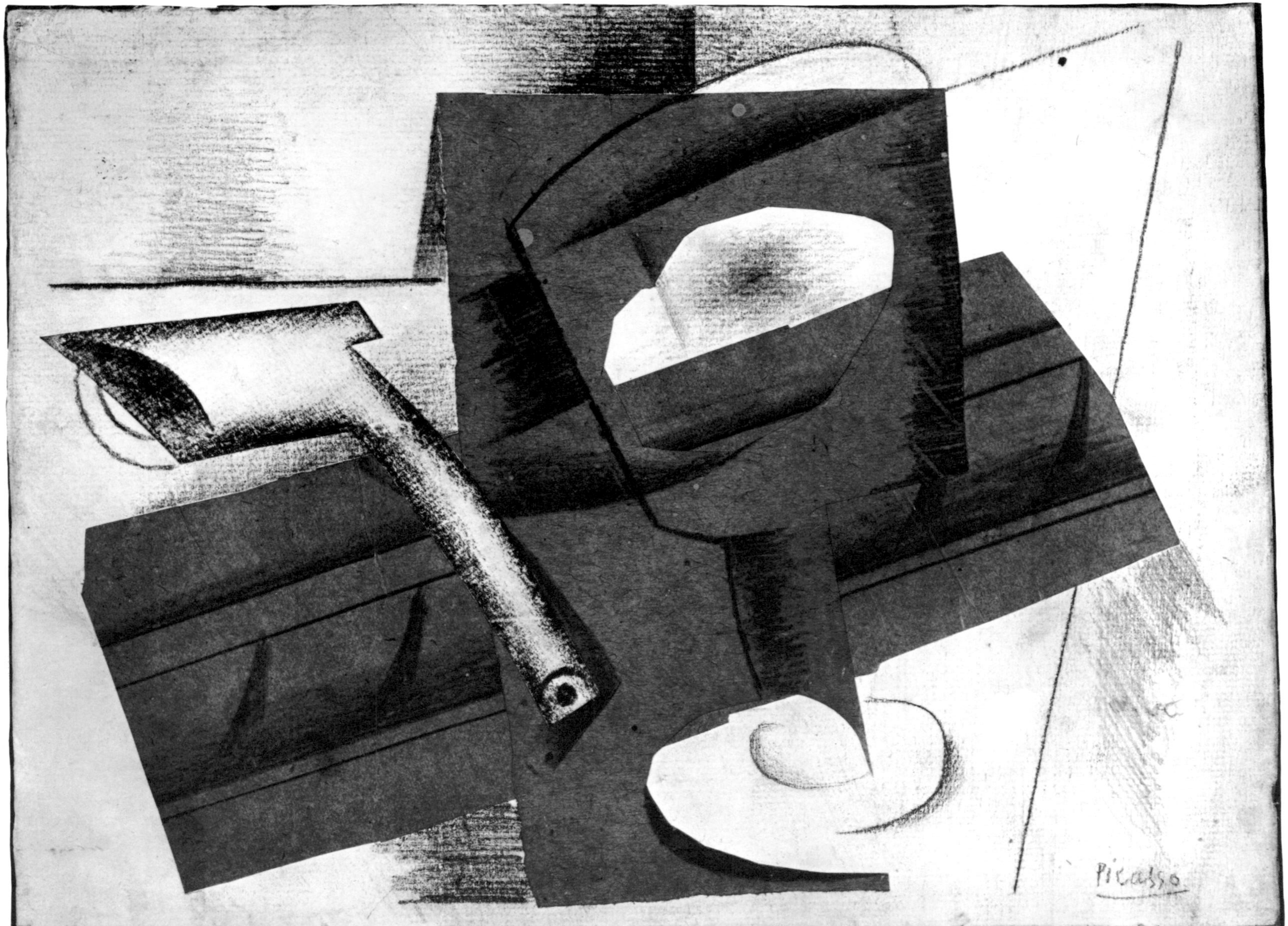

62 Pablo Picasso *Pipe and Wineglass*

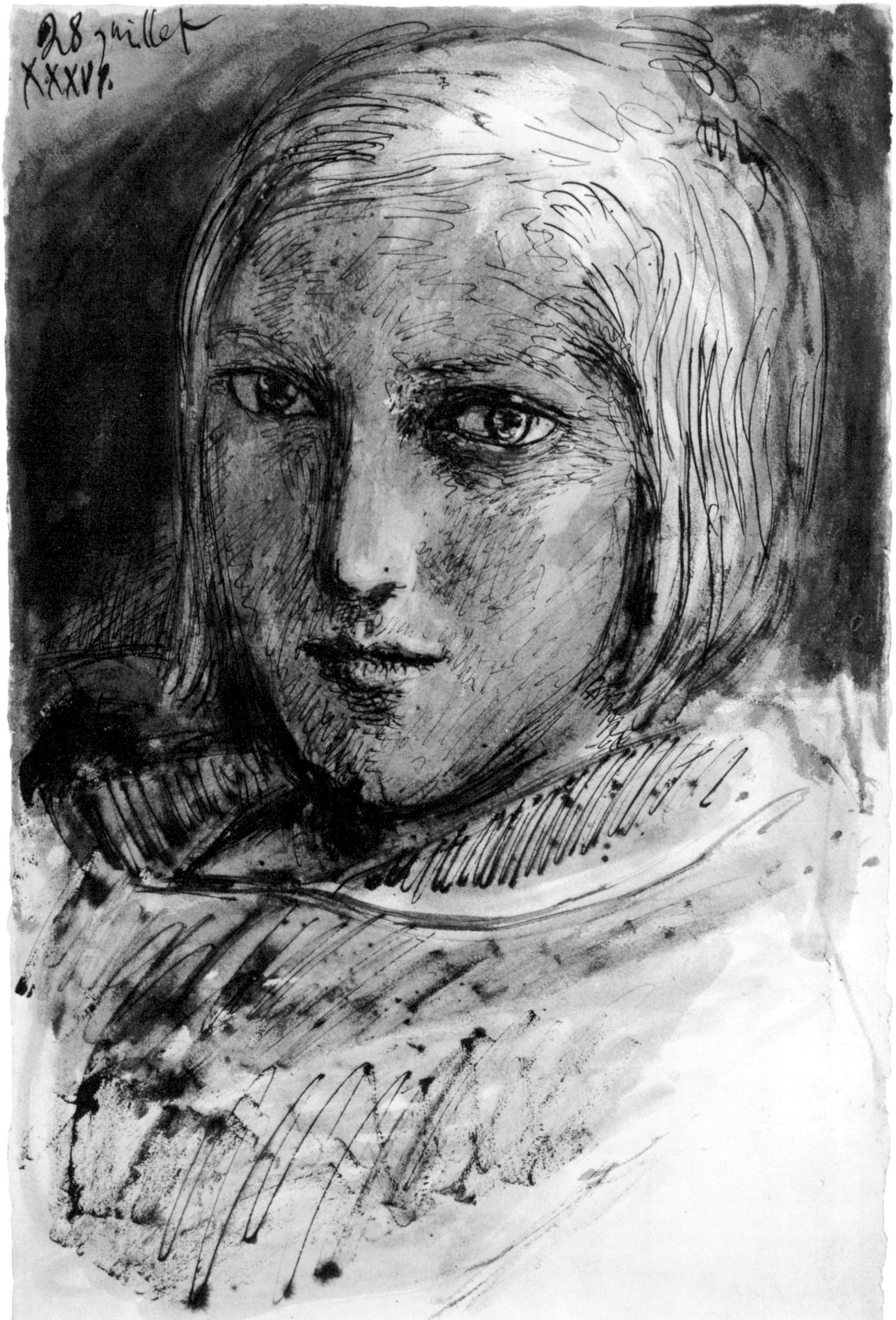

63 Pablo Picasso *Portrait of Marie-Thérèse Walter*

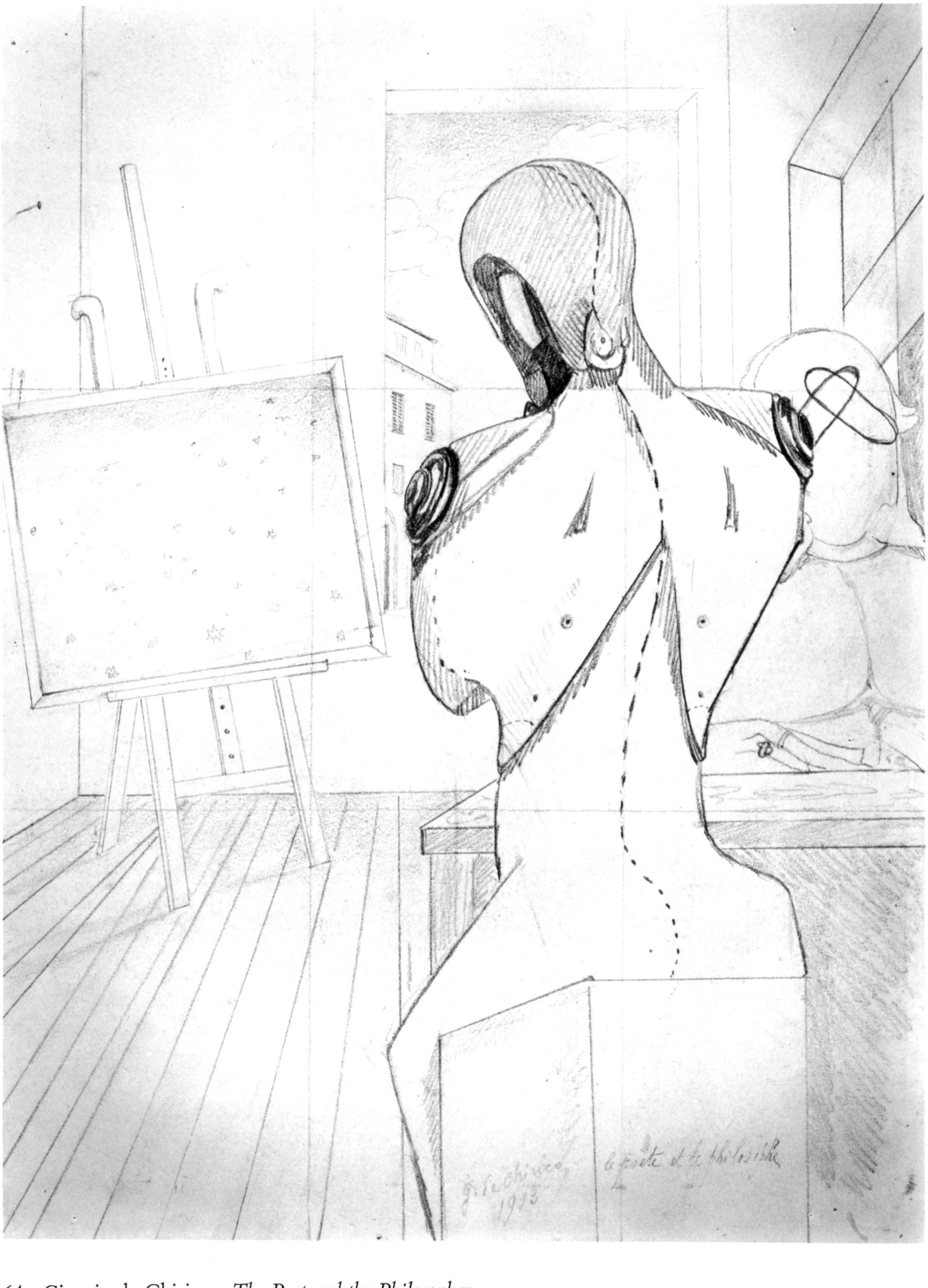

64 Giorgio de Chirico *The Poet and the Philosopher*

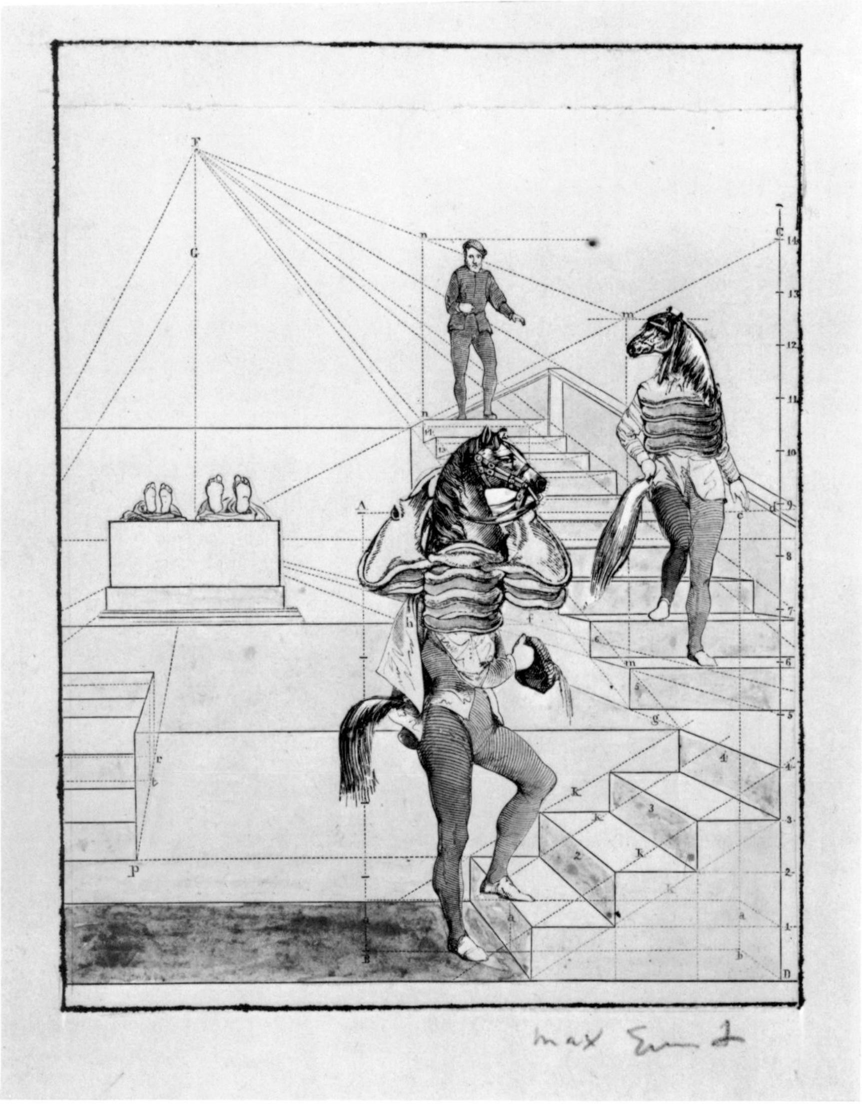

65 Max Ernst *Collage*

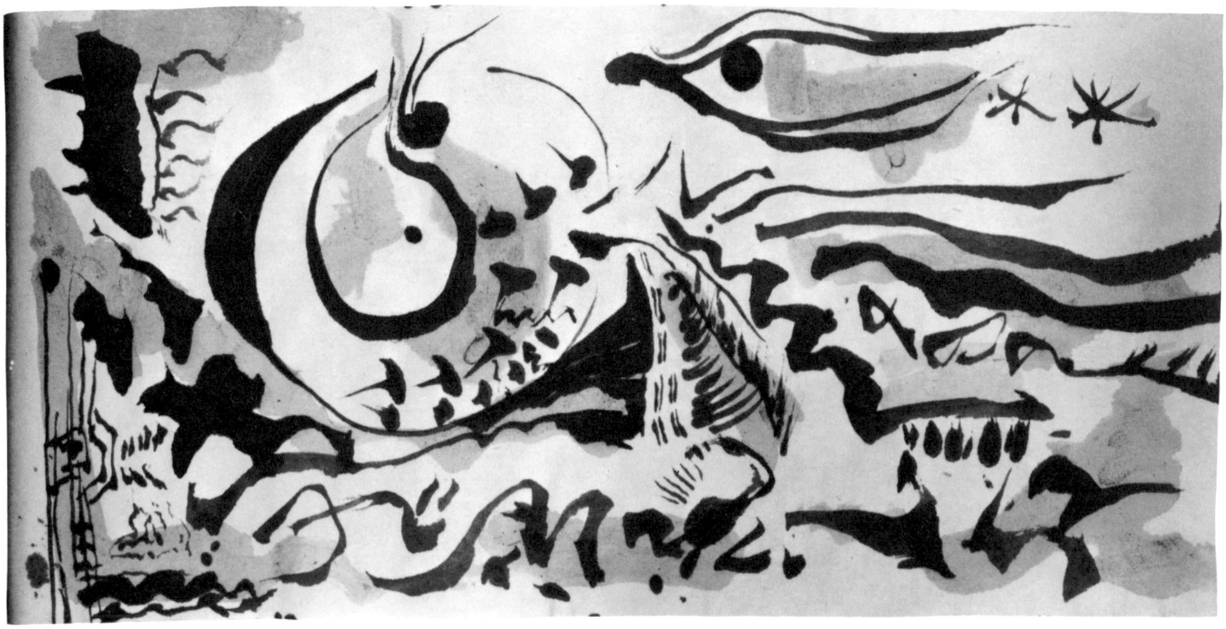

66 Jackson Pollock, Sketchbook, fol. 25

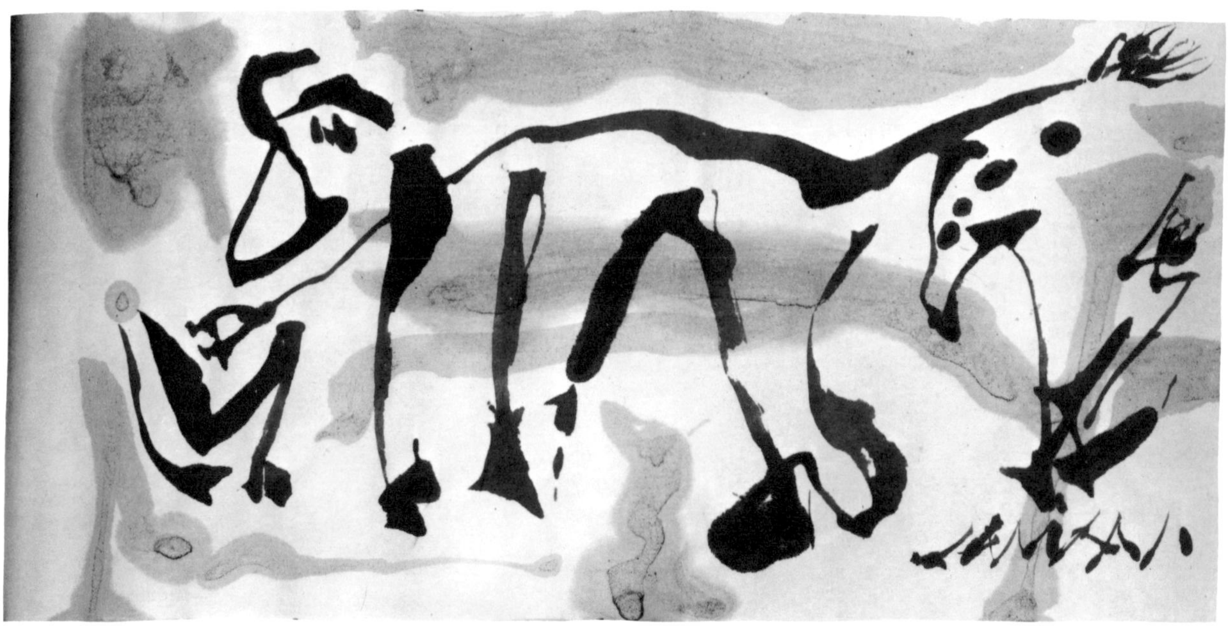

66 Jackson Pollock, Sketchbook, fol. 27

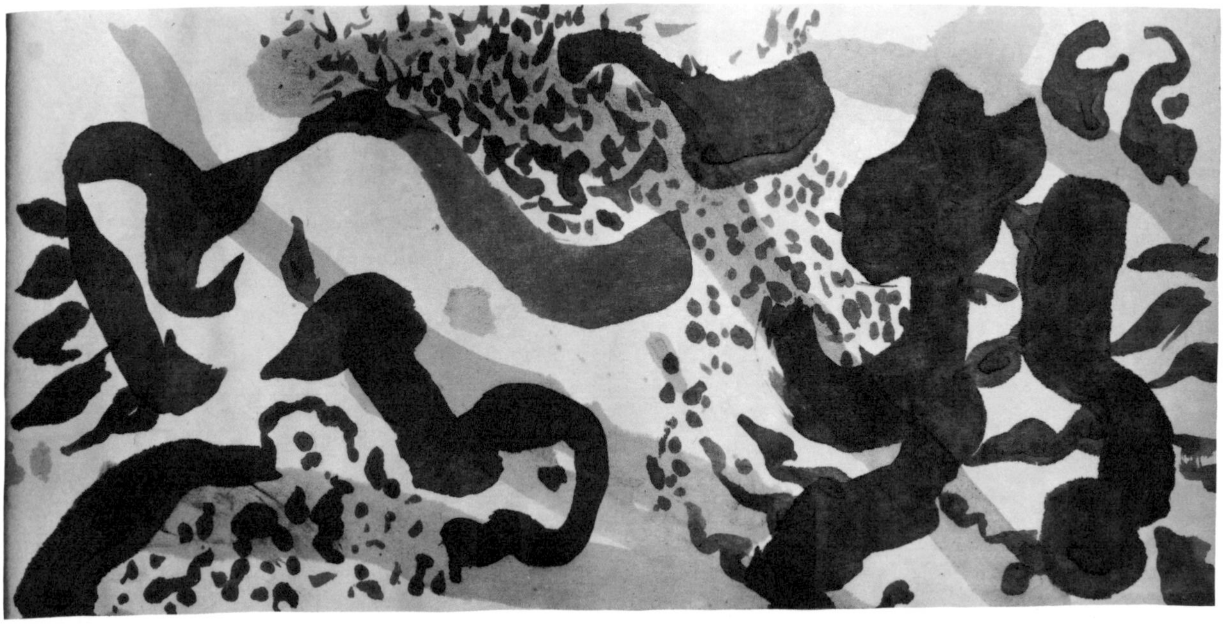

66 Jackson Pollock, Sketchbook, fol. 30

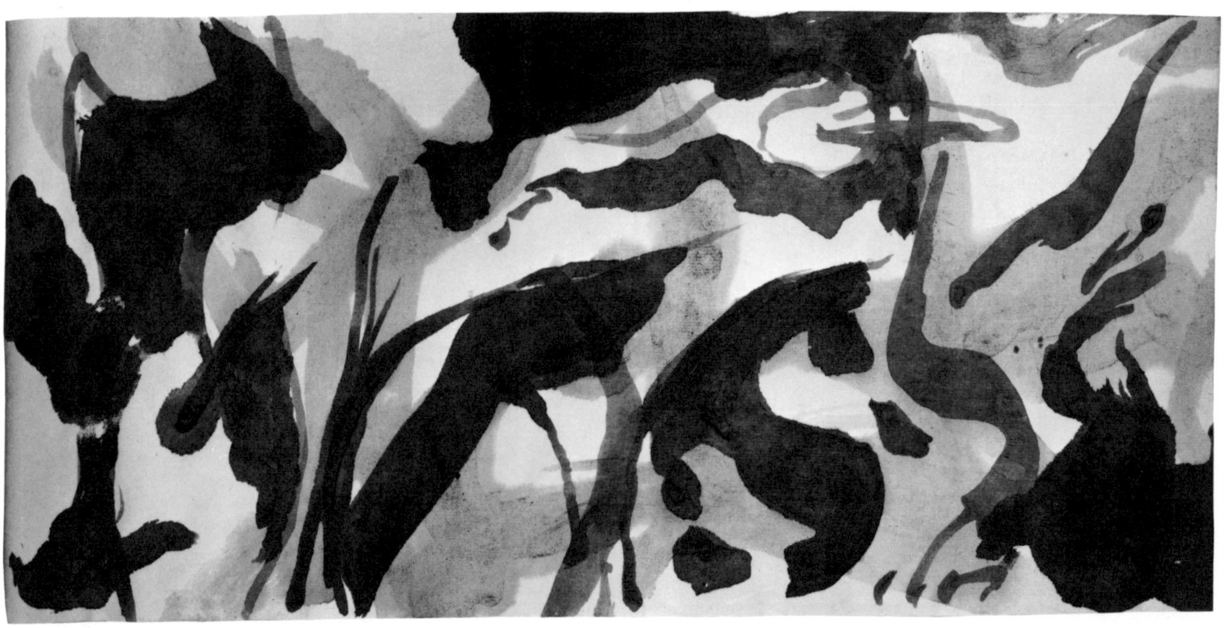

66 Jackson Pollock, Sketchbook, fol. 37

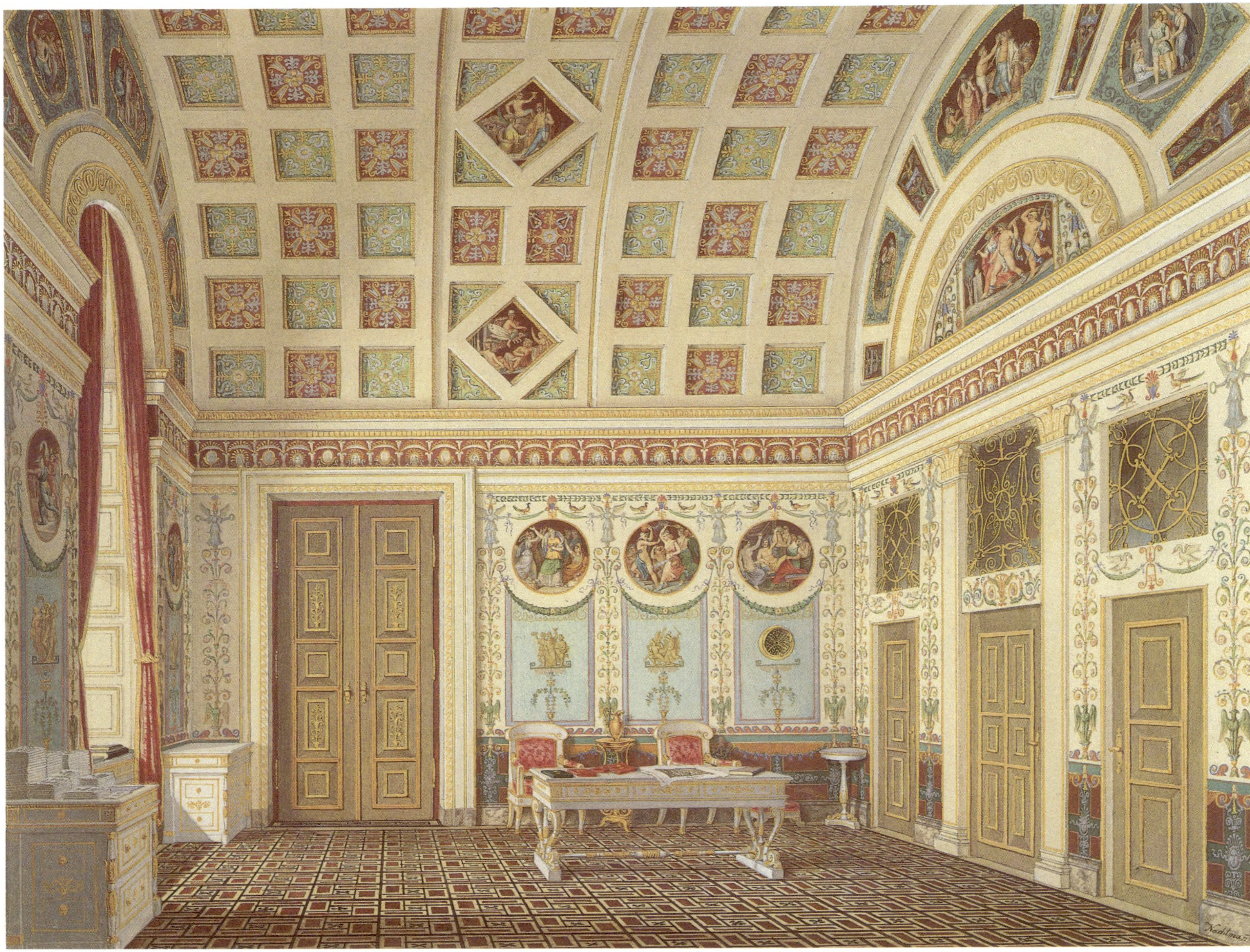

67 Franz Xaver Nachtmann *The Dressing Room of Ludwig I of Bavaria, 1836*

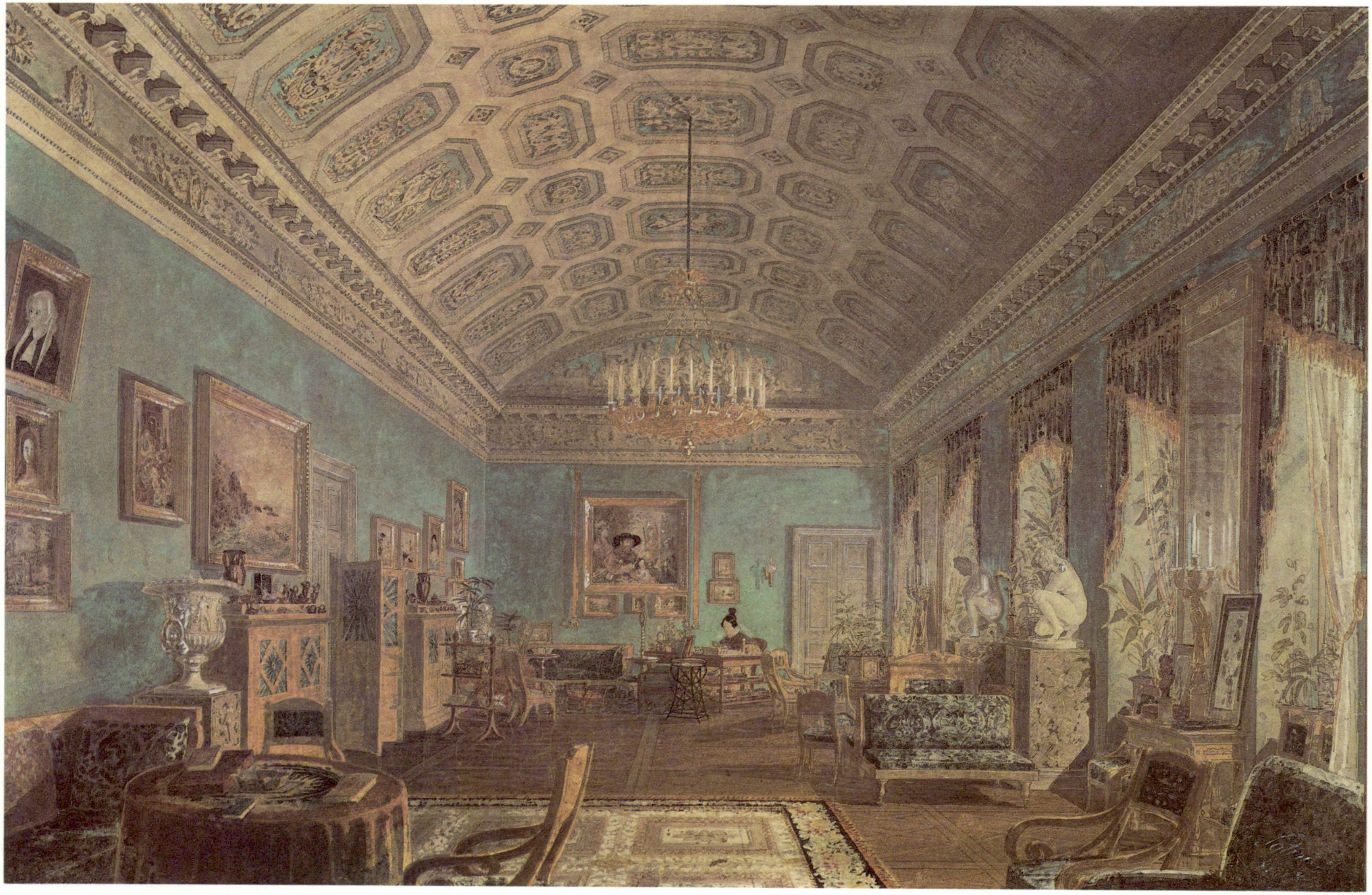

68 Sotira *The Salon of Empress Alexandra of Russia, 1835*

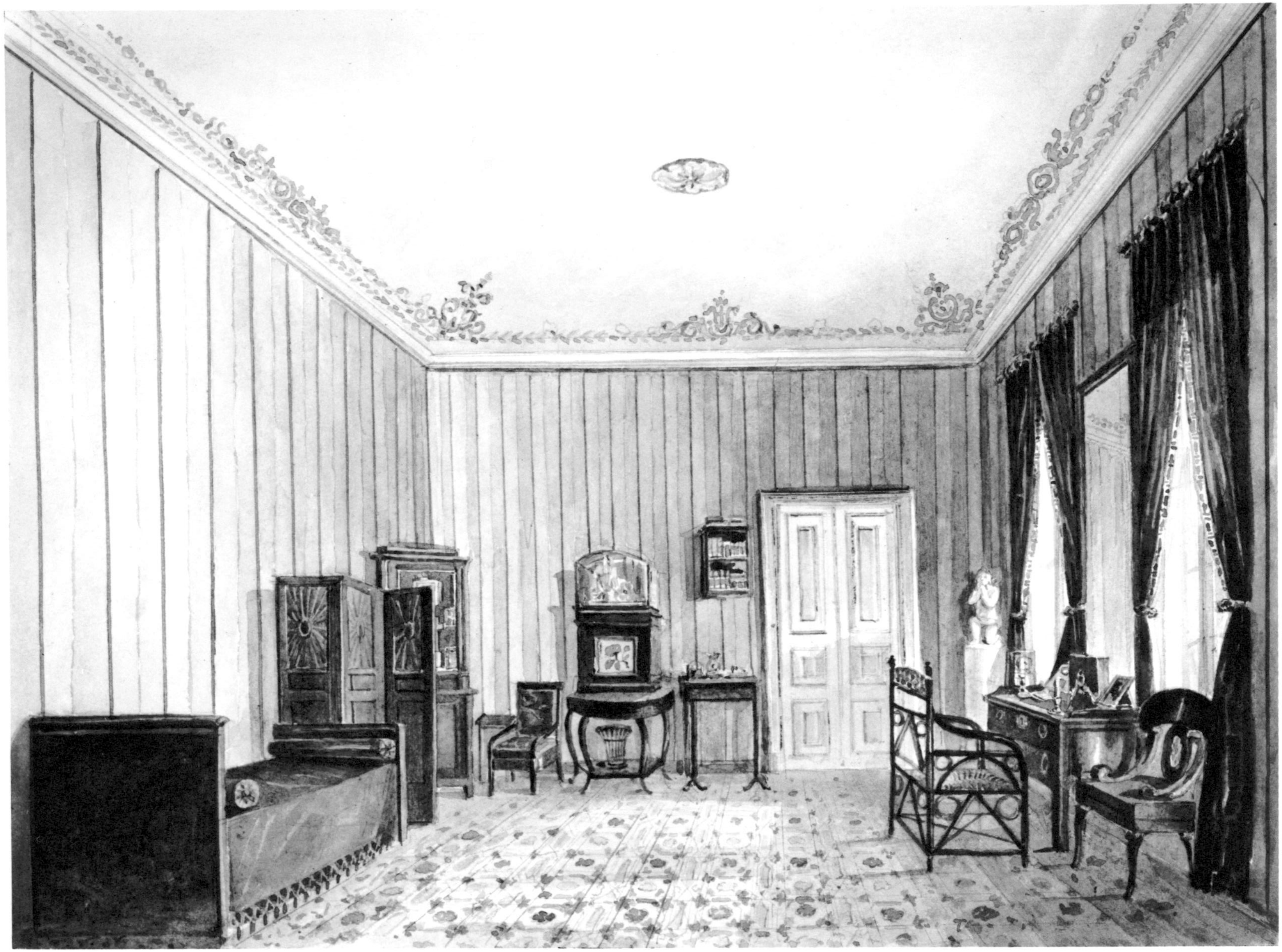

69 Russian School *Bedroom*

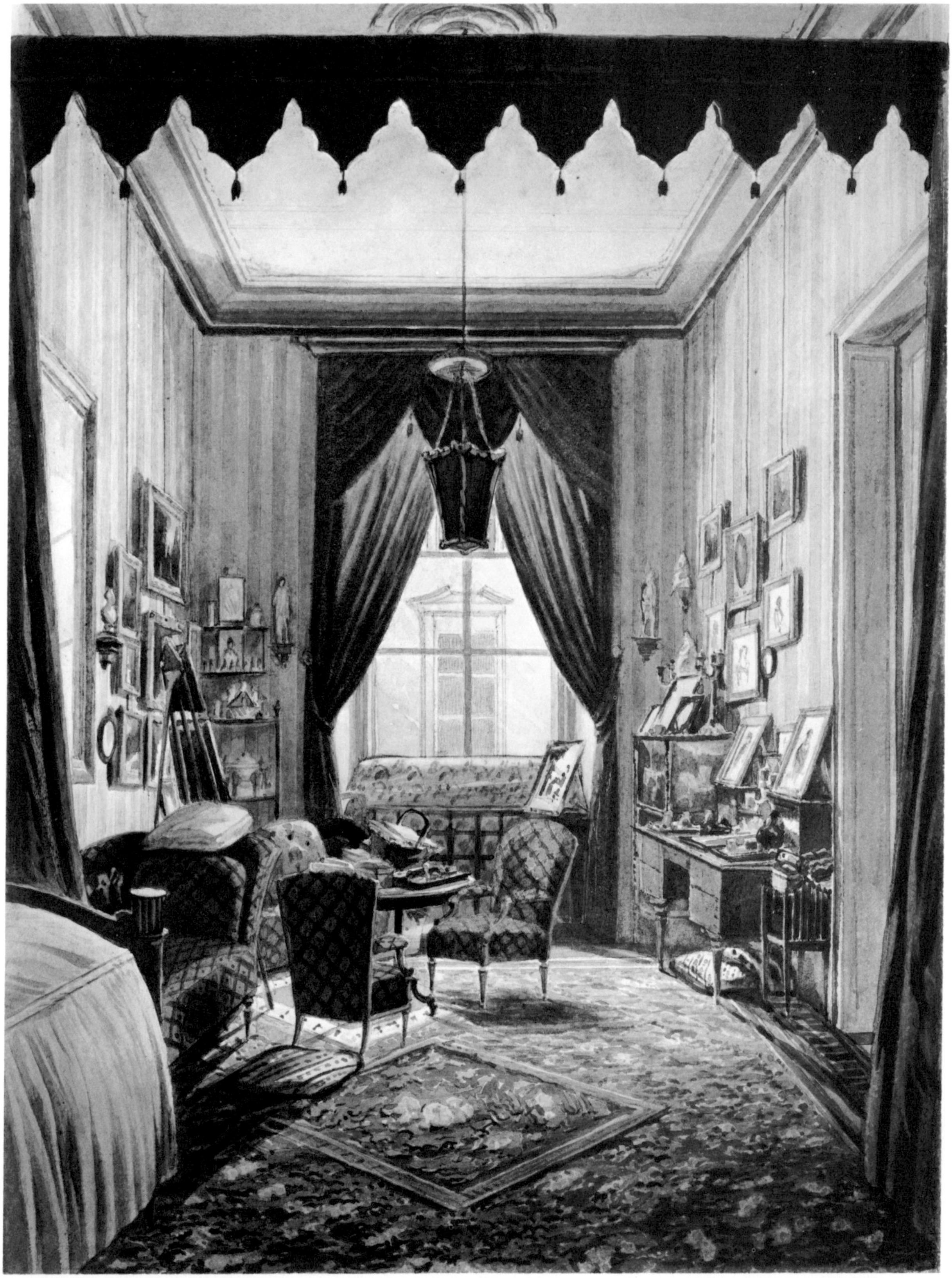

70 Austrian School *Interior*

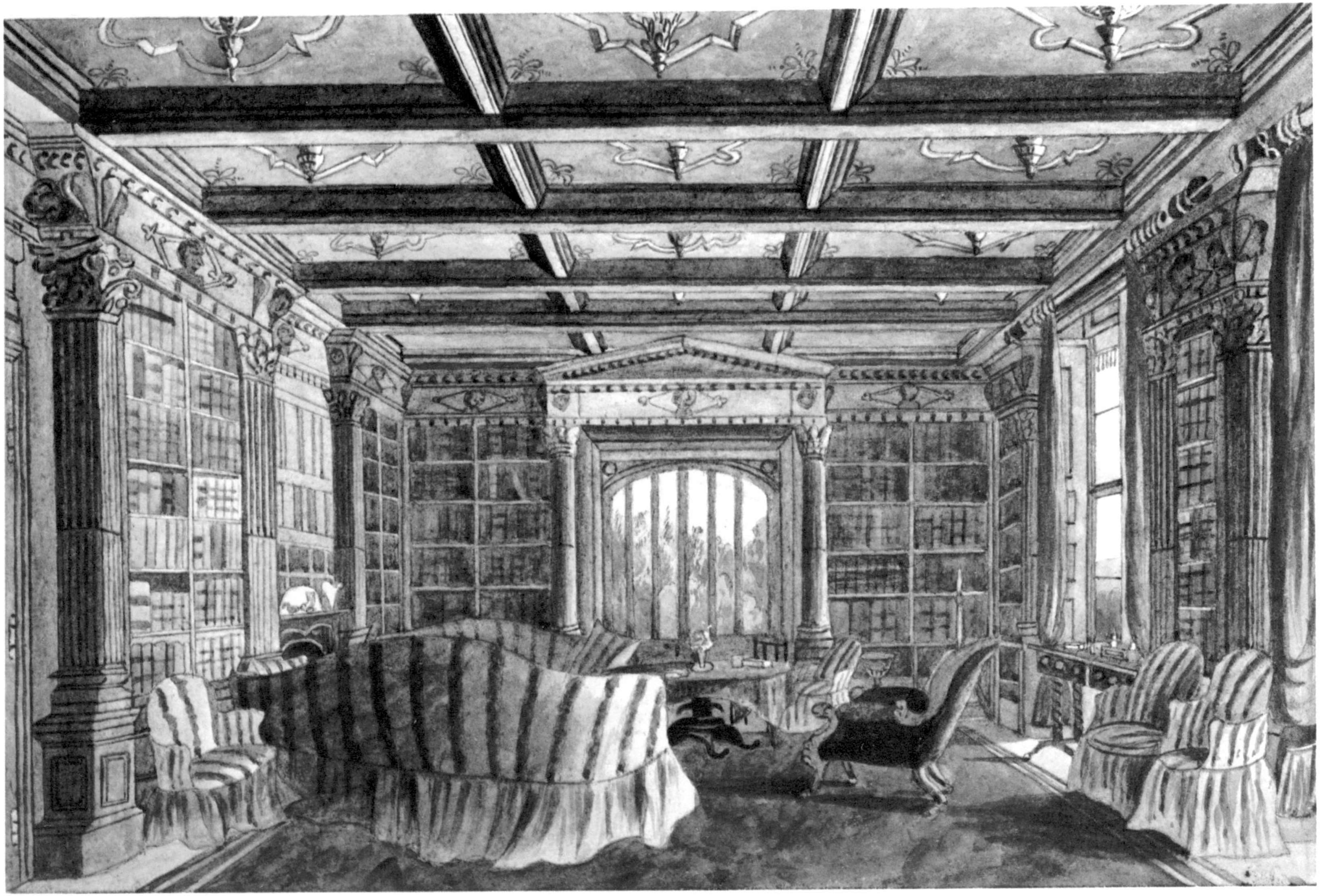

71 Charlotte Bosanquet *The Library at Dingestow*

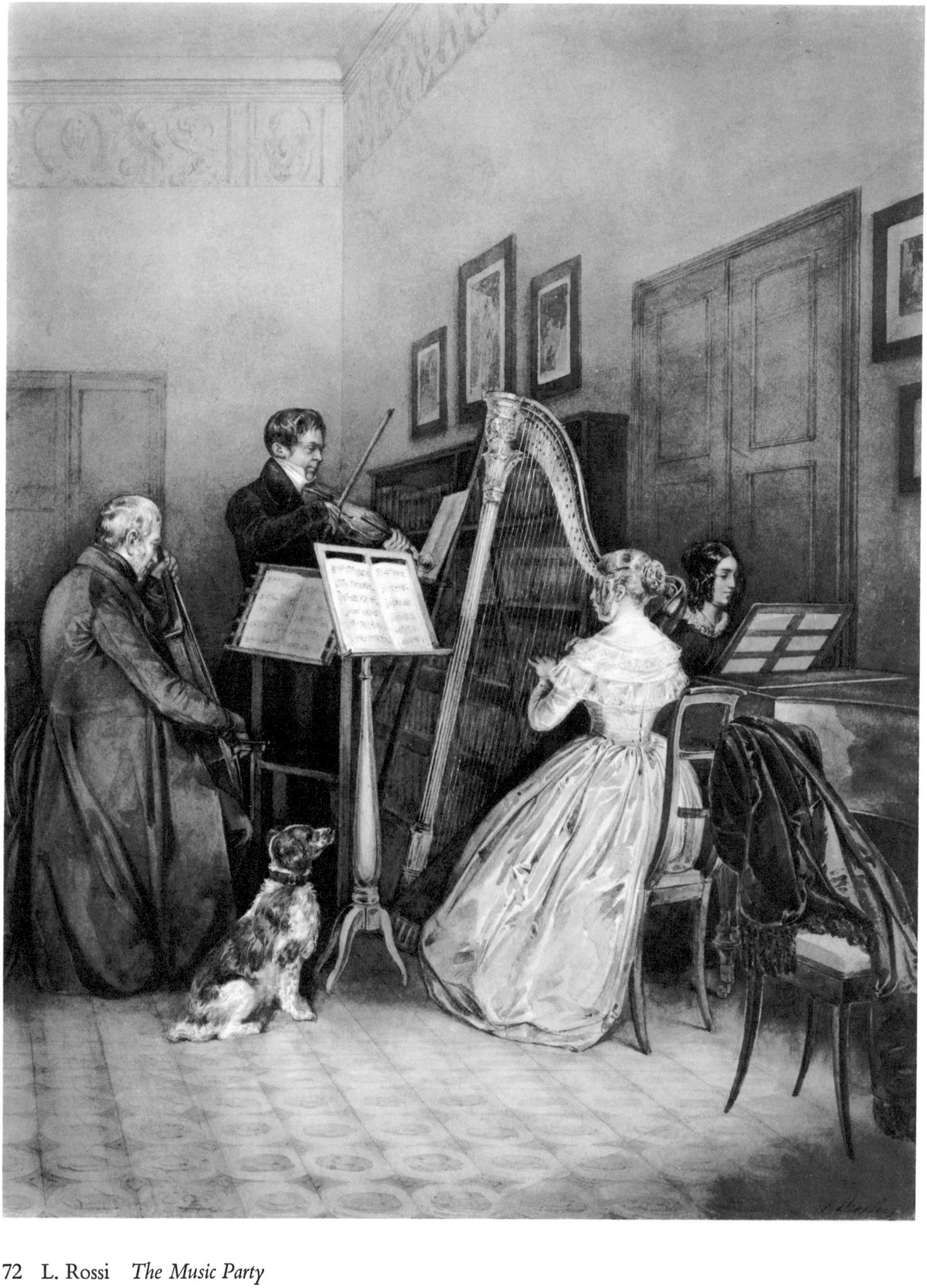

72 L. Rossi *The Music Party*

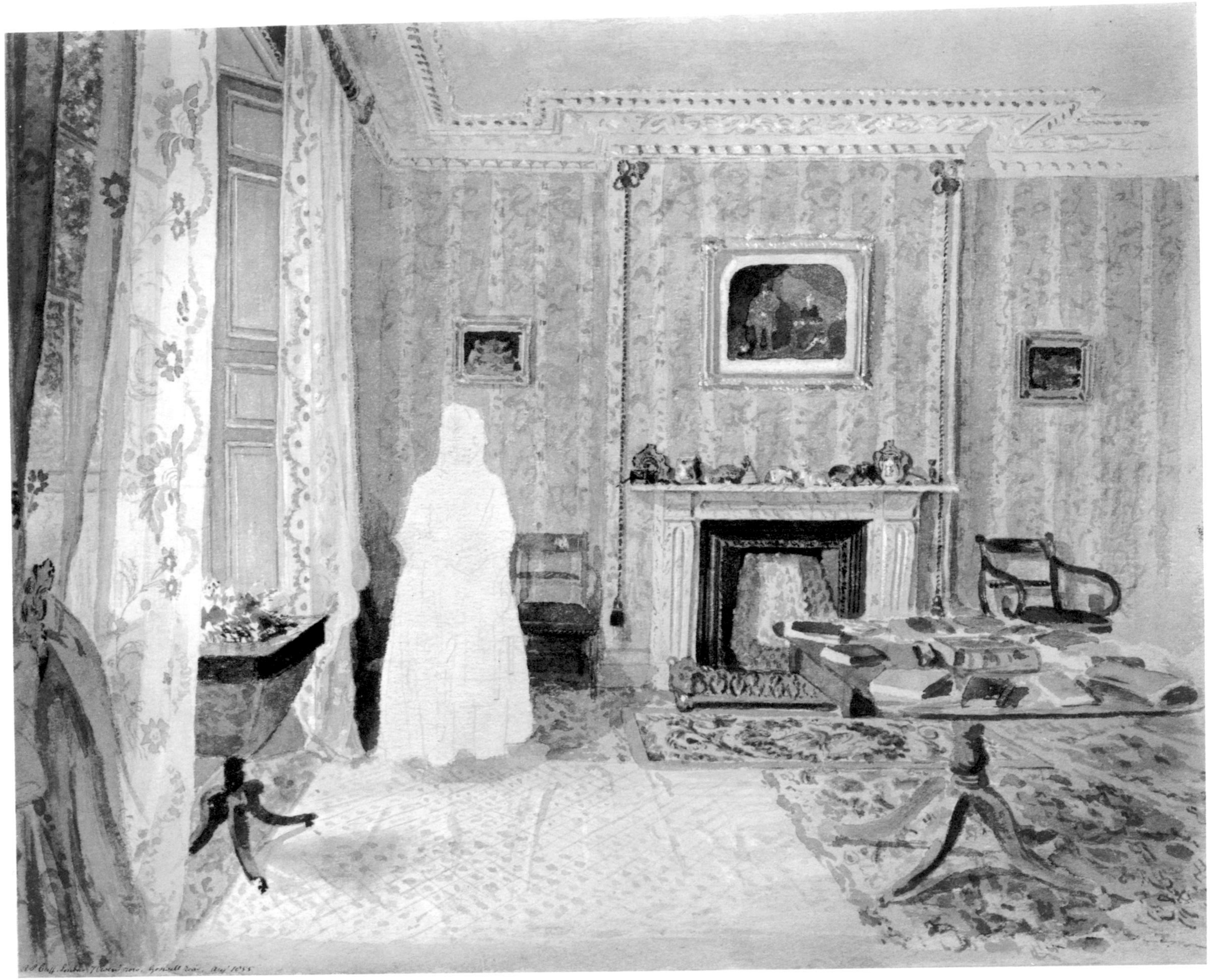

73 R. Parminter Cuff *Sitting Room*

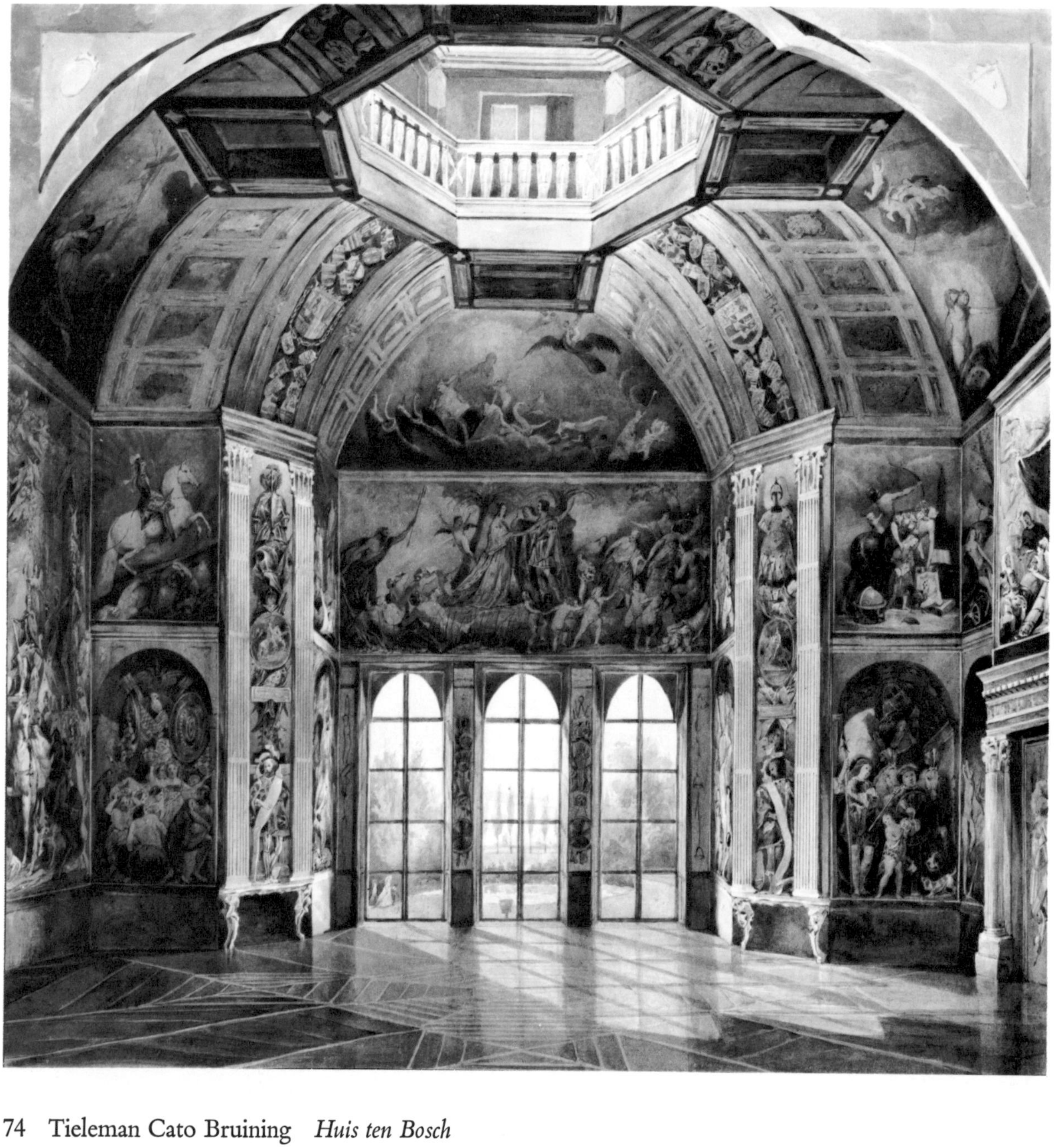

74 Tieleman Cato Bruining *Huis ten Bosch*

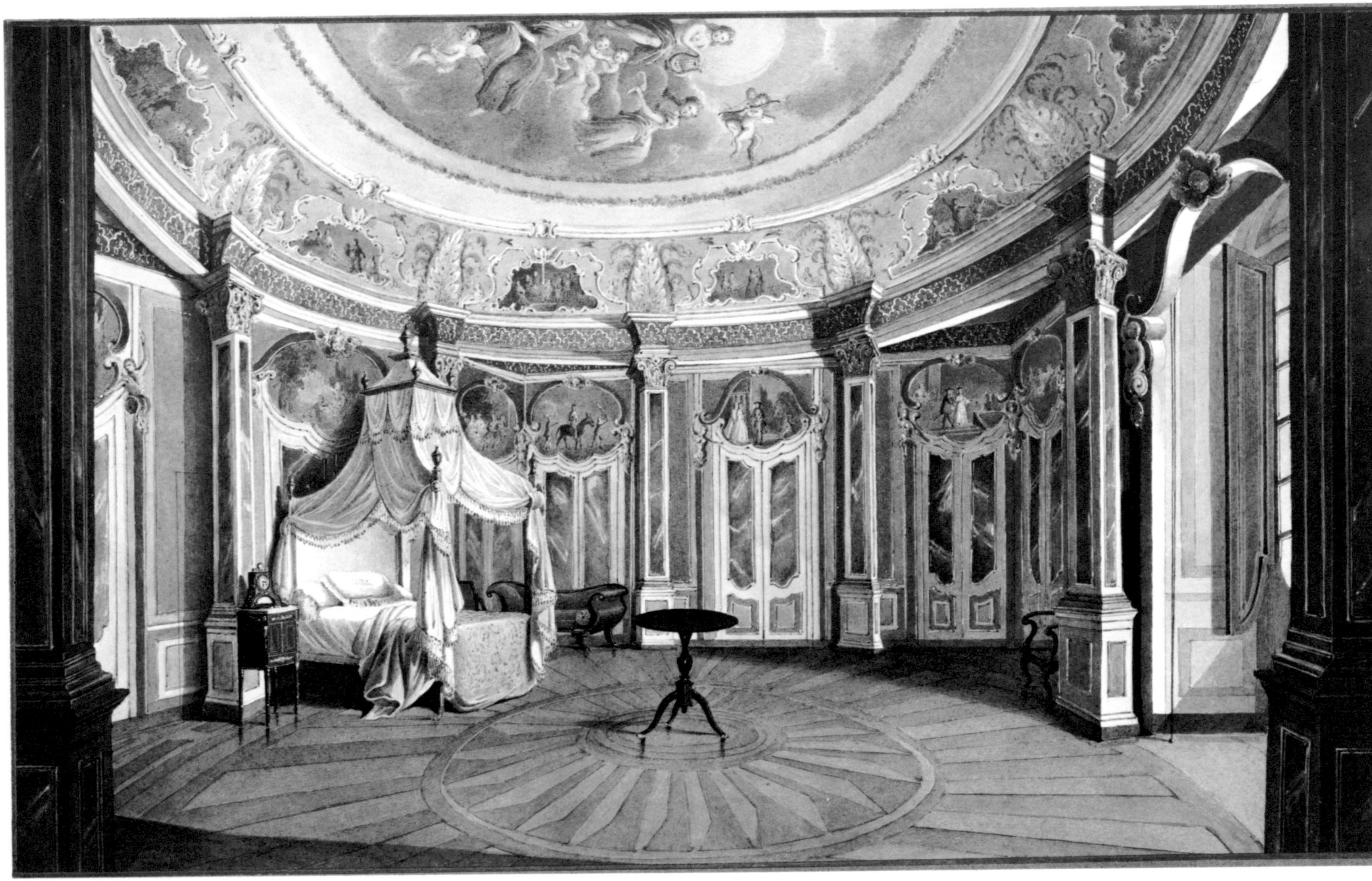

75 Ferdinand Le Feubure *The Bedroom of the Emperor Dom Pedro I, Queluz Palace*

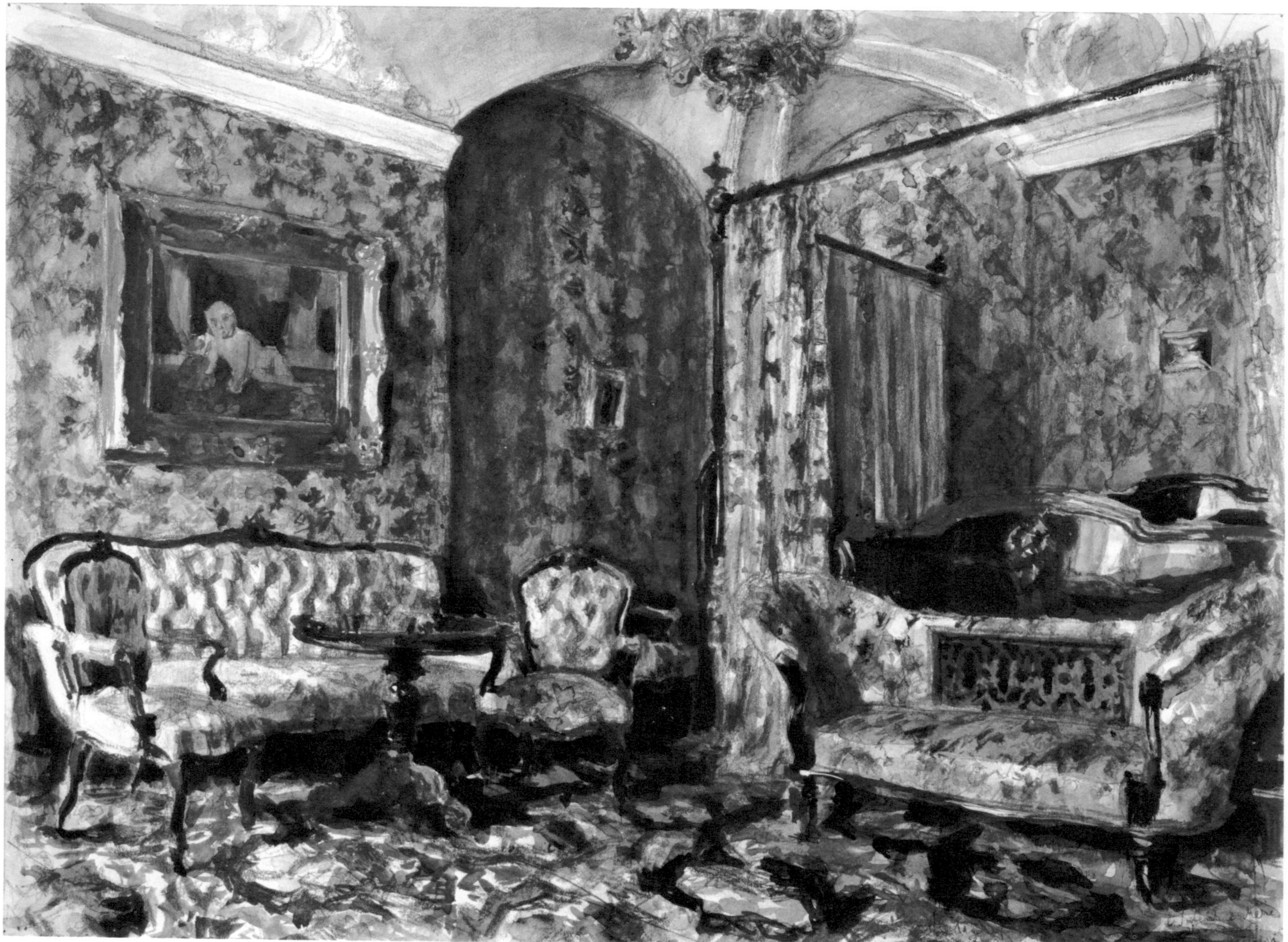

76 Alexandre Benois *Bedroom of the Empress, Gatchina Palace, St. Petersburg*

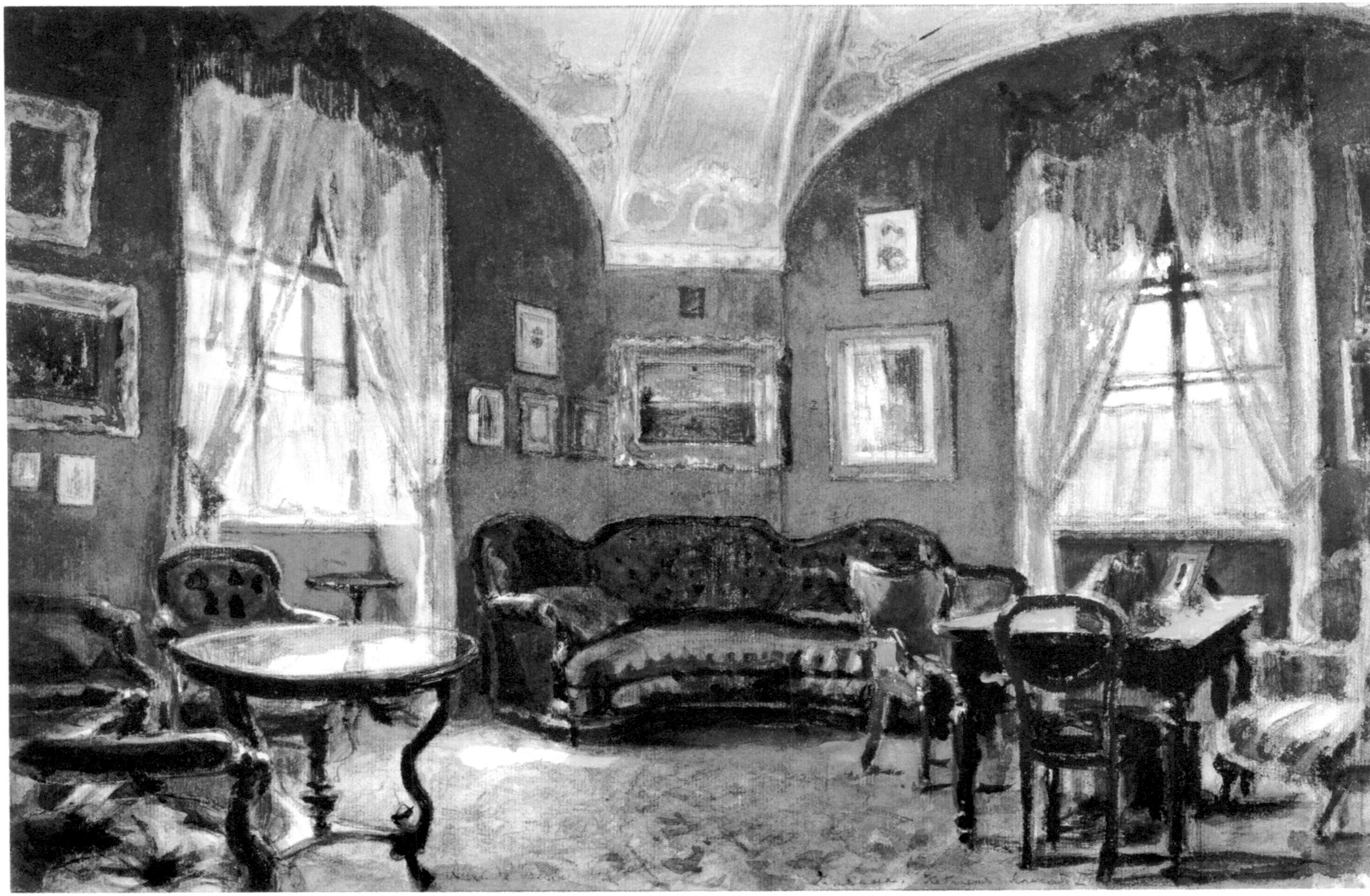

77 Alexandre Benois *Study of Czar Alexander II, Gatchina Palace, St. Petersburg*

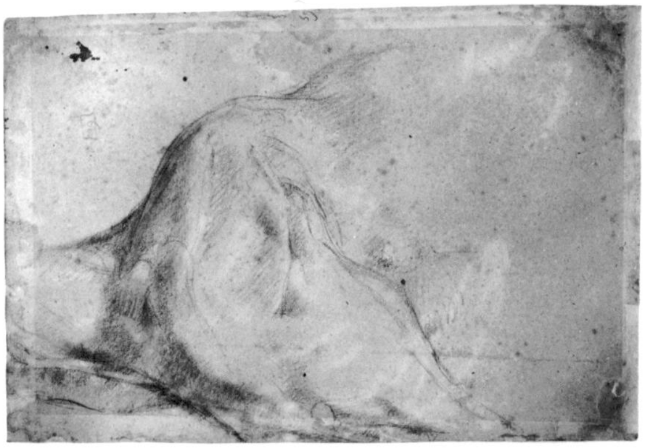

4 (verso) Hendrick Goltzius

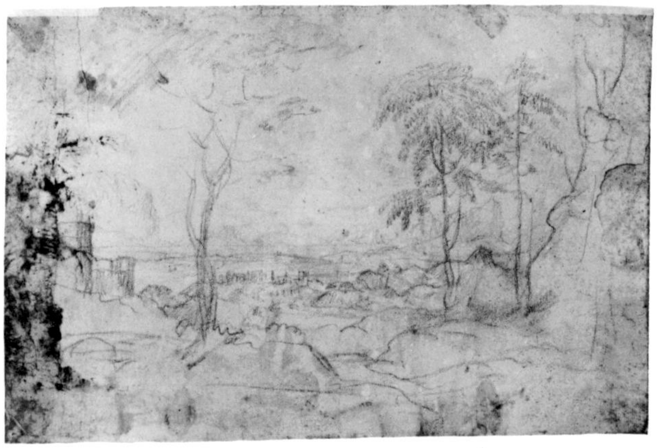

6 (verso) Claude

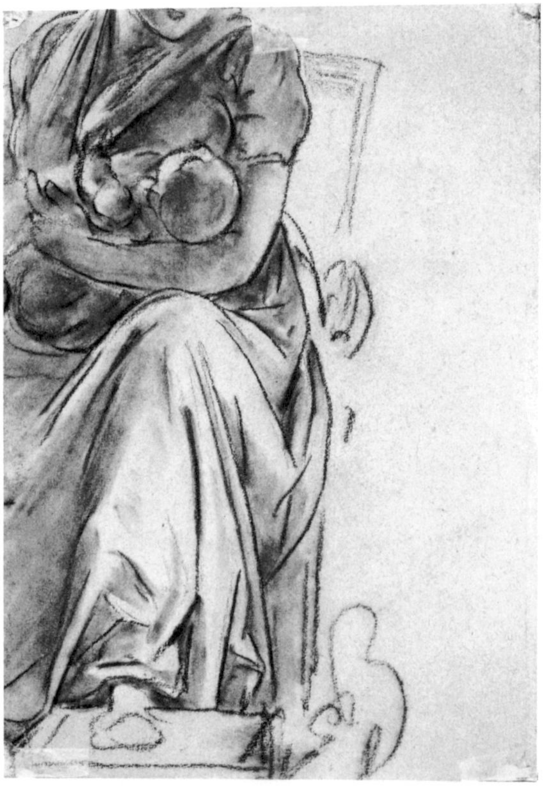

20 (verso) Louis Léopold Boilly

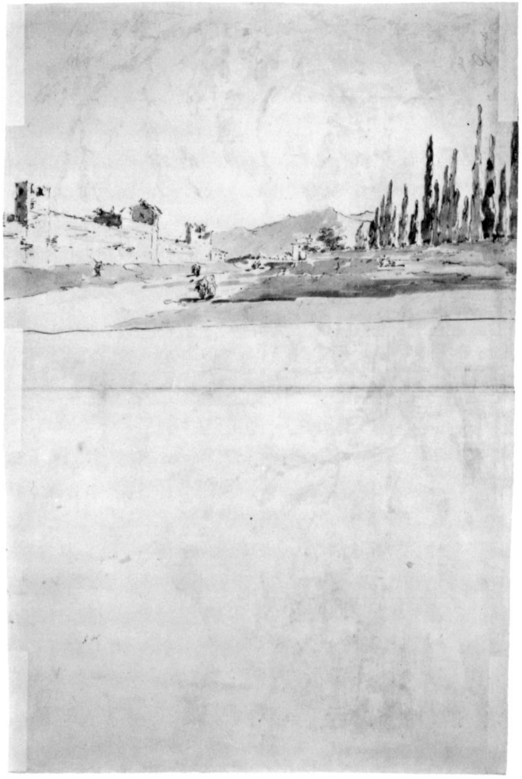

22 (verso) Francesco Guardi

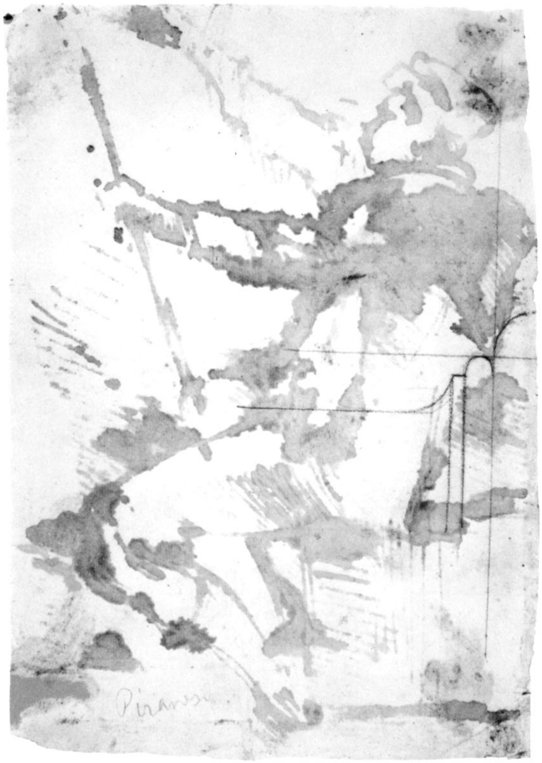

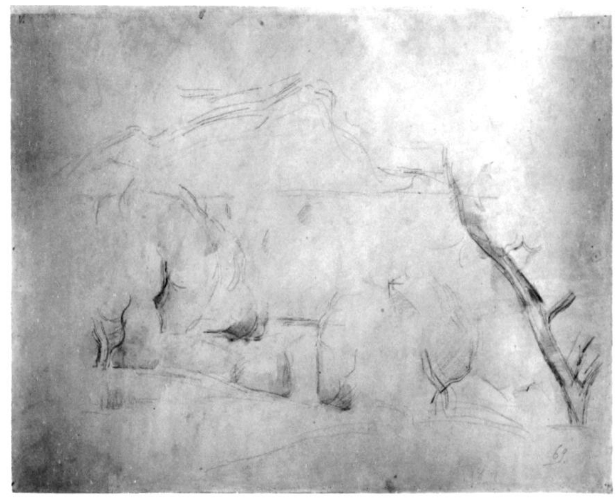

49 (verso) Paul Cézanne

23 (verso) Giovanni Battista Piranesi

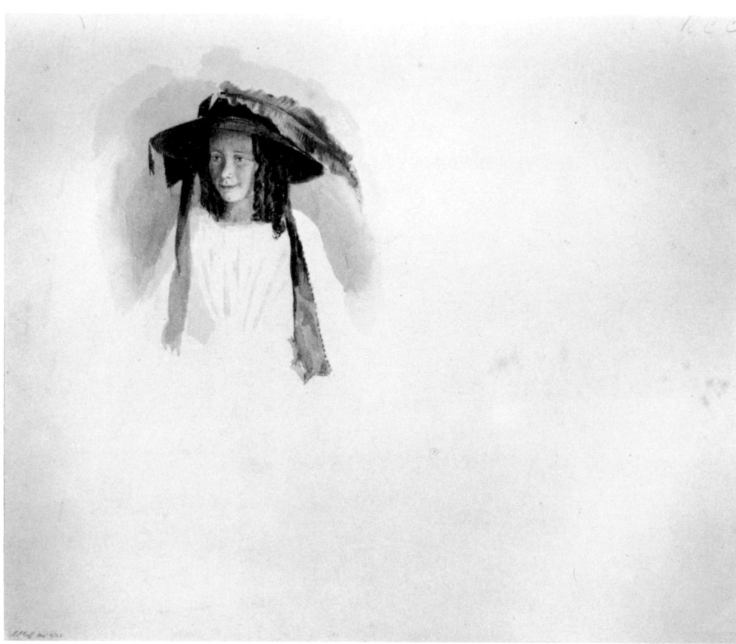

73 (verso) R. Parminter Cuff

INDEX OF ARTISTS

PRODUCED BY

MERIDEN–STINEHOUR PRESS